Writing Inventions

Writing Inventions:

Identities, Technologies, Pedagogies

Scott Lloyd DeWitt

State University of New York Press

Published by
State University of New York Press, Albany

© 2001 State University of New York

For information, address State University of New York Press,
90 State Street, Suite 700, Albany, NY 12207

Production by Judith Block
Marketing by Michael Campochiaro

Library of Congress Cataloging-in-Publication Data

DeWitt, Scott Lloyd
    Writing inventions : identities, technologies, pedagogies / Scott Lloyd DeWitt.
        p.   cm.
    Includes bibliographical references (p.) and index.
    ISBN 0-7914-5039-2 (alk. paper — ISBN 0-7914-5040-6 (pbk. : alk paper)
        1. English language—Rhetoric—Study and teaching. 2. English
    language—Rhetoric—Study and teaching—Technological innovations. 3. English
    language—Rhetoric—Study and teaching—Data processing. 4. Report writing—
    Study and teaching (Higher)—Technological innovations. 5. Report writing—
    Study and teaching (Higher)—Data processing. 6. Hypertext systems. 7. World
    Wide Web. I. Title.

PE1404 .D425 2001
808'.042'0285—dc21   00-061922

10 9 8 7 6 5 4 3 2 1

Contents

Figures

Author's Note

Writing Inventions: Identities, Pedagogies, Technologies uses student writing and interview transcripts extensively as data. A few points need to be clarified about the methodology:

- I have chosen *not* to note errors in writing samples and interview transcripts with [sic].

- Readers should assume that errors in writing samples were part of the original text (most were collected on disk).

- Readers should assume that "errors" in speech patterns and grammar in the transcripts of face-to-face interviews were as spoken.

- I have used student writing and interviews as data. Because of promised anonymity, I have changed the names of all students whose work I cited within.

Acknowledgments

I belong to a writers' group. An amazingly successful writers' group. The players are affectionately known as "Crazed Researchers," a group of colleagues . . . friends . . . who get together on a regular basis to share writing and offer constructive feedback to each other. We have been working together now for just over eight years. We usually meet over some kind of food, either in someone's home or at a favorite coffeehouse. We laugh—a lot. We gossip—a little. We show off new clothes and new hair cuts. We catch up on the parts of our lives that get lost in our busy work schedules—movies we've seen, restaurants we've been to, family, dates. Until recently, when we added a new member, I was the only man in the group of five; I often thought that if our conversations were archived in a hypertext, we'd see an incredible number of links through the word "uterus." We are a group where a lot of talk takes place.

Throughout our four-year existence, we've used e-mail to schedule or cancel or reschedule meetings—"business." We've never attempted to use the technology in our *real* business, our creative work. There hasn't been a need, really. Mostly, though, I think we have avoided the idea of a virtual writers' group because we like to be with one another, so much so that we're compelled, driven to carve out a chunk of time in our lives to share a physical creative space, complete with animated body language, loud laughter, a cushy couch, and spilled food.

This book would not be in your hands now if it were not for these dear people: Lynda Behan, Anne Bower, Marcia Dickson, Beverly Moss, and our recent addition, Thomas Piontek.

A number of other colleagues deserve recognition: Stuart Lishan, Timothy McNiven, Jacqueline Spangler, Michael Lohre, H. Louis Ulman, Jacqueline Royster, Les Tannenbaum, Andrea A. Lunsford, F. Dominic Dottavio, Greg Rose, Beverly Carpenter.

I also need to thank my teachers, especially those who have engaged me in the work that shapes who I am in the classroom today: Douglas Hesse, Janice Neuleib, James Kalmbach, Ron Fortune, Gail Hawisher, Elizabeth Crowley, Robert Seufert, Catherine Peaden, Anne Rosenthal, Lois Sisler, and Deb Bendis.

I also remember Richard McGuire and Phil Decker, two very gifted teachers who will be deeply missed by their students.

This book would be empty if it were not for my students who so graciously allowed me to use their work.

Friends cannot go unrecognized: Angela Wall, Andrew Rivera, Penny Visser, Anne Wysoki, JoEllen Brannon, Pete Howells, Vince Constabileo, Dan Henry, Kris Harrison, Gina Cronley, Jeffrey Cox, Pam Takayoshi, Mark Cunningham, David Ward, Gary Grubler, Dave Dierks, Doug Zelinski, Jim Francis, Tony France, Jeff Rosa, Lance Adams, Joe Rutan, Danny B. Stout, Cray Ferguson, Robert Thompson, Brian Laird, Greg Kirby, Nate Payne, Brent Bell, Jim Ressa, Nancy Carlson, Peter Warsaw, Linda Ketcham, Kim Fisher, Nancy Speir, Donna Murrow, Lisa Thoennes, Mary Wildenradt. I also need to thank my parents, Stuart and Janet DeWitt, and my siblings, Sharon DeWitt and Stuart DeWitt, and their families. Kip Strasma deserves much recognition for saying "yes" when I wanted to write a book and who just convinced me to do it one more time.

The research in the book was supported by Illinois State University's Department of English, The Ohio State University at Marion's Small Grant Program, and The Ameritech Faculty Fellowship of The Ohio State University.

I also need to thank The Coffee Table at Buttles and High in Columbus, Ohio, for never once saying "no" when I needed to plug in.

More often than not, life's most important lessons have nothing to do with school. I offer my deep gratitude to Stephen "Monica" Lippi for teaching me that "it ain't always pretty," both on and off the court.

Finally, I dedicate this book to Jim Ryan, my dearest friend, confidant. Your vision, courage, passion, intellect, and humor have guided me since the day we met.

Introduction:
Inventing Ourselves

This is a book about teaching writing. Usually, I don't feel the need to make such plainspoken claims about my work. Yet, I grow increasingly uncomfortable with the ways both my work and I have been named, as of late: "His work is in computers. . . . He teaches computers. . . . He's a computer specialist." I don't necessarily disagree with these tags. They are not erroneous, nor are they purposely misrepresentative. In fact, I'm sure that I have made these very statements about my professional identity at one time or another. These characterizations, however, allow people to forget what it is that I do: I teach writing.

Professionally, composition has been a field forced to specialize. The reasons, both scholarly and practical (and all of which are political), are many. But few areas of specialization have had such widespread appeal and such identity-forming effect as have "computers and composition studies." Quite rapidly, a large cross section of the profession has been more than willing to accept computer technology into its departments, programs, and classrooms. At the same time, however, compositionists whose scholarship explores computer technology have become so narrowly defined that their identity as teachers of writing, in the eyes of others, is obscured by the appeal of the technology itself—often resulting in, "His work is in computers. . . . He teaches computers. . . . He's a computer specialist."

The widespread appeal is easy to understand. Consider why writers use computers in the first place. Computers relieve some of the tedium of composing. Technology has given us access to new forms of research previously nonexistent or out of reach. We have discovered opportunities to use computer technology for communication in ways we had never before imagined. Of

1

course, computers are fun—when they work. And we must admit that computers have allowed us to recast our introductory courses for students who don't like taking writing classes, not to mention for teachers who are less than eager to continue teaching them. Computer-enhanced writing programs become a public relations asset for our schools, too. When learning institutions require students to take writing courses that just happen to be taught using computers, administrators can promise computer literacy among all of their graduates.

The reason that computers have had such an extreme identity-forming effect on those who use them to teach writing and on those who conduct research on computers and composition is a bit more difficult to understand. Perhaps it is as simple as novelty: The glitz associated with the technology still overshadows our pedagogical purposes. Perhaps our early years teaching writing with computers, when we sometimes spent more time teaching computer operations than we did teaching writing, are more pervasive than we would like to believe. Or maybe what we are looking at here is a lingering reaction to the technology that, for many, *still* seems so out of place within the humanities. One cannot help but understand why certain administrators associate us so closely with the machines; certainly, never before in the history of the humanities have budget requests been so focused on the implementation of computer technology.

Regardless, my association with these machines—as teacher and as researcher—has forced me to be acutely aware of others' perceptions of me and my work. At times, events and circumstances surrounding the use of computers cause even me to question my own professional identity. I just recently completed a temporary stint as technical support for our campus after the resignation of a key player on our computer staff. I found myself scheduling labs and equipment, teaching basic software operations, fixing faulty wiring, and assisting with the repair of a campus-wide network crash. On my drive home at night after a day that had much more to do with "tech" than it did with "teach," I would find myself asking, "What did any of this have to do with why I'm here?" When I feel backed into a corner, fielding endless questions about hardware and software that are truly devoid of any consideration of teaching and learning, I gently remind those in my company, "I teach writing." And when I find myself wrapped up in the bureaucracy of computer committees, or having spent an afternoon circling an empty room of humming computers trying to figure out just what went wrong with the LAN or the LISTSERV during the class before, I gently remind myself, "I teach writing."

I remember as a graduate student being assigned Andrea Lunsford's published CCCC chair's address, "Composing Ourselves: Politics, Commitment, and the Teaching of Writing," in which she urges the profession to discontinue its trend toward narrowly defining itself "according to rigid meanings grounded in preexisting, fixed categories" (Fontaine and Hunter, 1993, 2). Lunsford's essay was included as a reading within a seminar discussion centering on academia and marginalized voices, primarily those of women and people of color. Our approach to "Composing Ourselves" allowed me to explore some questions I had begun to raise about my role as a gay man categorically set "outside" and restricted by various academic boundaries. Yet, as invaluable as that learning experience was to me as a student, a scholar, and a teacher, Lunsford's essay spoke volumes to me on another level: I left the immediate conversation of the seminar to consider—for possibly the first time—how I was composing myself professionally and, subsequently, how I had allowed others to compose me.

Understanding this composition of my identity actually became an exercise in understanding how specific choices and experiences had led to a creation, an *invention* of sorts. I was nearly ABD and just under two years away from a tenure-track job offer. I no longer saw my graduate studies as mere coursework; instead, I recognized I was inventing a professional identity that would traverse coursework, dissertation, and the job market. I pursued my degree in a nationally recognized Doctor of Arts program that emphasized the training of undergraduate teaching professionals; many of the courses offered included a strong pedagogical foundation, where the content itself was pedagogy. My department required that I complete a cognate to my composition and rhetoric degree; I chose computers and composition studies, not only because of interest and expertise in the technology, but also because I could form an attractive job persona in an extremely tough market. I was expected to write an empirically researched dissertation that grew from this cognate where I designed a classroom-based study that would yield some type of data that I could examine and analyze: This study became *Hypertextualizing Composition Instruction: A Research Study*. My training in teaching writing occurred in a program where 100 percent of lower division writing courses were taught in computer classrooms. I also spent one year as the coordinator of computers in the department, a job that required me to manage and maintain ten computer classrooms and provide continual support and training to new and seasoned teachers.

I carefully examined this invention of my professional identity and, without question, deliberately composed and pitched myself on the job market as a *computer specialist*, responding vigorously to job announcements that requested candidates who could bring technological and pedagogical expertise to their departments. Really, I shouldn't be surprised by the composition that has become my professional identity, for I am its author. Today, however, years into the tenure track of my first job, I find myself *re*inventing and *re*composing myself in many of the "practical, concrete terms" that Lunsford's agenda forwards:

> [W]e will situate ourselves in the complex, problematic history of writing, trying to find ways to tell and retell that story around and through us. . . . [W]e will continue our often unspoken commitment to resist the temptations

> of binary oppositions—between research and teaching, theory and practice, composition and literature, teacher and student, between playfulness and seriousness. . . . [W]e will tell our stories, stories of students . . . and of teachers of writing. . . . [W]e will insist, as we compose our stories, on combining the private and the public, the personal and the professional, the political and the social. . . . Most of all, we will refuse to be or become composed or static. (1990, 77–78)

Reinventing and recomposing myself takes on new importance as I struggle to simultaneously embrace and resist the sometimes accurate, yet "often limiting and constricting" label, *computer specialist* (Lunsford, 1990, 72). As I continue to negotiate and find commonality between *writing teacher* and *computer specialist*, I continue to see the weight of understanding not only how I have invented and composed myself, but also in how others will *read* how I have invented and composed myself.

Nothing, I believe, keeps me more grounded in those gentle reminders ("I teach writing") than the reflexive activity of writing about the various roles that computer technology plays in the craft of teaching composition. Such activity moves well beyond simple narration in scope: It propels me to consider the history of both the field of computers and composition studies and my own place within that historical context. That sense, then, of knowing where the profession has been enables me to question where it is at this moment and where I, for one, want to go next. (I've learned that the trend toward *predicting* where computers and composition studies will go next, with the quickly and always changing technology of computers, is not nearly as useful as *directing* where it will go next.) This active interrogation of the field helps me to avoid reducing the complex acts of both writing and teaching to mere "how to" lists and prevents me from forgetting that my own writing, my teaching, and my research all inform each other. Finally, writing about my work also gives voice to the stories of my classroom that make an ever-important contribution to a culture of teaching and learning.

These are the considerations that motivate this book, *Writing Inventions: Identities, Pedagogies, Technologies*. As a way of describing what is amassed here, let us begin by examining my title. As with Christina Haas' *Writing Technology* and my own research study entitled, "Defining Links," I intend a play on words in my title. The first meaning, the most obvious, might be a way to describe a technology: computers are writing inventions, machines used to compose. Yet throughout the book, *invention* becomes a theme, a controlling idea. I use *invention* to mean a rich collection of processes, both systematic and chaotic, that leads to discoveries of what is not yet known: topics for papers; new pedagogies; personal and professional identities. I believe invention, in practice and in its rich history in rhetorical theory, touches more in composition pedagogy than does anything else. This is especially true in the sense in which I use this term throughout this book—as a complexly intertwined impression of the often separated acts of reading, writing, exploration, discovery, and research.

The act of writing itself is immediately tied to invention, as is evidenced by current practice in the field of composition and rhetoric. Much of the instruction implemented in composition courses provides opportunities for students not only to find topics about which to write, but also to move beyond a superficial treatment of a particular subject, to find an interesting angle on a particular subject, or to internalize difficult content, making the knowledge their own. Frustrating for our students (and sometimes for us) is the realization that much of the resulting writing (and much of the learning) never "appears" in a final product. But couple these inventions with *writing* as a present participle, a verb form that describes the act of doing something, and the phrase comes to mean committing these discoveries to written text, the act of composing that which each of us discovers and creates. As awkward as it sounds—especially on the printed page—in this book, I am *writing inventions*.

No volume can address how to use every type of computer technology available to teach everything we need to accomplish in our writing courses. So I have deliberately chosen to narrow the lens through which I view composition pedagogy. Focusing on the notion of invention, I model how computer technology and certain instructional goals can be connected. Because this book explores the pedagogical implications of technology, it is concerned with various writing courses I teach, some of which are representative of other university writing programs, some of which are not. These courses teach students the conventions of academic writing. They concentrate on topic formation and development, including types of evidence and strategies of argument, as well as intense investigation of audience and purpose. These courses, in short, intend to foster students' development as active writers within various academic and public intellectual communities. Some of these courses link writing instruction closely with in-depth explorations of academic subject matter. In other words, they offer instructors the opportunity to develop a particular course topic so that the subject is supported by a seminar course format. At the same time, students learn the role that writing can play in academic endeavors where a focus on one subject is maintained throughout the term.

Immediately, readers will see that nothing in this volume assumes a "one size fits all" approach to computers and teaching writing. I scrutinize the interrelationships of pedagogical applications of computers with educational settings, student populations, hardware/software configurations, and institutional technical support. I recommend that anyone inventing instructional approaches to computers and composition do the same. Teachers who use writing in a variety of courses across the disciplines, as well as those who direct or mentor in

Writing Across the Curriculum programs, will find much that applies to their classroom work.

Inventing Audience

I find that writing about computers and composition forces me to consider audience differently than does other writing. Of course, the basic questions for analyzing one's audience still exist: What attributes define my audience? What does my audience need to know, and what does my audience want to know? Yet years of studying the texts of techno-compositionists—classroom idea exchanges, published research, conference papers—lead me to believe that the field's attempts to reach a wide variety of professionals have been less than inviting and inclusive.

Research today—in general—tends to be written to "the highest common denominator," or, in other words, to those who are not only well entrenched in the published literature, but also to those who have an understanding of the history of the field, including where it has been, where it is now, and where it may be heading based on calls for future research. Sometimes, when writing in a field of study that is either teeming in publication or is growing at a phenomenal pace (both are the case in computers and writing), writers grasp, out of necessity, for ways to narrow the scope of a particular project. Likewise, writers find their research is sometimes shaped by institutional pressure to be on "the cutting edge" (this is most evident in the "publish or perish" world of the tenure track). Unfortunately, the deepest cut made is often that of the audience.

Writers choose their approach toward audience for many reasons, yet most share a common call for continually questioning our approaches toward and agendas for using computers in our classrooms, usually reminding us to avoid treating the technology as "just a machine." I am reminded of Nancy Kaplan's appeal to carefully consider the questions

> that foreground the tensions between what teachers teach and what teachers use to teach with. . . . Teachers' concerns . . . should extend well beyond the confines for their daily work, leading them to examine the situatedness in a full field of ideological constructions, for theorists and practitioners alike need to understand that both the tools that come to hand and those they seek to create may come with ideological price tags. (1991, 35–36)

Hawisher and Selfe emphasize the importance of these questions for the field: "By examining questions that must still be answered and by exploring ways in which we might begin to gather needed information, we avoid the danger of using electronic technology haphazardly. We avoid making decisions without carefully considering the issues affecting our students and ourselves" (1991, 2).

However, few writers allow an inclusive (and complex) vision of audience to guide how we write about computers and composition. I believe the field has been, in many cases, guilty of a limiting approach toward addressing audience, for what we often refer to as a community of teachers and/or scholars is actually many different communities that form themselves around the domains of knowledge, experience, and access.

When I talk to teachers, the ones who are "out there" with the students in the classrooms, it becomes clear that such an approach to audience when writing about computers and composition fails to address and include a significant number of people. Consider this list of questions by a group of middle- and high-school English teachers who are facing the introduction of computer technology into their curricula. I have included here about one half of the questions that they generated for me when I was a guest speaker in their class on methods of teaching English.

Hardware/Software

- How do we decide what programs are good? Do we have to pour over endless catalogs?

- How do we convince parents, voters, administrators, school boards, etc., that purchasing computers is important for our students' learning?

- How do we continue to be current with computer information in addition to other imposed (or self-imposed) duties?

World Wide Web

- The Web takes time—what about class time constraints (forty-eight minute periods, for example)?

- What practical use of the WWW can I make for and with my students?

- How do we monitor students who try to access inappropriate materials?

- Is there a site where teachers share their ideas on teaching literary selections? How do we put our information on the Web?

Internet

- Is e-mail the same as the Internet?

- How do we get addresses of people?

- Could I do interactive book reports?
- Can e-mail messages be intercepted by others?

Reading and Writing

- Is it possible/practical to read short stories, novels, etc., on the computer?
- Should or could the technology change our approach to the traditional research paper?
- Is there a simple booklet of step-by-step word processing instructions?

Research

- How do our students get to the *Readers' Guide*? How can they pull up a specific article?
- How can students determine the quality of information received?
- How do they document sources they find on the computer?

Other

- How do you assign homework?
- What about plagiarism—turning in papers found on the WWW as their own?
- Can I require work to be done on computers?
- How do I grade student work on the computer (some have better abilities and/or access)?
- How do we find time to learn so we can teach the technology?
- How do we keep up with all of the new data on computers?
- How can we measure student achievement/success while on-line?
- Is it possible or necessary to "stay ahead" of the students?

Now consider this list of questions that these same teachers would find if they turned to Selfe and Hilligoss's title, *Literacy and Computers: The Complications of Teaching and Learning with Technology*:

- What model of literacy will guide our discussion of technology? What conceptual framework for literacy, teaching, and learning does this software (hardware, etc.) imply? Does technology enhance or limit the model of writing instruction in this setting? (Zeni, 1994, 79)

- How does technology change the social relations in writing and in research communities? (Zeni, 1994, 84)

- How does a computer network promote or inhibit the process of social construction and social interaction? That is, how does it promote or inhibit collaboration and interaction among individuals, collaborators, discourse communities, and the larger community? (Duin and Hanson, 1994, 99)

- How do network configurations reflect distributions of power? That is, how do they reinforce or resist existing models of authority? (Duin and Hanson, 1994, 98)

- In what ways do [telecommunications] projects take into account special issues—such as equitable distribution of resources and sensitivity to cultural differences—that may arise when students communicate across distance and social class? (Bowen, 1994, 115)

- How do instructors' and institutions' definitions of literacy influence the ways that technology is introduced and used? (Forman, 1994, 143)

Perhaps, quite simply, *Literacy and Computers* is not written for the teachers I met. But Selfe and Hilligoss say that they attempted to reach a wide audience by "avoid[ing] technological jargon in favor of language that teachers share because of their involvement in literacy education" (1994, 2). Their approach, they hope, reaches a broad range of teachers with varying backgrounds in technology. Yet, the striking differences in these lists are easily attributable to the differences of the composers themselves: one group made up of teachers who have intensive classroom expertise yet limited computer experience from which to draw when asking questions; the other, teacher/scholars with a great deal of background in both the technology and the theory, connections between which actually generate the questions they ask. Perhaps there also exist differences in immediacy and exigency in their questions as these two groups feel the pressures of the technology and the other concerns of teaching bearing down on them.

I find that those who attend workshops I conduct on computers and writing fall into several communities of teachers and scholars. The first I have already mentioned—those who have been part of and are familiar with the movement of the past fifteen years or so toward using computers in writing instruction. (It is important to note that not all of these folks are conducting and publishing research. Many direct their energies towards developing teaching methods and putting those methods into practice in their own departments and classrooms without the desire or pressure to publish their classroom stories.) Another community is made up of those who do not have access to computers for the purpose of teaching writing, but really wish that they did. These teachers tend to be well read in the theory of teaching with computers and can articulate why they believe their school should invest in the technology (many of them have had to do just that with their various administrators). Others really know nothing about computer technology and teaching but really want to know more about computers on a personal level before ever considering using them with students—which seems to be a safer move than trying to learn technology and teaching at the same time. Still others are being literally dragged into the "techno" age. They see "the machine" as an intrusion into the humanities curriculum and feel that computers distract from the real purpose of their courses. Yet, they realize that computers are not going away and they let their guard down, willing to give them a try.

One more group of teachers consists of those who were in on the ground floor of the early computers and writing movement. They had state-of-the-art computers in their classrooms and embraced them as an integral part of their teaching practice. Unfortunately, state-of-the-art equipment can quickly seem about as useful as Paleolithic clay tablets, laden with malfunctions and broken parts and unable to run the simplest software of the day. Departments that received large sums of money to develop computer-enhanced writing programs five to ten years ago are told to wait their turn for upgrades; others who have waited patiently for their first round of computers are offered hand-me-downs from departments who are "more deserving" of new hardware, where spending seems "more appropriate." Nevertheless, there are a whole lot of really old machines in a whole lot of our writing classrooms under the direction of teachers searching for new, exciting ways to use these digital dinosaurs.

Experience and dated computers are not the only signifiers/designators of computers and writing communities. I find a significant disparity in the number of computers that teachers have access to as well as the frequency with which they have access to computer facilities. Ideally, a computer classroom should have at least one computer per student (actually, *ideally*, that would include one for the teacher, too). A one-per-student classroom design offers the most flexibility for teaching, the most important facet of which is working individually or collaboratively on the computers *depending on what effective pedagogy dictates*. But many teachers report anywhere from one computer to a small cluster of computers for their entire class. Such limited access forces teachers to fragment their teaching, preventing whole-class instruction, and adding yet another chore to class maintenance. Others report fighting for time in a classroom (usually designed more as a "lab" than a "classroom") that is shared by other disciplines, usually math or computer science; these teachers are sometimes lucky to get one class meeting every two weeks in the computer facility.

Inventing Myself

I have worked in many of the communities described above. My first teaching assignment thirteen years ago was in a computer classroom—at the time, this advanced technology had dual 5 1/4" drives, monochrome monitors, and ran nothing other than simple word processing. From that point on, I have never taught a writing course that was not computer supported in some way. Since writing my dissertation on the use of hypertext in a developmental writing class, my research has continued to focus on computers and composition studies. While I try to consume as much scholarship in the field as I possibly can along with hardware and software reviews in the popular press of the computer world, I have surrendered to the fact that I *really* can't read everything, given the fast pace at which computer technology and its respective research change.

My current teaching setting on the Marion Campus of the Ohio State University, though, has over the years relocated me to two new communities in computers and composition studies. Although my program still teaches 100 percent of its writing courses on computer, for years we did so on machines that were so dated that we feared many of our students were taking a significant step backwards from the computers they had access to at home or at work. Whereas this writing program is pedagogically parallel to my first, my previous department upgraded hardware and software once every two to three years. Budget constraints prevented my current program from replacing antiquated and malfunctioning computers for over five years. Up through the mid-1990s, I continued to pet and rub and whisper softly to our ailing 8086s and 286s, "Boot, just one more time." Then, we were given funds to purchase eight new, powerful machines, leaving us with thirty-two computers that could hardly be called stable. We decided to place the new machines in a classroom directly next to some of the oldest machines on the entire campus which did not make for technological continuity.

I would be less than honest if I said this technological setting allowed me to do the work with my students that I would have liked. Research seemed to indicate that to be on "the cutting edge" of computers and writing, my students should have immediate access to the World Wide Web and other Internet technologies such as electronic mail, on-line discussion groups, and GOPHER research data bases. This research led me to believe that my students should be gaining valuable experience in writing through real-time, on-line discussion spaces where they could converse with their classroom peers as well as with students around the world. In addition, researchers were convincing me that advanced technology should be sending students with problems, via their computer, to an on-line writing center rather than asking them to trudge across campus to sit face-to-face with a tutor.

What I was reading and hearing at conferences and seeing at workshops was all very exciting. Yet, I present here no blanket acceptance of these applications. Instead, I find it necessary to identify a tension comprised of two realities—the realities of enticing possibilities and the realities of limited resources—as a place to *begin* questioning the current nature of research in computers and composition. Of course, this problem runs deeper than conflict between the haves and the have-nots. Researchers and teachers like myself find ourselves struggling with what could be self-defeating circumstances. Plainly and simply, some teachers don't have the necessary resources to journey with their students to the writing experiences they currently see reported in published and presented research. So, immediately, not only is their practice questioned as "dated," but they begin to question themselves, wondering just what they could possibly contribute to a dialogue that seems to have left them behind and that, with each upgrade, moves farther and farther away.

I had, for some time, resisted acknowledging my own role in these conditions. As a faculty member in a department with rigorous, demanding research expectations, I worried about how such conditions would affect my approaching tenure decision. I had composed myself as a computer specialist, and my senior colleagues expected that my *research* would reflect the *researcher*, that the research would be undeniably tied to the technology. Could I actually articulate compelling research problems that, although obviously tied to "old" technology, didn't seem to mirror "old" research? Would my research be unequivocally dismissed because of its seeming datedness? I also worried for more practical reasons: If I proved to my administrators that I could both teach and produce effective research on teaching writing with obsolete computer equipment, what would there be to push them toward updating our technology?

After years of teaching writing and conducting research with antiquated technology, my department was given two new computer-supported classrooms: fifty Windows-based computers capable of running any market software for many years to come; powerful word processing, desktop publishing, presentation, networking, and Internet software; sharp laser printers; Web authoring capabilities. With additional grant support, we were able to purchase a powerful departmental Web server. These upgrades, however, did not come easily. I attended endless campus computer committee meetings at which I justified the expenditure on the new technology by arguing that because all students enrolled in at least one composition course on our campus, we could boast computer literacy across our entire student population (the argument I continually pitched toward my administrators). I presented formal proposals in which I outlined theoretical concerns, classroom designs and schedules, equipment requisition forms, technical support, elaborate budgets, and faculty training sessions. One of my arguments resounded at every meeting where computers were the topic of discussion: We are doing our students a disservice by educating them on equipment that more than likely will no longer be considered "viable" outside our classroom walls.

In retrospect, I see that many of my arguments for acquiring a new computer classroom furthered the disparities that exist among numerous educational institutions today. While my professional colleagues at a private institution less than an hour away would give the world for the opportunity to begin working with technology in the classroom, I was actually requesting the world. And one simple fact of privilege remained: While I had to work hard to convince my administration to spend the money on my department, in the end, the money existed. It was there, and it needed only an application.

Denying economic as well as scholarly inequities does little more than secure their continuation. Yet, what will enable us to turn the tables on these disadvantageous situations, so common to many teachers and researchers?

I argue that we need to change a current, wide-reaching trend in our approach to research—one that delimits and hinders—in order to create a space where we can truly compose ourselves, resisting the boundaries and privileges that all too often technologies themselves impose. Such a change will not come easily, especially when our research is so often tied exclusively to hardware and software. We can begin by shifting our gaze away from "the machines" and back to the situations arising from real writing instruction that perhaps utilizes computer technology as a means to an end. To do so begins to level the playing field by lessening the research privilege of those who have the loosest purse strings and, thus, the most powerful machines. I am certainly not suggesting that we ignore the presence of computer technology in our teaching and learning environments. Instead, the technology needs to be regarded in a new light that allows the teacher running WordPerfect 5.1 on a 286 and the teacher guiding students to instructional Web pages on a new Pentium III equally legitimate voices that are valued by a multitude of audiences.

Also, we need to continue to study the reciprocal nature of theory and practice not only in our teaching but also in the role that computer technology plays in our teaching. Writing teachers who use computers in their classrooms face a vast array of theoretical and pedagogical problems that need to be solved— problems that do not necessarily exist in the traditional classroom setting. Our first and foremost task is rigorously challenging the assumptions behind the question, "Will the use of computers make our students better writers?" Underlying this question exists the misconception among many that adding technology to our classrooms creates a simplistic cause-and-effect equation: computers=better writers. In their concern with the unreasonable expectations that technology will "solve" our students' writing problems, scholars and teachers in computers and composition studies, the pioneers in this field, stood firm on one point: We need to ensure that the focus of our composition classes remains on the study of written communication and that the teaching strategies we bring to the classroom to make our students better writers continue to be informed by what we know about teaching writing, not by what the computer can do. In other words, they believed that we should always start with good teaching practice and find ways to bring computer technology to it.

While I embrace this belief as a guiding vision, especially for those new to using technology in the classroom, I want to push beyond this boundary, too. I propose that new technologies can help teachers to *imagine* new pedagogies, that teachers' actual hands-on experience with particular computer applications can lead them toward the development of teaching practice. Such reciprocity allows us to remain true to sound pedagogical practice in its many forms but, at the same time, opens up possibilities for the creation of new practices. Of course, we need to remain critical in our view of developed pedagogies. I'm not suggesting, for example, that we support as sound pedagogy a "back-to-basics" approach to writing instruction based on the fact that teachers may still have access to drill and practice grammar software. Yet, I am equally critical of any theory that limits rather than expands the possibilities for how we might change what we know about writing and writing instruction. Finally, this reciprocity supports a change in the current, global trend in our approach to research by allowing theory and practice to grow from experience with computers regardless of the technologies to which teachers and researchers have access.

◆   ◆   ◆

I've struggled with the form this book should take. Actually, I tried to resist "the book" as a uniform image because this text employs many forms: narratives, theory, classroom practice, histories, empirical research, interviews. Often these approaches and forms run right up against one another; at other times they are easily separated. In many ways, this book tells stories. While I want these to be instructional stories about computers and writing—to me, the story is an excellent way to present instructive work—I also intend for them to speak on a deeper level, one that includes my own reflections on the subjects at hand. It's strange to think of myself as a storyteller after having only taught thirteen years. But then again, these are stories about teaching writing using computers; my subject matter has a relatively short history, and I've been present through a major portion of that history.

Realizing the likely diversity of technical knowledge readers will bring to this book, I have tried to assume very little in terms of how particular technologies work. First of all, the research presented within was supported by a wide range of computer platforms and capabilities. Also, most technologies in our classrooms are rarely used as they were created by the computer industry (a close look at the capabilities and graphic interfaces of any modern word processing program reveals more about corporate America than it does about today's classrooms and the students who populate them). Instead, we shape and mold the technologies to fit specific needs and purposes; we invent ways to use the invention. So for me to say that my students conducted an e-mail discussion is really meaningless without a description of the configuration of the software and how I directed the students to use the software, so to speak. Many will find descriptions of the technology boring at best, while others will welcome some straightforward writing about terms and concepts that are dropped all too casually into discussions about teaching with computers.

In chapter 1, "Inventing Invention," I articulate a theory of invention that draws somewhat from classical rhetoric but mostly from instructional/cognitive psychology and collaborative learning theory. Specifically, I look at three mental processes, or domains, while constructing this theory of invention, all of which, I claim, are a part of "what writers do":

- *Noticing* as an integral process of discovery

- *Forming and shaping* relationships and connections that are created from the disorder of writers' discoveries

- *Reflecting* on the disorder of invention.

Much of this theory is, on the surface, not necessarily grounded in technology studies. However, I conclude that carefully reading cognitive and learning theory forwards new possibilities for regarding the use of computers in our writing classrooms.

Chapter 2, "Inventing Discussions, Inventing Pedagogies" unveils two important areas of inquiry in this book. First, I introduce Computer-mediated Discussion (CmD) and its use in facilitating invention processes for student writers. I have gathered here numerous portraits of students' computer-mediated discussions, both effective and ineffective, to illustrate the collaborative communities that did and did not evolve from them. My experience working with CmD technologies enabled me to see three benefits important to writing teachers. First, students begin to see writing and discussion as shared experiences. Students also gain contextualized writing experiences that will feed into other writing they complete. And finally, students increase their participation in class discussions and in the overall amount of writing they produce. Besides exploring CmD, this chapter also introduces a theory of inventing new pedagogies while working with technology. Current convention promotes an approach that merely fits existing teaching practice into new technology. However, I counter this position by showing how my own experience using the technology allowed me to imagine new pedagogies that met goals I had for my student writers.

The next chapter in the book pulls together the experiences my students had with the World Wide Web and with computer-mediated discussion. In chapter 3, "Inventing Hypertext Reading," I explore possibilities for teaching invention using the World Wide Web. I argue that we need to bring a method of invention to this new technology if we expect our students to use it effectively in our writing classes. Utilizing the discoveries I made observing students' experiences with hypertext and computer-mediated discussion, I created a working definition of instructional Web sites:

- Their purpose is teaching a particular subject.

- They act as an information resource.

- They serve as a virtual meeting space for students and teachers.

- They facilitate specific pedagogical goals of a course.

- They provide a space for students and teachers to make sense of their experiences with virtual worlds.

- They give teachers a glimpse into students' learning processes.

The chapter illustrates these defining qualities by providing examples of the Web site used to teach composition at the Marion Campus of the Ohio State University.

Chapter 4, "Inventing Hypertext Writing," focuses on an extensive research study that examines students' work from multiple perspectives to provide a profile of student thinking and learning as enriched by computer technology. I present an elaborate classroom portrait of how developmental college writing students created hypertexts that later served to support their invention processes while writing a required, traditional academic text. I also explore how students' self-constructed definitions of hypertext influenced their use of and experiences with the technology. Although the software and hardware configurations students had access to were relatively simplistic, I argue that hypertext provided students with a concrete, sophisticated illustration of not only the goals of the course, but also of their own cognitive strategies for learning.

The final chapter of the book lays out an entire course where various invention technologies are used. Chapter 5, "Inventing Scenes," describes a second-year composition course where students studied documentary films. Early in the course, students completed a number of traditional writing assignments about the films they were viewing. However, the course concluded with a class project where students were asked to create "documentary Web sites." Instead of looking at assignments and technologies in isolation of the course in which they are implemented, as I have done in previous chapters, this work examines an entire course. My reading of students' work not only looks at their invention processes, but also it raises questions about teaching new text forms in traditional academic courses.

1

Inventing Invention

I grew up around invention and inventions. My father is an engineer who, for over forty years, worked in the area of refrigeration at major appliance companies before retiring from a small company that made thermostats for household electronics. Everything in his world is a "part" that, when put together with another "part," might become something. Growing up, my friends and I used to call him "The Gadget Man." He is a continual inventor, yet, at first glance, he appears to be much more a pack rat than a mad scientist. His garage has been stocked complete with strange items accumulated over a period of forty-eight years of marriage and raising a family: wires, tool handles, broken toys, thermometers, an ice bucket, lamp switches, an intercom system, the first microwave oven ever manufactured (an Amana Radarange), odd pieces of Plexiglas, sheet metal, wood, and screen, a cracked wooden bowl, an old trash compactor (the "compactor" went down and never came back up, preventing the trash drawer from ever opening again).

Surprisingly, the garage is quite neat, always space for two cars and room to get in and out of both the driver's and passengers' doors. In my opinion, the garage has never really been dirty or messy, so I wasn't sure what he was doing when he claimed that he was "cleaning," a process of taking everything out of its place and putting it back, or removing items saved in four baby food jars and relocating them to an old road salt bucket. All the while he makes a sort of whistling noise that isn't quite a real whistle but that has enough tonal quality to it that the sound coming from his lips is recognizably songlike.

Well into my adult years, I learned that his ritual was more surveying than it was cleaning, a way of recalling what's there and what's where, of keeping in touch with what may or may not be of use at some time. It's been an interesting process to watch over the years, especially when I realized that, as far as he is concerned, everything may be of use some time. He never throws anything away. At times, he labels items or creates short directories, but his mental impression of the garage that is created and recreated with each "cleaning" is more true than anything he might record on paper. His mental text is an authentic, real representation of the artifacts stored in his garage.

Recently, it came to me that this surveying of the garage, oddly enough, has something to do with the way my father walks through a store. Like many of us, often he heads to a store because he needs something in particular, something very specific. List in hand, he gathers what he set out for, rarely deviating from his agenda. When his errand list is short, however, and he is not pressed for time, he adopts a different mode, less forced and driven, more relaxed and observing, yet all the while purposeful. His posture changes greatly, from literally leaning forward to read his list, moving directly toward the items he needs, to one which, at first glance, is a rather strange practice: he walks with one hand in his pocket jingling keys and change (a habit formed early in his career as an engineer—keeping his hand in a pocket was assurance that he wouldn't "complete" an electrical current through his body), the other lightly touching and handling items as he walks down the aisles. Sometimes he looks at what he's touching, sometimes not, always making that same whistling noise, the song of his garage.

Occasionally, during his perusal, something will bring him to stop—the texture or weight of something surprises him, a line of tools he has known for years changed the design of its grips, a small kitchen appliance for which he designed a thermostat has finally hit the market, someone has mistakenly mixed flat-head screws in the round-head screw bin. Usually, this cause for pause is momentary, and he moves on. Every so often, though, his contact with something— with his hand or his eyes or with any of his senses, for that matter—is more substantial, bringing together or connecting somehow various items collected in the garage. The mental register, a mental text of sorts, breaks down into fragmented items that begin to shift and reorder. These found bits, either abstract concepts or very physical "pieces," connect with the garage and allow him to envision a process of creation. Sometimes this thinking through of problems and questions and steps, at least for the moment, remains nothing more than a process. However, on other occasions, his mental exercises result in inventions— some rather odd, some rather mundane—that usually solve specific problems that have come up in the house. (And depending on the invention at hand, sometimes when the "light comes on," a light really does come on.)

I'm a bit concerned about possible genetic makeup, yet unknown to the world of science, that may have been passed on to me. I recently moved from an apartment where there was little room left in my attic where a lot of yard sale treasures went in but almost never came out. All of them were purchased because they somehow connected with something else in the attic. I'm not as good at completing inventions as my father is; most never make it beyond "process" into "product." I just bought my first house. With a garage. It is filling quickly with a rather strange collection of items. And more than once I've caught myself lightly touching center-aisle sale items as I walk through Home Depot (though I do *not* whistle). I approach libraries and stacks of magazines and friends' CD collections in much the same way, leapfrogging from one item to the next, browsing with no agenda then suddenly focusing intently, quickly losing track of where I was while also recognizing influences and making connections. I do cherish the eye of the inventor that has grown with me over years of watching my father. Although my inventions currently tend more toward the abstract—these days, ideas and scholarly pursuits—than the gadgets and gizmos that are the artifacts of my father's thinking, we share a way of looking at the world, one where creativity, problem solving, vision, and most of all, process are highly valued activities.

Contexts of Invention

If I were to categorize how I spend my hours teaching writing, I'm certain that I would find that I concentrate most time working with students on invention. In order to develop instruction in an area of writing pedagogy that I believe to be essential for my students, I try to better understand invention in its multitude of shapes and forms, from a history of rhetorical thought to watching my father invent an emergency Christmas tree light shut-off the day after our new puppy almost took down the tree. I have to admit that more than once, I have wished I could find *The Complete Yet Concise Handbook of the History of Rhetorical Invention* as I surfed library stacks. I remember when I was a graduate student taking surveys of classical and modern rhetoric, I attempted to make a neat and tidy chart of "invention throughout the history of human kind" to use for class discussions and as a study guide for my comprehensive exams. What I soon discovered as I tried to write seminar papers for those courses was that my charts were pointless; I had decontextualized "invention" from the study of rhetoric as a whole to the point where I basically had rendered it meaningless. An orderly taxonomy or a handbook of sorts, at least an adequate version of such, will never exist because invention shares a complexly intertwined union with its complete rhetoric. If we attempt to isolate invention and its complicated variations from its time in place and history, its perceived cultural value, and its role in rhetorical education, we will end with a practice that is vacuous at best.

That said, I was to issue a "disclaimer" for my readers. For the moment, I want to dissociate a discussion of invention in writing from a discussion of writing inventions. In other words, I want to examine the act of invention—finding content for writing—independent of the emerging technologies one might use for the purpose of invention. Such a separation, however, won't be possible to maintain for long. For now, though, I want to begin by laying a general foundation, a starting place, for what I mean by this term—*invention*. Invention is contextual, both as a practice and as a subject of inquiry, and a useful study of invention must remain contextualized with particular attention paid to how it is defined, how and when it transpires, with whom it occurs, and how it is taught.

Folks are usually surprised when I let them know that I love teaching first-year college composition. The reasons are many, most of which have to do with the growth and change so visible at this level. At the same time, I think the course keeps me grounded in who our students are. By "our students," I mean those who we see entering our schools and programs and colleges and universities—the specific institutions where we teach. With certain exceptions, first-year college writing courses represent a true cross section of who is entering college at a given moment. First, these students typically choose a section of the course because it fits into their schedules (at some schools, students don't choose at all—they are randomly placed in sections). And in most cases, students aren't aware of teachers' reputations to guide their decisions, nor are they signing up for courses en masse with their friends. So throughout an academic year, where it is not unlikely for me to teach this course every term, I can't help but get a good sense of who our students are.

Over the past ten years teaching this course at two different institutions, I see that the makeup of our student body continues to become increasingly diverse as more and more different types of people have the opportunity to attend college (although I fear this trend might end as various constituencies chip away at affirmative action and certain scholarships with no regard for the positive outcomes of these programs). At my campus, this diversity is represented mostly in age and economic background, as well as in an interesting mix of first- and multigenerational college students. A friend at a private college sees almost all eighteen-year-old, affluent students whose parents are almost all college educated, yet who are vibrantly diverse in race and religion. So I'm cautioned at this point to think that I can paint a context for invention that I have called for that easily and neatly extends to "our students." My discussions of students in this text are intended to invite multiple contexts for thinking about college writers—my writers, your writers, our writers.

Even after recognizing such diversity among our students and between our student populations, I think there is a common context where we all can begin to think about invention. Like all of us, our students seek models, both indirectly and directly, as a way of recognizing and making sense of the world. Cognitive psychologists refer to this as schema theory, the idea that individuals store frames of reference used to organize and understand experience. Writing scholars have been particularly interested in this phenomenon because they believe that readers and writers look to the world for models of written communication, internalizing their forms, their structures, and their conventions (Beach and Liebman-Klein, 1986, 64–65). They call on content schemata to interpret the meaning of a text while relating the text meaning to prior knowledge and experience. On the other hand, they call on formal schemata when they arrange structures in order to make sense of the meaning of the text (Kucer, 1987, 31). Although it is possible for readers and writers to fail to relate information to a known structure, and also possible for readers and writers to generate text without knowledge of any structure, competent readers and writers allow these internalized structures to guide their written language processes (Flood and Lapp, 1987). Typically, teachers who subscribe to this theory involve students with the discourse of the academy, hoping that these are the forms, structures, and conventions that are internalized. Schema theory, however, is hardly limited to the study of academic written discourse. In fact, schema theory may be more applicable to our students' difficulties with written discourse if we begin to take into account the many other-than-academic textual world models that students internalize.

Currently, I find that the discourse models presented to my students are overwhelmingly fragmented, legitimizing the sound bite in their view; for many, this is the dominant communication system they know. The criticism that greets them at every turn in the academy asserts that they are heavily influenced by, if not completely entrenched in, a sound bite mentality pervasive in their worlds: the color-coded *USA Today*; the music video that not only tells a story in under three minutes but does so with hundreds of fractional images; the evening news that scans international hotspots in under thirty seconds; "Just say no." Condemnation of this world, most often from the likes of would-be education reformists, implies a chargeable cause and effect: Students can't pay attention for any sustained amount of time; they can't maintain interest, or worse yet, they have no interest to begin with; they tend toward the superficial; they don't read books; they are addicted to screen-feeding; they opt for easy answers and quick fixes. Unfortunately, these charges usually land square on my students' shoulders rather than on their environment that, for example, devalues reading or force-feeds the screen.

I unequivocally resist the scornful reproach that faults students and holds them responsible for what they fail to bring to our classrooms. Our students *do* come to our classes with worldviews, with textual experiences, and with developed schemata, even if these stem from sources outside those that the academy tends to value. I argue that we, as teachers of these students, fail to recognize their schemata and, as a result, fail to effectively use what our students know—their prior knowledge—in our pedagogies. In many ways, we are confronted with a simple power struggle: Whose world is valued? Or whose world is more pervasive where? But I contend that the questions shift and the power struggles dissipate when we ask: In what ways can writing instruction pull our worlds together? How can we take what we know about teaching writing—the complex theories of our field—and apply them to the conditions of our students and their worlds, and vice versa?

In *Fragments of Rationality: Postmodernity and the Subject of Composition*, Lester Faigley points out that "there are very few calls to celebrate the fragmentary and chaotic currents of change" in composition studies (1992, 14). I would add that there are few calls to celebrate the fragmentary and chaotic worldviews and learning approaches that many of us are seeing in our composition students, too. I am not suggesting that we begin treating the sound bite as legitimate student research, as legitimate exploration for their work. (Interestingly, a good sound bite in the eyes of, for example, the advertising industry, is not an easy text to write. The process almost always entails beginning with the complex, the big picture, and then reducing it while maintaining rhetorical elements such as audience, purpose, message, image, etc. Yet, the sound bite is intended to be easy to read. The sound bite does not invite exploration or criticism. It invites its consumer to accept and believe and be done with. It rarely suggests relationships and connections.) We could continue working in ways that writing teachers have been for years: Introduce students to a learning culture that involves them in complex written texts and extended discussions that move beyond sound bite, surface conversation. In many cases, I embrace this as one of our teaching goals. However, in light of what I see in my own students, I think we are falling short of the complete picture if we stop there. To only value written culture (as academics typically do) implies that our students have failed themselves and that they come to our classes as empty vessels, lacking the abilities and experiences necessary for academic success. If the sound bite or other aspects of fragmented postmodernism form the texts of our students' worlds, then we need to offer purposeful, alternative writing instruction that teaches them to make connections between sound bites, thus creating more complex texts. Furthermore, we need to teach students to deal with—describe, analyze, criticize—the fragmented texts they confront and that confront them and define ways that these texts can be both explored and connected to others so that students can learn the nature of in-depth examination. Of course, such a pedagogy means we as teachers must become familiar with and, as difficult as it may seem, accept as a reality the fragmented textual worlds of our students.

Moments of Invention

Investigating the textual worlds familiar to our students offers us a way to begin looking at invention and invention instruction. Compositionists generally see invention as the art of "gathering information about a problem and asking fruitful questions" (Young, Becker, and Pike, 1970, 120). Much like my father's process of invention, this includes recalling that which is already known and finding something new (D'Angelo, 1984, 202). Emphasized throughout a history of rhetorical invention are *systematic* methods, or heuristics, with which one discovers ideas for writing. In this book, I am less concerned with systematic tasks than I am with the multitude of ways in which discoveries are made and are later materialized in a written text. I'm not dismissing heuristic methods; quite often, discoveries—good ones, at that—occur because of orderly, methodical procedure. And whereas very little of my teaching practice could be described as heuristic in approach, much of what I am going to describe in this book employs detailed method. My wish is to explore the bigger picture of invention, one that complements the systematic approach with more whimsical, haphazard, at times playful, accidental, and random methods of discovery. Like the bits and pieces found in my father's garage, the fragmented textual worlds of our students are often situated in this picture.

Invention, orderly or not, in most cases can be described as a recursive series of events whose surface features can be described:

- Invention in writing occurs when a writer makes a connection between two or more initial discoveries. At least one of these initial discoveries is external (what the writer encounters), and at least one is internal (what the writer recalls from within). Even if the writer sees a new connection between two internal discoveries, both of which were recalled from within, he or she was able to do so because of an encounter with something external—however small, sometimes not even discernible—that allowed that connection to be made. Likewise, if the writer makes a connection between two external discoveries, something internal—possibly nothing more than basic interpretation—pushes the connection.

- The connection itself is formed into and becomes something new to the writer—an invented discovery. However, this invented discovery is still just that—a discovery—and belongs only to the writer; it exists in a rather chaotic and scrambled form—thought—in the writer's mind.

- As the writer commits the invented discovery to writing, external and internal discoveries continue to be made. He or she is confronted with rhetorical consideration of role, purpose, audience, additional information and insight, and the use of a language system. This written invention forms and re-forms along the way, a process of maturation.

In a great deal of composition instruction, invention often has been treated as a single art form, or a single act of creativity, something that comes first, before writing. Some of my early training as a teacher of writing insisted that students needed to follow a unified process of prewriting, writing, and rewriting. "Brainstorming" was often coupled with techniques of clustering, freewriting, and branching, but all of this activity, I was told, was "prewriting," which was to take place early in the step-by-step process called "writing." As demonstrated by the model above and throughout this book, I reject the notion that invention could be monoexperiential, let alone the idea that it is not a part of "writing." Instead, I see invention as a layering of episodes, with each episode becoming what I will refer to as a "moment of invention." These moments occur when students notice something and when they see relationships and make connections. Furthermore, when students make connections between two or more moments of invention, they experience yet another, richer moment of invention as they create a mental text of sorts, a link between two or more moments, that begins to pull together their fragmented experience. (One might imagine water drops merging—tiny ones combining to make small ones, small ones to medium, medium to large, finally becoming a pool.) The goal, then, is to teach our students to seek out multiple and diverse moments of invention in order to see productive connections that will result in rich, elaborate, and plentiful written inventions that are real in purpose.

Unfortunately, descriptions of invention, including the one above, are often less than effective because they imply a level of proficiency that excludes many of our students. I believe, beginning in the tradition of Aristotle and carrying through to current convention in composition pedagogy, that the art(s) of invention can be taught. However, in order to be taught, the process needs to include a theory of learning and a theory of instruction. For example, experienced writers often complete a process of invention automatically. One might argue that automaticity, as learning theorists call it, is a signifier of proficiency. I argue, though, that it is not the *only* sign of proficiency. For many students, and for a very long time, this process may not become automatic. (How many times has a student come to us with, for example, two ideas and said, "I don't know what to do with this," when the connections between the two discoveries and the ways to move into invention are more than obvious to us?) The process outlined above can also be effective when the writer, rather than functioning "automatically," is highly self-aware. In other words, an awareness of *invention processes* and the ability to articulate *specific acts of invention* also signify proficiency. This latter kind of proficiency is within the grasp of many of our students. Therefore, implicit to a theory of moments of invention is metacognition, an awareness of mental processes involved in the act of learning. Moments of invention require that writers are aware of the connections that they see while constructing knowledge. Therefore, the more numerous and diverse the connections they make, the richer these moments of invention and our students' learning experiences will be.

A Point of Invention/Contention

My own college composition instruction becomes more and more vivid to me the longer I teach writing and the more my students share with me stories of their own English education backgrounds. I attended a liberal arts college of about six hundred students supported by a small, almost completely full-time and tenured/tenure-track faculty. First-year English consisted of a full year of coursework: one semester of introductory composition and another semester divided evenly between research paper writing and speech. I remember approaching this sequence of courses with great enthusiasm. Based on a placement essay, entitled something like, "Bullshit Makes the World Go 'Round," illustrating the evils of gossip, I was enrolled in an advanced composition class, which we affectionately referred to as "the honors rejects"—we didn't quite make it into the honors section, we were told, but we showed a skill level that surpassed the rest of the entering freshman class and therefore required a more challenging level of instruction.

I didn't know better at the time, but really, that course was anything but "challenging" in terms of truly involving students in their investigations of writing topics. Most will recognize my composition instruction as nothing more than the five-paragraph theme in a most reductive sense. *Writing to the Point: Six Basic Steps* (Kerrigan, 1979) was the text adopted by the department of English, and its formulaic philosophies and methods were adopted in every course in every discipline at my college (except for one radical history professor who refused to conform). Students, in their course syllabi from English to sociology to biology, were repeatedly faced with variations on this theme: "You will be expected to write papers according to the methods taught by the college's Department of English. If you did not take your freshman English courses in this department, you should purchase *Writing to the Point: Six Basic Steps* from the campus bookstore." Faculty and students alike referred to these six basic steps as "the Kerrigan method," named after the textbook's author, William J. Kerrigan (1979):

Step 1: Write a short, simple declarative sentence that makes one statement. [Also called a "sentence X."]

Step 2: Write three sentences about the sentence in Step 1.

Step 3: Write four or five sentences about each of the three sentences in Step 2.

Step 4: Make the material in the four or five sentences in Step 3 as specific and concrete as possible. Go into detail. Give examples.

Step 5: In the first sentence of the second paragraph and of every paragraph following [the second and third sentences from Step 2], insert a clear reference to the idea of the preceding paragraph.

> Step 6: Make sure every sentence in your theme is connected with, and makes clear reference to, the preceding sentence.

As absurd as this list seems, I'm afraid that I have not simplified the method at all. This is the Kerrigan method. It further prescribes an awkward format on writing essays that is bizarre at best. Students were instructed to turn in final essays that followed this format and could be penalized for any mistakes in their presentation:

> X. Step 1 sentence goes here.
>
> 1. Step 2 sentence goes here.
>
> 2. Step 2 sentence goes here.
>
> 3. Step 2 sentence goes here.
>
> -
>
> X. Repeat Step 1 sentence here
>
> 1. Repeat Step 2 sentence here. The paragraph made up of Steps 3 through 6 would follow.
>
> 2. Repeat Step 2 sentence here. The paragraph made up of Steps 3 through 6 would follow.
>
> 3. Repeat Step 2 sentence here. The paragraph made up of Steps 3 through 6 would follow.
>
> A short, rounding-off sentence would conclude the essay.

To reinforce this formulaic method, students were asked to respond to assignments from the text, like this one following a chapter on Step 4:

> Carefully make up a sentence X for yourself, and keeping in mind the requirements of Steps 2, 3, and 4, write a theme on it. Don't forget to add a short rounding-off sentence at the end of your theme. (Kerrigan, 1979, 82)

At times, students were given a little more direction in topic and a little less in formula, although certainly, by the time they saw an assignment like this, they were able to recite the "six basic steps" with ease (in fact, I remember a pop quiz or two that tested my ability to state the steps):

> Write a theme on the following sentence X: "A student must have a regular schedule of study." (1979, 60)

The text also asked students to complete exercises that would help illustrate its prescribed writing instruction:

> Go to any two articles (but not news stories in a newspaper) and examine the beginnings of the paragraphs. Prove to yourself that the writers have followed Step 5, and notice the various ways they have done it. (1979, 120)

And in a chapter entitled, "A Breathing Space," student writers were presented with a list of summaries and reminders of what they had learned thus far, which included:

> - Steps 1, 2, 3, and 4 are not rules that someone has decided on, like the rules of a game. They can't be changed, as in the case of the elimination some years ago of the center jump in basketball. No, they arise out of the very nature of writing, and are as necessary for writing as heat is for cooking, cloth for clothing, fuel for a motor.
>
> - Do not hope to find either a sentence X or any topic sentences in all that you read, especially in articles of information. You will rarely find a sentence X or topic sentences in stories, of course. But when you read, always try to follow any writer's *explanation*.
>
> - No one can write a theme on a topic. You must write a sentence about a topic, then write the theme strictly on that sentence. Once that sentence is well written, the theme nearly writes itself, because that sentence dictates what must be said.

> • Students' themes should not be written on their opinions, nor
>   on vague notions they have picked up from their reading on
>   "Pollution," "Communism," "The Energy Shortage," "Infla-
>   tion," "Capital Punishment." Students should write on what
>   they have observed first-hand, or on what they are learning in
>   an orderly and detailed way in their other classes. Comple-
>   mentarily, students should be encouraged to be gaining
>   knowledge and understanding, not forming "opinions."
>
> • Do not attempt to be interesting. (Remember, that is not your
>   purpose.) You will not be called on to write for a reader who
>   is not already interested. And what your reader is interested
>   in is a good, clear explanation of something, backed up by
>   real clear, convincing details and examples. (Directly quoted,
>   1979, 98–99)

The Kerrigan method professes a notion of reading and writing contra-
dictory to what most of us practice as sound composition instruction today. In
fact, it professes a notion of reading and writing that often contradicts itself—
just what *is* the point of *Writing to the Point*? One need not struggle to see the
messages students (myself included) were forced to grapple with after a semester of composition, only to be reinforced throughout four years of academic
study: Writing is not a complex process, but rather an algorithm in six easy
steps; all writing looks and behaves in the same way; student writing that does-
n't fulfill Steps 1–6 is not good writing, yet "other" writing may not fulfill all
the tenets of the method; the writing that students produce has little or nothing
to do with the writing students will read; topics are easily reduced to a simple,
declarative sentence; students' opinions don't matter and therefore should not
be expressed or developed in writing; students have superficial experiences and
know little and should continue to know little about pressing issues; information and knowledge exist in a vacuum and should not inform student opinions;
student writing should not attempt to engage an audience.

Ironically, the college called this course *Rhetoric* 101.

Little changed in philosophy between a semester of introductory composition and the course on research paper writing. Yet two differences in these
courses posed an even more significant problem than the apparent incongruity
in the Kerrigan Method: First, I was expected to write longer papers, casting
aside bizarre formatting for what most would recognize as an academic paper;
and second, I was expected to consult outside sources and incorporate them effectively into my writing, but only after I had stated my sentence X and turned
it in for teacher approval. We didn't have a text for this course other than a

packet of information on library resources and styles of documentation. This course was not centered around any particular seminar topic. There were no common reading assignments that gave the course any uniform content to explore. Instead, we were expected to find something that we wanted to write about—the theory, I suppose, was that students would be more inclined to write well when they were allowed to choose topics that interested them (yet another contradiction of the program). As in all other courses we would take, we were told that the Kerrigan Method would serve us well; there was no need to consult any other text about writing.

"I don't understand how the Kerrigan Method works in a ten-page paper. Won't those be really long paragraphs?" This seemed like a legitimate question at the time that I asked it. Today, it sounds more like one of those questions that makes teachers think, "Where did I go wrong?" With some practice, I had mastered the formula: Given a topic, I could write a sentence X and fill in Steps 2–6 better than anyone on that campus. My papers were taken to English Department meetings as models of how well the Kerrigan Method was working, and I was soon hired in the writing center to help struggling freshmen who had no idea what to do when their teachers stamped, "You need details and examples in this paper. See Step 4." I could tell them how to "do" Step 4. But ask me to write a ten-page research paper, and I was at a loss, faced with cognitive dissonance at every turn.

Once I was assured that I must have more than five paragraphs in a ten-page paper, my next battle was finding a topic for my paper. In conference with my professor, I told him that I wanted to write about the Moral Majority. He told me that I needed to choose a topic about which I knew something so that my paper would be more than a patchwork of quotes. But I did know something about the Moral Majority. They were responsible for canceling my favorite television program, "Soap," for its sexual content and religious satire, and I wanted to learn more about how this group of people operated and how they had the power to influence the television industry. My professor asked me if I had a thesis in mind, and I told him that I strongly disagreed with what the Moral Majority had done, but that I didn't know too many of the details. My professor told me that such a thesis would be too opinionated, and that I needed to develop a strong sentence X, simple and declarative, before I began to conduct my research. He strongly suggested that I find another topic.

After many pained hours of sitting alone in my dorm room trying to develop a sentence X that met all the requirements that I had been told were hard-and-fast rules of all writing, I finally reworked a topic on the Moral Majority that my professor approved of. I clearly remember being less enthused about writing it than any other paper I had written thus far in college. The paper I wrote had more to do with Jerry Falwell than it did with what made "Soap" so offensive to his followers that it led them to target an entire television network. The paper had more to do with a history of Falwell's organization than it did with the manipulative tactics of an organization that was developing significant political strength and stamina at a time when I was developing significant political interest and identity.

I was less than satisfied with the grade I received on that paper, but even more confused by the rationale for the grade: My paper lacked development. I had treated the topic too superficially. Just as I had begun to develop a topic, I moved onto the next. In Kerrigan-ese, I suppose that meant that I needed more Steps 3 and 4. My professor, recognizing my difficulties, decided to stray from the tried-and-true six-step method and copied a number of pages from a text that perhaps would give me a different framework for looking at my writing than Kerrigan had. He also thought that a different view of writing might help me when I was tutoring students who also were having trouble with development. *The Lively Art of Writing* (Payne, 1982) offers guidance in "The Shorter Paper" and "The Longer Paper," which consists of the ever-so-popular introduction as inverted triangle, body as a series of rectangles, and conclusion as opposite from the introduction. Both examples illustrated how to arrange a paper and suggested that with "The Longer Paper," there was more flexibility in organization granted to the writer when he or she had more text to work with, but in the end, an essay should still "look" like the figure.

Today, I am not surprised that *The Lively Art of Writing* really didn't help me with my problems of topic development. My difficulties didn't lie with how to organize my writing. If I knew anything, I knew how to organize a paper. What I didn't know how to do was to participate in purposeful acts of invention in order to create meaning out of a "suitable" topic for an academic paper, how to research that topic effectively, and how to develop that topic as fully as possible within the constraints of an assignment that asked for a ten-page paper.

What Writers Do

The writing instruction I received as a first-year college student privileged form over content. Interestingly enough, the evaluation of final written products, both by the professor and by myself, privileged content in a manner inconsistent with this pedagogical practice. Invention, exploration, and topic development were viewed as skills that follow or are secondary to proficiency in form and structure and, therefore, don't necessitate instruction. In her discussion of why basic writers are prone to produce "underdeveloped or meaningless texts," Marcia Dickson refers to formulaic writing instruction as a possible culprit: "The student merely has to fill in the blanks with information. This example of textual construction . . . not only encourages the student to fill in the blanks in a *correct* form—introduction, body, and conclusion—it implies that all good writing will fit this pattern. Writing is a simple matter of formula over matter" (1995, 70). As much as teachers think that such forms provide students with a structure that will help their writing, Mike Rose found in one study that students who suffer from writer's block were writing under a set of "rules or with planning strategies that impeded rather than enhanced the composing process," thus inhibiting their growth as writers (1980, 390). In the case of the Kerrigan Method, the six-step form was such a planning strategy, dramatically limiting the vast possibilities students could encounter and utilize to develop their writing.

Writing instruction that espouses rigid forms and formulas over discovery and exploration allows, and perhaps pushes, our students to compose coherent yet empty themes disguised as academic writing. The pedagogy outlined above is certainly extreme but is the kind that Dickson warns "is more representative than we would like to believe" (1995, 70). The problem here runs deeper than asking students to fill in the blanks, and it runs deeper than asking them to fill in the blanks correctly. Such writing pedagogy disregards the need students have for instruction in how to *look for* the blanks, how to *find* the blanks, how to *recognize* what the blanks are, and how to *make* the blanks. This is the essence of what good writing *process* is because these are the problems of writing.

Most well-seasoned writers understand this. Their processes, though, may have become so rooted in automaticity that they are unconscious of what they are doing when they write. Interestingly, many proficient writers claim that they were never "taught" how to invent, how to find topics, at least not in the way we think about teaching writing today. Rather, they were and are tireless consumers and producers of written texts of various shapes and forms in a variety of settings who have absorbed a range of processes from their readings and struggles. Furthermore, experienced writers understand the important role that disorder plays in discovery. They have found the benefits of disorder, which, by its very nature, may uncover what lies beneath the surface, below what is only apparent at first glance. And clearly, most experienced writers possess an urgency for writing in the first place that comes from their awareness of and an engagement with their surroundings.

Our students, though, are often less than seasoned. They require instruction that not only teaches them how to find and solve the problems of writing, but also how to do so with the capacity that proficient writers employ. Where should our instruction begin? Does such instruction have a discernible starting place?

It would be tempting at this point to exclaim, "The computer!"

Tempting indeed, but somewhat premature. I will commit, however, to the claim that computer technology is an undeniable player in the context of students' writing today and, as I stated earlier, any discussion of teaching invention and student writing must include an examination of the worlds where our students live. These worlds include technology, and, more and more, the worlds where they write and *learn* to write include technology. Yet, I'm still not prepared to couple invention in writing with the technologies we may use to write. I believe we first need to flush out some of what we know about proficient writers—their behaviors and habits, their experiences, their abilities—and bring this to articulating a theory of computers and writing instruction.

In an attempt to understand how experienced writers invent, I want to begin by briefly looking at two areas: *noticing as exigency*, and *disorder and reflection*. These areas, I would argue, are interdependent and devoid of particular order or importance. The distinctions I make in the discussion that follows may seem to imply a hierarchical linearity I do not necessarily envision. However, each of these areas seems equally important to the process of invention; they are rarely as separable as presented here.

Noticing as Exigency.   Creators—visual artists, composers, writers—depend upon their ability to notice. This concept of noticing is difficult to define, partly because noticing appears to be small, quick. The act of noticing is often, unfortunately, slighted at the expense of the more thorough processes of perception and observation. For example, Rudolf Arnheim contemplates visual perception:

> A difference between passive reception and active perceiving is contained even in elementary visual experience. As I open my eyes, I find myself surrounded by a given world. . . . It exists by itself without my having done anything noticeable to produce it. But is this awareness of the world all there is to perception? Is it even its essence? By no means. That given world is only the scene on which the most characteristic aspect of perception takes place. Through that world roams the glance, directed by attention, focusing the narrow range of sharpest vision now on this, now on that spot, following the flight of a distant sea gull, scanning a tree to explore its shape. This eminently active performance is what is truly meant by visual perception. . . . The world emerging from this perceptual exploration is not immediately given. Some of its aspects build up fast, some slowly, and all of them are subject to continued confirmation, reappraisal, change, completion, correction, deepening of understanding. (1969, 14–15)

Although he mentions "the glance," Arnheim's concerns lie with the ability to actively focus. Ann Berthoff continues in this vein,

> Any composition course should begin, I believe, with exercises in observation. . . . The reason for a writer to have a lot of practice in looking is not to gain skill in amassing detail to be deployed in descriptive writing. . . . The real reason for beginning with observation is that looking—and looking again—engages the mind, and until that happens, no authentic composing is going to take place. (1984, 3)

Demetrice Worley found that students excel in writing when they are taught to visualize, a skill left behind very early in school curricula (1994, 139). I know of no writing teacher who would argue that students don't need extensive experience in perception, in recognizing and interpreting, becoming aware and coming to understand. Nor do I know of any compositionist who would find what Berthoff calls "exercises in observation" out of the ordinary in a writing class, where students learn to sustain their gaze both to gain insight and to engage deep thinking. Yet Arnheim, Berthoff, and Worely speak of something larger than I am concerned with at this point. These writers' texts indicate how little attention writing teachers give the act of *noticing*. It is a difficult act to define, which may be why it is not often taught.

I define noticing as allowing one's eye to be caught. My use of the passive voice here is intentional, for I wish to impose a certain level of passivity in noticing. Paradoxically, though, such passivity requires activity of sorts. Noticing can occur when one suspends or lets down one's own guard. It is a matter of allowing oneself to be unfocused and inattentive and pervious, of widening the scope of one's purview and dissipating the boundaries that limit that scope. (The difference I am making here is mirrored in my father heading to the store with list in hand versus him strolling down the aisles, waiting to notice something he comes in contact with.) In other words, it is a matter of actively deciding to become passive so that one's eye can be caught.

Many teachers of writing may be alarmed by this suggestion, that passivity of any kind could actually become a part of writing pedagogy. As a profession, I feel we are near obsession in seeing a dichotomy between the active and the passive, when such a distinction is not as clear as one may think. Teachers claim we want our students to be *active*, not *passive* learners, as if our students are either one or the other because of a simple change in cognitive processes. I would argue that our students are active creatures in many regards and that what we consider to be their passivity is instead quite deliberate. Our constant push toward what we consider active learning may fail our students in an important part of problem finding.

A distinction between active and passive behavior is not nearly as telling to teachers of writing as is the distinction between productive and nonproductive. I once asked a sophomore composition class to write a critical response to a representation of a group of people or a social issue found on any popular television program. One student's response to the assignment still resounds in my mind: "I watch television for entertainment. I don't want to think about it, I just want to sit back and enjoy it." Such resistance on his part is not uncommon; those teachers who incorporate current popular cultural studies practice in their writing classes are often told by their students that their assignments "ruin" the entertainment value of television, film, music, etc. Many would be quick to label this student's attitude as "passive," a label that stems from the student watching television passively. I would disagree with this assertion. This student's attitude is an example of the active passivity I describe above, but it is also *nonproductive*. The student has actively chosen how he wants to view that television program. And whereas he may not be engaged in active, critical thinking about the program, he has certainly and quite actively defined the act of viewing for himself. He has built up his guard, limited his scope, and prevented his eye from being caught.

A new conflict arises for the student with a writing assignment such as that described in the above scenario. In many ways, the student's resistance toward noticing might stem from the fact that he was in a position where he had to respond to a writing assignment. I had directed him toward a very specific type of noticing. Whereas I expected his writing to grow from what he noticed, the assignment—an academic essay requiring description and analysis—loomed overhead. The assignment provided the exigency for writing more than anything the student could have noticed on his own. For writers who are not writing under the constraints of some type of assignment, noticing implies an interest, not only in a subject but also in the act of noticing itself; one notices because he or she becomes engaged by the act of noticing. Writers' dependency on noticing, however, is derived from their ability to use it as exigency. Noticing might be a beginning, but it is not *only* a beginning. In other words, noticing isn't a starting place in that all invention grows from one instance. (It is at this point that we move closer toward Arnheim and Berthoff's thoughts about perception and observation.) Noticing is a continual process because of the questions that writers ask themselves when they notice something. In fact, noticing may very well be a question in and of itself. The very moment one notices something, one begins asking, "Have I ever experienced anything like this before?" The question is implicit in the act of noticing. One only notices something that is different or similar or peculiar or problematic, making comparisons and seeing relationships between what has been noticed and what is already known.

Relationships and Connections: Disorder and Reflection.

The questions of noticing help writers to establish relationships, to see commonality between two or more things. When writers can make connections between two or more ideas or pieces of information, they are making meaning and creating knowledge. The more seemingly different the ideas or information linked, the more complicated the relationship, and thus the knowledge, constructed. David Bleich relates this to cognitive stereoscopy:

> Knowledge is always a re-cognition because it is a seeing through one perspective superimposed in another in such a way that the one perspective does not appear to be prior to the other. Because the perspectives are different, or heretofore unrelated in our minds, the new knowledge is sometimes described as the "aha" experience, or surprising and satisfying at once. (1986, 99)

These relationships are drawn from connections between what is already known, prior knowledge, and what is new, although the prior knowledge often remains invisible during this process. In other words, if I see a connection between two facts that I did not know, new knowledge is constructed by bringing these facts together; however, the relationship is supported, often unconsciously, by what I already know, for prior knowledge in some way has allowed me to make the connection in the first place. (This helps to explain why some connections that seem obvious to the instructor sometimes are not available to the student.) Similarly, contact with an external idea often brings together two or more internal ideas, yet the external entity is often dropped or lost, serving as the occasion for the connection but adding little in information to the newly created knowledge.

Writers' connections can only be as rich as the opportunities that make them possible. The more complicated the approach toward a particular topic, the greater the opportunities for seeing relationships and making meaning. In their study of children writers, Bereiter and Scardamalia found that children who had difficulty generating text were typically having difficulty inventing (1987, 62). In addition, they also state, "All the evidence we know of indicates that children's main problem with content is in getting access to, and giving order to, the knowledge they have" (1987, 64). Bereiter and Scardamalia reveal two areas of concern when considering invention in writing: finding content and dealing with discovered knowledge.

In order to find content, proficient writers purposely place themselves in disorderly situations where relationships and connections can become possible, recognizing the value of a scattered and jumbled perspective. If those disorderly situations don't appear to exist, or are not easily visible, they take painstaking steps to create disorderly situations. As writers find content through disorder, they use the act of writing to bring order to and thus create their newly discovered knowledge.

Writers often seek out collaborative situations—the chaos of working directly with other human beings—in order to bring various perspectives to the act of problem finding as well as problem solution. Not only can collaboration reveal missed or unexplored content, but rich collaborative experiences can provide the tapestry of connections writers need to create knowledge. Collaboration can aid in the search for content both as deliberate situations (writers' groups, brainstorming meetings, feedback to written texts) and unplanned occurrences (casual conversations and heated arguments). To illustrate, we can consider the writing behaviors of my colleagues and myself who teach English on our small campus. We work on writing projects that are both individually authored, where only one name is listed as the author, and collaboratively authored, where all names are listed. However, anyone who has watched us write understands how artificial these labels are and, thus, how uncomfortable I am using them. The nature of the writing task dictates what type of collaborative experience is used, but in all cases, our meetings occur on a continuum of what could be considered deliberate to haphazard. If we are assigned a writing task, our collaboration usually begins with some type of a scheduled meeting—in the faculty conference room, over Chinese food, on the Internet. Other writing projects, those that are not charged to us, for example, by our dean or by the chair of our campus computer committee, arise out of corridor conversations where one of us begins to tell the others about something he or she noticed, where sometimes tempers flair or loud laughter resounds, and where colleagues from various disciplines come out of their offices to add, "It's not like that with my students at all. I think students' misperceptions of, for example, geology come from. . . ." These collaborative situations enrich our writing by disclosing to us a disorder that subsequently allows us to invent content. Regardless of how collaboration looks, key to all collaborative situations is that multiple world views are being brought to the table in what John Trimbur calls "intellectual negotiation," where engaged individuals make a commitment "to take their ideas seriously, to fight for them, and to modify or revise them in light of others' ideas" (qtd. in Wiener, 1986, 55).

Contact with others is not the only means writers use to create disorder and to find content. Contact with other written texts is integral to understanding the role of disorder in finding content for writing. One's purpose for writing may often dictate the type of disorder one searches for or is willing to create for oneself. Likewise, the purpose for reading a written text dictates the role it will play in the disorder of finding content. For example, the differences between an Associated Press story reporting recent Center for Disease Control statistics of HIV transmission and Michael Bronski's "Magic and AIDS: Presumed Innocent" are apparent (1993). The writer of the AP story avoids chaos; his or her purpose for writing is to present statistical information succinctly and concisely. The goal of this author's writing process is to find order as soon as possible—if not to begin with order. Bronski, on the other hand, formulating his thesis that society finds comfort in labeling people with AIDS either innocent or guilty, needed to consider metaphors of illness, construct a history of AIDS, pore over interviews with Magic Johnson, and read other writers' perspectives on Johnson's disclosure that he had contracted HIV (1993). Although I cannot be certain, my sense is that his goal was to bring as much disorder to his invention process as necessary in order to find complex content and to use composing as a way of bringing order to that content without reducing the content's multileveled nature. Similarly, the reader of an AP story probably would not experience disorder by processing the text alone, though if the text were aligned with conflicting statistical data presented in similar types of texts, disorder in a reader's thinking about AIDS might occur. No careful reader, however, could find Bronski's analysis of "innocent" and "guilty" simplistic. The very experience of reading Bronski's elaborate arguments, at least reading the text carefully, would bring about a sense of chaos in the reader. If the reader looked at the two articles together, where Bronski takes statistical data like that represented by the AP writer to task, a different experience with disorder would probably ensue. Consequently, the contact that readers have with these two texts would result in very different opportunities for disorder, and thus for finding content.

Once they find it, proficient writers and our student writers often differ in how they deal with complex content. Bereiter and Scardamalia admit that "there could be large differences in outcome depending on the writer's knowledge of the topic of discourse and on the writer's sophistication in the literary genre" (1987, 10). They point to the difference between *knowledge telling*, a composing model where writers offer "readily available knowledge" and "[rely] on already existing discourse-production skills" (1987, 9), and *knowledge transforming*, a model where writers participate in elaborate meaning making by discovering connections, making inferences, and drawing conclusions (1987, 10–12). Bereiter and Scardamalia are adamant in their stance that these models "refer to mental processes by which texts are composed, not to texts themselves" (1987, 13). In other words, one cannot tell which model of composing was responsible for the production of a text by looking at the text alone.

However, there are striking differences between our students' and more proficient writers' texts and composing behaviors when it comes to finding and dealing with complex content. When given a general topic with which to work, typically our students are willing to settle on simplistic approaches to content for writing whereas more proficient writers are more willing to explore more complex content in their writing. Research reviewed by Birnbaum shows that skilled readers and writers exhibit highly developed reflective abilities, mostly in their willingness to pause and deliberate while reading and writing. Kagan et al. term this difference the "reflective-impulsive dimension" (Birnbaum, 1986, 32). Reflectiveness is rooted in success, with writers pausing and deliberating in hopes of finding the best possible solutions. Impulsiveness, however, is rooted in failure, with writers' "anxiety over failure [leading] them to seize the first possible solution to a problem and give it public report" (Birnbaum, 1986, 32). Reflective readers and writers are better able to hypothesize, ask questions, recognize when to abandon a topic or an approach to processing a text. They also characterize reflective readers as those who are willing to reread a text when their interpretation isn't working and reflective writers as those who are willing to suspend their push toward a final product prematurely (Birnbaum,1986, 30–31). And finally, more proficient writers are able to sustain both complexities in subject and structure, not only because of prior knowledge and experience, but also because of their willingness to tolerate uncertainty, ambiguity, and interference while solving the problems of writing (Birnbaum, 1986, 33–40). When less proficient writers do adventure into more sophisticated approaches to topics, their writing often breaks down. In other words, as they struggle with difficult ideas, the formal structure of their writing often suffers. As a result, they are more likely to experience anxiety when dealing with difficult content and exhibit impulsive behavior by seizing the first possible solution to a problem.

What Students Do—or Don't Do

When we begin to think of "what writers do," no matter what research we cite or what processes we subscribe to, it is easy to compare "proficient" writers with our students. Perhaps this comes from a desire to have students participate in "real" writing acts that address "real" audiences in "real" rhetorical situations. At times I grow uneasy with the comparison as it often suggests that our students' abilities are somehow "artificial," or it implies a "deficiency" in our students that can quickly elevate to the damaging rhetoric of "a nation at risk," or "why Johnny can't read." When approached sensitively, though, a comparison between what experienced writers do and what our students do—or don't do, as the case may be—can further a context for teaching invention in composition.

I have been teaching introductory college writing, in its various forms, for thirteen years. In this time, I have made a number of observations not only about the students in my classes, but also about the "profession at large," if you will—the vast range of communities, knowledge, and practices that amount to this thing we call *composition*. When considered alone, my observations, I'm afraid, are hardly revolutionary; anyone who has spent even a short time working with college writers will recognize these profiles.

Observation:
Reading and Writing

Many students coming to college don't read and write much in their everyday lives. The reasons are many. For some it is a choice, while for many others it has more to do with the nature of literacy practices in their home cultures and communities. Consequently, they are relatively uncomfortable with and underprepared for the reading and writing tasks we ask them to take on in the classroom. This discomfort and lack of preparation has as much to do with experience as it does with proficiency. Regardless, a number of fundamental reading and writing problems surface regularly: erratic grammar, mechanical, and structural usage; an inability to summarize; a failure to distinguish between main points and supporting examples; a limited capability to move on a continuum from concrete to abstract to concrete again. Also, when faced with a problem while reading and writing, they fall back on formulaic approaches to writing (if, that is, they have these to fall back on in the first place) or look for easy, quick-fix solutions (again, that is, if they know where to find them). Furthermore, because of a lack of deep and continual experiences with reading and writing, students have difficulty discerning the conceptual notions that are the foundation of our courses: they have relatively no experience writing for situations that necessitate a studied understanding of audience; they do not regard writing

---

or reading as conversation; and they have great difficulty comprehending "situation" and "context" in writing. Finally, they have a superficial understanding of the connections between reading and writing and little to no awareness of the powerful potential of written text to simultaneously reflect, shape, and construct reality. In other words, they lack critical abilities and, thus, critical experiences, and this limitation prevents them from becoming truly engaged with written texts.

If students have such difficulty with reading and writing itself, it should not be surprising that I find student writers have limited experiences with, and, consequently, narrow definitions of research.

Observation:
Research

Research, in our students' minds, has very little to do with discovery, inquiry, and invention. In fact, they know very little about what it means "to research" a subject and, as a result, end up knowing very little about that which they are supposed to research for their coursework. They don't look at themselves as researchers who truly will develop expertise on a topic. Research to our students still means finding information that will make them *sound* like an expert on a particular topic. In addition, students see research only as a way to support claims, not as a process of discovery. In other words, they see research as finding information about a topic they have already decided upon, not a process of finding a topic or discovering a narrow angle on a topic. With topic firmly in mind, they push forward, failing to see connections between unseemingly similar ideas. At the same time, as much as students complain about assignments where they are forced to write on a particular topic, when they are asked to use research as a means of discovering a topic to write about, they resist, falling back on that stock list of general research paper topics (capital punishment, abortion, gun control, gang violence). Often, our students have "systematized" their perceptions of research (i.e., filling out notecards correctly or following "Turabian") to the extent that when they write, they are more apt to think about meeting assignment requirements and following a system of documentation so that they don't "lose points" when the paper is graded.

I, myself, have generated a number of responses to these two observations, the most obvious of which is, "Well, students are coming to college to become better readers and writers and explorers, to become a part of the academy where, we hope, reading and writing and discovery will become a part of their everyday lives. Let the work begin!"

Such work needs to grow from the belief that students' abilities with reading and writing are contingent upon multiple, diverse, and continual experiences with reading and writing. And for whatever reasons, and there are plenty, they are coming to the college classroom without these experiences. The best thing I can do is to immerse my students in a multitude of learning and instructional opportunities that allow them to see the ways that reading and writing feed into and enrich each other, as well as the ways that reading and writing can enhance and enliven their academic and nonacademic worlds.

I am certain that nothing bridges gaps between reading and writing as completely as does the process of research. In this sense of the word, I define research as a collection of rich, complex processes that includes a wide range of activities: library work, notetaking, introspection, testing, data collection, debate. Research is generation and creation. Exploration and discovery. Invention. In fact, I have come to see research and invention as inseparable concepts, virtually synonymous. Burkland and Petersen write:

> We want our students to learn not only how to do research, but also how to understand the process of research and of responding to reading in ways that make them active composers of meaning. . . . Research is a twofold process. On one hand, it is a search inside of oneself, what Donald Murray calls "recollecting." On the other hand, research is a search outside of oneself, a discovery and integration of what is known with what is not yet known. . . . Such research is not done only in the service of a "research paper," but is rather a way of thinking about both reading and existential experience. (1986, 189–90)

Burkland and Petersen charge that emphasis in research instruction is all too often placed on discovered facts rather than on discovery of the process of research. They suggest the usefulness of getting students to focus on research narratives, "a record of their associations, questions, and thoughts as they read" (1986, 194). In this way, students will come to see that reading, writing, and research are interconnected meaning-making acts.

Unfortunately, though, I find that our students routinely perform research activities in the noninventive manner that they have been taught. No surprise here: If students possess a reductive view of research, perhaps it is because we have taught them, in practice, this view. Considering the pervasive notecard mentality of research instruction in much English curriculum that I myself have experienced and witnessed, it is not difficult to see why students don't like research, and why they are not very good at it. Doug Brent describes his early accounts of teaching "the research paper":

> In the composition class, it typically occurs as a poorly understood, rather orphaned form when it appears at all. My own early attempts to teach students to write papers based on research were fraught with a profound sense of failure. My students learned how to use quotations, more or less: that is, they learned how many spaces to indent and on which side of the quotation marks to place the period. They learned how to find information in the library and how to document it when they used it. But their research papers, by and large, remained hollow imitations of research, collections of information gleaned from sources with little evaluation, synthesis, or original thought. They approached research as they would gathering shells at the beach, picking up ideas with interesting colors or unusual shapes and putting them in a bucket without regard for overall pattern. I was tempted to dismiss the research process as unteachable. (1992, xiii)

When rescued from "its ghetto in Week 7 of freshman composition" (1992, xiv), as Brent characterizes current practice, the research process is teachable, but only insofar as the research projects we assign in the first place are equally instructional and engaging. Such assignments, I would argue, then must mirror *real* research projects that require *real* research processes. My experience with students has led me to assert that they actually *like* the processes of exploring and discovering and inventing. But most are rarely offered the opportunity to participate in these learning activities in their courses to the point that they can become truly engaged. When they are encouraged—without limitations—to explore, while at the same time given instruction in systematic approaches and strategies toward research, they thrive.

Already alluded to, one other observation begins to simultaneously complicate and address a notion of students' experiences with reading, writing, and research.

Observation:
Awareness of Learning

Students are, in essence, unaware of how they learn. They certainly do learn, and they can tell us what they have learned. Also, they can articulate what may translate into "helpful hints about learning," like, "Try to avoid distractions when you are learning something difficult," and "I find it best to make an outline when I am studying for a test." What they don't understand is how those hints are related to real learning theory and vice versa. They are unaware of why, for example, distraction prevents them from learning something considered difficult, nor can they closely relate a process, such as outlining, to a task they are completing, such as studying for a test. It's not necessarily that they are incapable of understanding learning processes. Instead, students are rarely asked to pay attention to their own learning and the learning of others. In fact, such a concept is so new to many college learners that when they are asked to do so, their initial reaction is to resist, frequently claiming that making them accountable for what is, or what should be, "natural" or "automatic" interferes with *what* they are actually supposed to be learning.

At first, we might think of basic writing students as the only ones who have trouble articulating their thoughts about learning. In fact, a great deal of basic writing instruction deals with getting students to be more cognizant of their learning. Yet, this inability to label the processes of cognition runs throughout most of our student body. In 1987, the English Coalition Conference was organized to decide the directions that English studies should take into the twenty-first century. The coalition included three sectors, the elementary, the secondary, and the college, and all three came to a similar, encompassing conclusion: Students need to be involved in educational settings in which they can and will become responsible for their own learning (Lloyd-Jones and Lunsford, 1989). The coalition report recommends three principles on which to base a freshman composition course:

> The principle of critical inquiry suggests that students are in active control of their learning—using, analyzing, and evaluating language within different contexts. The collaborative model suggests that the teacher acts as an informed and challenging coach, offering multiple perspectives, while students practice and experience the kind of cooperation all citizens increasingly need. The concept of conscious theorizing about their learning and about how language works . . . allows students to understand the principles they follow and so enables them to transfer what they learn. (Lloyd-Jones and Lunsford, 1989, 28)

Further, in the forward to the coalition report, Wayne C. Booth cites the college sector's report: "We seek to prepare students . . . who are active learners and who are able to reflect critically on their own learning. . . . In an information age, citizens need to make meaning—rather than merely consume information" (1989, x).

The Technology of Invention

Thus far, I have deliberately isolated a discussion of a theory of invention with *the* invention that is the subject of this book: the computer. It has been an artificial separation, as my varied experiences with computer technology have significantly influenced how I perceive invention. One more observation will begin to connect the notion of invention I have thus far constructed in this chapter with computers.

Observation:
Computers

Many students come to college with a multitude of computer experiences and knowledge. For our traditional, right-out-of-high-school students, computer technology, of some sort, has been directly or indirectly a part of most of their academic and nonacademic lives. Many, for example, have had some kind of hands-on experience, from arcade video games to elaborate multimedia systems. Many were curious children and the first to learn to operate the "simple" remote controlled on-screen programming VCR in their homes. Others had some type of computer training, probably in high school (and as time goes on, perhaps much earlier in their education). Yet, access to technology obviously determines experience with technology, and access varies tremendously from school to school, from home to home. Thus, some students come to us with little experience and virtually no training in computers. They have waited on the sidelines, rather impatiently, for their chance to use that which they have been watching from a distance. Interestingly enough, they show little fear of the technology itself. Our nontraditional-aged students (at my school, these are students who are returning to college after the age of twenty-five) come to school with even more varied experiences. They are returning to school after a long time away from the classroom. But many have access to computers at home or work, are self-taught, and have had contact with a wide array of applications, including word processing, desktop publishing, computer networking, spreadsheets, and databases. Other nontraditional-aged students, though, are returning to school perhaps after raising a family or finding themselves unemployed and unemployable as the nature of the economy, and thus the workplace, changes from a labor-centered one to an information-centered one. The computers present an unavoidable challenge; these students' approaches are either enthusiastic, certain that knowledge of the computers will secure their success in the academy and beyond, or cautioned, certain that computers will be the cause of their demise, proving that they weren't college material in the first place. For all our students, however, traditional and nontraditional alike, a certain leveling begins as they all learn how to use a computer in discipline-specific coursework: word processing in English, SPSS (statistics) in psychology, spreadsheets in business management, ERIC in education, etc. And any trip to an academic library usually requires contact with some type of computer system. Because the technology is so much a part of the university-learning setting today, by the time students graduate, they have all had the opportunity to become computer literate. However, as much as the computer has been a part of how students learn, they don't know how to use it as a *complete* tool for learning. Instead, they tend to use the computer as a fragmented tool to attack what they view as fragmented tasks: to write papers, to surf, to game, to communicate, to search, to compute, to correct, to analyze, to organize. They have very little experience in making these computer operations coalesce into a useful, complete tool with academic purpose.

The role of computer technology in university life grows immense as it becomes increasingly necessary to graduate computer-literate students into the workforce. But what roles should computers play in our writing instruction as we try to engage students in real writing projects and processes that require a purposeful, complex notion of invention? Richard Young notes, "As new and significant methods of invention emerge, we need to develop a more adequate terminology which distinguishes various arts or methods of invention from *the* art of invention" (1976, 17). Technology, or more accurately, its use in the writing classroom, creates distinct methods of invention that necessitate our attention as computers become more commonplace in a diversity of pedagogies.

Computers, in theory and practice, have been a part of invention instruction for close to two decades, their use in the classroom becoming more complex as the technology has advanced (see Hawisher, LeBlanc, Moran, and Selfe, 1996). Early on, as theory in composition continued to subscribe to process-oriented instruction, word processing allowed teachers to encourage students to revise their writing. Students were taught to compose directly at word processors, using them to move, add, and delete text with ease. As the software developed over time, word processors included tools such as spell checkers, on-line thesauruses and dictionaries, and grammar checkers that allowed students to address surface-level matters in their writing. Therefore, the process of invention was originally taught through word processing by inviting students to see writing as a fluid process at both macro- and microstructural levels. Theorists believed that the fluidity of the act of composing with computers allowed students to expand their texts and delve deeper into their subjects. Although word processing was the earliest computer technology embraced by the field, it still remains an important part of teaching writing today.

Computers certainly allow for a free space where students can brainstorm about their topics—where they can generate text that can easily be manipulated. Even though teachers gained much by promoting good revision strategies and illustrating the concept of fluid versus fixed text, they found word processing alone didn't systematically push students to think about their topics—especially early in an assignment. Invention, or heuristic, programs were created to allow students insight into their topics through a computerized line of open-ended questions that encouraged open-ended, student-generated responses (Kemp, 32, 1987). The most widely recognized of these programs was Hugh Burns' TOPOI, based on Aristotle's central topics for invention. Such programs appear to be responding to students' input by utilizing a keyword system: If a student enters her name, "Vivian," and her paper topic, "charter schools," the heuristic program would ask questions like, "That's a great topic, Vivian. What do you already know about charter schools?" or "Who might be interested in a paper on charter schools?" If Vivian's response to a question were short (the computer would only know this by a word count), the program may respond, "That's a great start, Vivian. Can you say more about charter schools?" After Vivian ran through the program's series of questions, she could print the Q&A for use while drafting her paper.

The goal of these types of heuristic programs was for students to internalize the questioning processes modeled for them (Kemp, 1987, 36), similar to the questioning students learn from their teachers when they work through a new writing assignment in a face-to-face conference (1987, 34). Fred Kemp argues that whereas the programming involved here is relatively basic,

> it is the simplicity of the operating concept that makes for its great strength. The beginning of wisdom is the questioning of that which we have already accepted in some form or fashion. The questions that Burns' software puts to students challenge every aspect of their own understanding of their specifically stated subject. But, because his programs challenge relationships only

and not content, his heuristic method empowers the student in ways which would be impossible for even those instructors who are acutely aware of the authority relationship between teacher and pupil. Burns' method, simple as it seems at first, is in effect a profound means of stimulating student self-questioning without implicitly or explicitly devalorizing the student's experiences or idea. (1987, 34)

Open-ended programs like Burns' TOPOI do not evaluate the quality of students' response, which Kemp argues is another strength of the software. Helen Schwartz, who also authored an open-ended heuristic program for student writers called SEEN, contends that her students "soon realize they cannot get answers from the computer. They soon revel in the fact that they are doing the thinking, not the machine. The computer doesn't really know—or care—what the user says. This can be liberating" (1984, 241). Kemp and Schwartz' reading of open-ended heuristic programs becomes an interesting take on what seems to run counter to the field's acceptance of collaborative learning but remains true to compositionists' resistance to technocentrism: the computer is not going to "make" our students better writers (nor should we want it to); and students become independent when they learn invention as a process of internal dialogue.

As much as students might collaborate in other ways while writing (peer response, teacher conferences, interviews, etc.), the open-ended heuristic programs developed by Burns and Schwartz presented invention as a solitary act, reinforcing students' pre-/misconceptions about writing. They could decide upon a topic alone and work through the question/answer program without ever coming into contact with another thinking individual. Furthermore, whereas students *may* become aware of their own cognitive processes while using these programs, they will *not* be able to observe and learn from the cognitive processes of others. Students who work collaboratively on assignments not only generate more solutions to problems (content), but they are also able to carefully study how others tackle various learning tasks, like invention. As students are working together, they can compare how they approach an assignment with how others approach the same task. As a result of this collaboration, they may abandon ineffective learning strategies and adopt more useful ones illustrated by their peers, or together they may invent new approaches to learning out of the give-and-take of their cooperation.

These shortcomings of the software are mirrored in how the profession has in the past dichotomized its theories of invention, inquiry, and exploration—polarized views of invention as either a cognitive process or as a social act. Well known in the field is the Flower/Hayes (1980) model of cognitive processes that focused on the basic processes of the individual writer who is constructing a written text. Other work has attempted to identify that which is present and common to all information processing acts. These theories emphasize general knowledge as problem-solving and "[define] expertise in writing as the ability to bring to a writing task certain rich, well-developed, general strategies that guide the process and increase the chances for success" (Carter, 1990, 266). Many cognitive theorists, for example, encourage the use of problem-solving techniques and classical and modern heuristic procedures (Aristotle's topoi; Burke's Pentad; Rohman's prewriting; Young, Becker, and Pike's tagmemics; cubing; looping). Problem solving is a means of viewing the ways in which writers process information to achieve their goals. Heuristics, on the other hand, help solve problems because they aid in the acts of "discovery." What is common to all problem solving and heuristic views of invention is a series of separate, definable steps that writers follow. Although cognitive views of invention are often criticized for their linear, discrete approaches, many heuristics teach student writers about hierarchical order, levels of abstraction, comparison/contrast, and means/end analysis (Flower and Hayes, 1980). Instruction in cognitive-supported invention will, therefore, help students to develop these universal strategies that will enhance their learning experiences.

Others view invention and exploration in terms of social context, the site in which a writer is inquiring and exploring, along with the influences of that site on the writer. A social theory of writing is necessarily concerned with writing in context. Its concerns lie with community, the influence of social situation, and intertextuality. Therefore, those who embrace social theories of composing have taken the writer out from the cognitive, individualistic room and broadened the spectrum to include a houseful of the social influences that the writer may experience. Knowledge in writing is now defined as "local"—not based solely in an individual act, but, for example, by participation in a discourse community. In other words, someone who has reached expertise in writing, according to a social view of composing, is "one who has attained local knowledge that enables her to write as a member of a discourse community" (Carter, 1990, 266). Karen Burke LeFevre, in *Invention as a Social Act*, examines how writers interact dialectically within social and cultural settings. Although the "Platonic" view, LeFevre believes, has been important in foregrounding the significant part invention plays in composing, its reductive view of the process does not account for "the inventing 'self' [as] socially influenced, even socially constructed" (1987, 33). A social view of invention considers that one invents with a socially created/accepted/utilized language system while "[building] on a foundation of knowledge accumulated from previous generations, knowledge that constitutes a social legacy of ideas, forms, and ways of thinking" (1987, 34). Intertextuality, the relationship between existing texts and works yet to be written, comes into play here as writers interact with, assimilate, integrate, and respond to written texts. Equally important is the fact that invention includes internal dialogue, collaboration, and audience interaction which "dialectically connects" the individual and the social, rendering them "codefining" and "interdependent" (1987, 36–37). Instruction in invention that supports a social view of written communication will benefit students as its application highlights both social influences on writing and the social contexts in which writing occurs.

Indeed, both cognitivists and social constructionists boast of their own theory's benefits and are critical of each other. Oddly enough, calls for bridging the gaps between the two and creating an interactive theory of student invention are few. For the most part, we see that both cognitive and social views of writing remain separate schools of thought "that try to polarize (or moralize) cognitive and contextual perspectives," often with one pointing the finger at or simply dismissing the other (Flower, 1989, 282). But recent inquiry and dialogue are attempting to bridge the gap between the two without subordinating one to the other. In a departure from her earlier work, Linda Flower calls for

> an interactive vision of the writing process that can address the hurdles student writers often face, that can account for the cognitive and social sources of both success and failure, and that can talk about the experience of writing by being adequately fine-grained and situated in that experience. (1989, 284)

Similarly, Michael Carter argues that we need to view "human performance [as] a complex interaction of general and local knowledge" (1990, 271).

Both Flower and Carter note that the multitude of acts responsible for composing are too complex to attempt to initiate a single "interactive vision of the writing process"; to do so would continue a reductive view of composing, and thus invention, that already exists with the cognitive/social split (Flower, 1989, 286). Flower argues instead that we need to begin exploring the elements of an interactive theory: how context cues cognition, how cognition mediates context, and how an interactive theory of cognition and context creates an interwoven purpose (1989, 286–95). And in order to accomplish an interactive theory, we must begin to employ observational research which investigates "real acts of reading and writing" (1989, 294). This, in turn, will force situated instruction: "We must recognize that all knowledge and learning is situated, an idea that demands that we make our writing instruction situated as well" (Carter, 1990, 283).

An exclusively cognitive view of invention suggests that one invents within a controlled system of exploration that follows systematic patterns. An exclusively social view of invention, though, considers that one invents with a socially created/accepted/utilized language system and that invention involves both audience interaction and internal dialogue that "dialectically connect" the individual and the social, rendering them "codefining" and "interdependent" (LeFevre, 1987, 34, 36–37). When framed by calls to bring the two views together by the likes of Carter and Flower, we can begin to see a productive tension: *How can we create dynamic, pedagogical experiences in invention that involve our students with others and that will, in turn, create abilities to recognize and articulate learning processes that have resulted from these social interactions?*

Network-supported writing facilities provide access to particular emerging technologies that allow for a blending of the cognitive with a social vision of invention. Careful integration of networking has quickly become the standard by which computer classrooms are designed because the technology itself supports, in a broad spectrum, current theory in teaching writing and pedagogical practice in collaborative learning. With networking in place, students can communicate and exchange texts with their peers via the network, and thus experience writing and learning in a social context. Also, while working in a networked writing classroom, that today almost always include a connection to the Internet, they can have access to a vast array of written/multi-media texts and can conduct research by accessing databases, global networks, and the World Wide Web. Because of the dynamic nature of the computer and its ability to branch information interactively, the Web and other types of hypertext enable students to access and construct texts in an associative, intuitive way.

My experience with computers has shown me that communications and hypertext technologies in particular destroy any previous notion we have that invention is some type of "monoexperiential" art form or activity, especially in how I am going to promote their use in this book. Communications and hypertext technologies allow students to make multiple and diverse, continuous and sustained connections between people and texts, which individually and collectively become moments of invention.

Computer-mediated discussion, or CmD, consists as multiple, continual written exchanges that are focused in topic and purpose between two or more people. I am concerned in this book with asynchronous CmD—literally, "not at the same time." This mode of CmD allows participants to create written contributions to a discussion, but their texts are "delivered" or "posted" to other discussants to be read and responded to always at a later time, often in a different place, and rarely in the linear sequence that occurs in a traditional, face-to-face discussion. E-mail and newsgroups as well as Web-based bulletin boards are often used for this type of CmD. Because of the way a computer displays these discussions, CmD alters traditional assumptions of communication with its disorderly nature.

Specialists generally agree that two main components constitute the essence of hypertext. The first is that hypertext provides for the user a nonlinear, hierarchical means of accessing and sequencing information. The second is that associations made between chunks of information can be linked together by users as they process the information they encounter. Because of the dynamic nature of the computer and its ability to branch information interactively, hypertext enables the user to create and access information, and, thus, construct meaning, in associative, intuitive, and personal ways. Fragmented chunks of texts are linked together as the user interacts with the stored information and restructures the data and, at the same time, his or her own knowledge.

In the next chapters, I discuss both technologies, arguing that a theory of moments of invention can be used to "bring together" the fragmented tasks that students use the technology for: to compose, to surf, to game, to communicate, to search, to compute, to correct, to analyze, and to organize. Also, the methods and instruction I have developed with these technologies can illustrate students' own invention processes for them.

But perhaps more important is a point that I introduced in the introduction to this book. The next chapter provides a portrait of my own invention of a pedagogy that developed out of my experience with communications technology. In this chapter, I hope to dramatize the many problems faced by my small department that charged itself with designing an online learning environment and pedagogy.

2

Inventing Discussions, Inventing Pedagogies

My first real introduction to computers and composition studies was in the summer of 1987. I had just completed my first semester of graduate school, but because I started the program midyear, I hadn't been given a teaching assignment during the spring term. The department offered me an assignment for the summer working with a seasoned graduate student; we would both teach a section of first-year composition while she mentored me through my first time in front of a class, which just happened to be taught using computers. I remember the excitement I felt as I prepared assignments and classroom activities. I was rather uninterested in the computers at that time, more than happy to let her teach students the tech-operations they needed. At that time, the computers were nothing more than typing machines to me.

I mostly looked forward to leading class discussions on the pressing issues of the day that we were addressing in writing projects and various assigned readings. After all, I had just graduated from a traditional undergraduate program in literature where almost all of my advanced courses were "reading" courses where class time was spent participating in engaging, lively discussion about the texts we read. (Writing assignments usually came at the midterm and at the end of the term and were always completed outside of class.) This was the world I knew and the world I brought to my initial work as a teacher in the classroom. I'll admit my romanticized image of teaching differed only slightly from an episode of *Room 222*: a young, engaged, enthusiastic teacher who relates to students' interests and concerns (I was a freshman in college when MTV began broadcasting, so I just *knew* I could relate), who inspires them to value learning, who guides them toward connecting their lives to their school work. I would ask perfect questions and be as deeply interested in their comments as they were in mine. Yes, perhaps a touch romantic, but still, for me, teaching was about human interaction, and my own experiences as a student told me that classroom discussions brought interaction to learning.

But now I wasn't teaching literature. I was teaching writing about mostly nonfiction texts. At the same time that I was trying to put my quixotic teaching narrative into play, wondering how Denise Nicholas or Karen Valentine would get students interested in rather mundane topics such as transitions and paragraphing, I was enrolled in a graduate seminar entitled, "Computers and the Composition Classroom," taught by Gail E. Hawisher. Actually, the course was a "Topics in . . ." course, a generic listing that allowed professors to try out new or experimental course ideas; computers and composition studies was still too young and unknown to have had its own dedicated course number. The seminar served as an introduction to a body of research that was just beginning to find its place among compositionists. We read theory, descriptions of classroom applications, and empirical research on the effects of technology on student writers. About three weeks into the term, Hawisher assigned "Paperless Writing: Boundary Conditions and Their Implications," by Edward M. Jennings (1987). Jennings described what to most in the course seemed to be "the classroom of tomorrow"—ed-sci-fi, perhaps—although his portrayal was of an actual writing class. Students, Jennings reported, used computers in central labs or in their dormitories hooked to a university mainframe. Teachers could "post" assignments to an electronic bulletin board, a space accessible through a computer network where computer files were stored and available to be read, and students did the same with their completed homework. This system could be used, too, to carry on classroom discussions, where contributions and responses were typed on the computer and posted to the bulletin board or sent using a "mail" program. The class met at most once a week, "almost socially, to talk over how things had been going and what we would work on next" (1987, 12).

Our quick reading of his conclusions, a reading informed by little theory and even less experience, was reactionary at best: Students no longer needed to come to the classroom in order to take a class.

Of course, the theory in Jennings' piece was more elaborate than our initial reaction revealed. Our reading of the article was technocentric (Hawisher, 1989, 44–45), focused almost entirely on the technology and not on the pedagogy he had laid out for his readers. Our classroom discussion hardly moved beyond the premise that the death of the classroom as we knew it was a certain future. The visionaries among us were completely absorbed by the possibilities of what we now call "the virtual classroom." Those whose humanities-influenced worlds were rocked by such prospects were adamant that Jennings' ideas about teaching would single-handedly bring down the university as we know it.

As my fellow grad students and I discussed Jennings' "future," I looked around the room, noting my peers' animated expressions and body language as they presented their gut reactions to these new ideas. I ran my fingers over the computer keyboard that sat in front of me, eager to find a machine like Jennings described on campus so I could try "posting." The concept was completely foreign to me at the time. At the same time, I recalled the class activity I had led just a week earlier, where first-year writing students gathered in small groups and attempted to come to consensus on what they thought a writer's intention was in a particular sentence from an essay they read. In my mind, the volume of young student writers' voices increased as their close readings grew in complexity. I gazed out the classroom window that looked out across a short walkway that led to a large residence hall, imagining my students in their individual rooms, eagerly hammering out a response to a flip comment made by one of their network peers.

I was jerked back into my graduate seminar when Professor Hawisher asked me to share my thoughts, trying to pull all of us into the class discussion. She was attempting to illustrate how the dynamics of face-to-face discussion differ from those that occur on-line, both for students and for teachers. I stumbled. I explained that I embodied "the middle ground," and although I couldn't describe, or hadn't really thought through, what "the middle ground" was, I knew that I was situated somewhere between enthusiasm for never being restricted by a "class" as a physical boundary defined by time and place, and concern for students (and teachers) who desire and need real, face-to-face human interaction in which to learn.

A Comfortable Middle?

Almost seven years after reading Jennings' article, and two years into my first professional teaching position at the Ohio State University at Marion, I received a grant from the Ameritech Foundation to find, or better yet, *create* this middle ground. I wasn't attempting to create Jennings' classroom of the future—by this time, the idea of virtual learning environments was a reality for many. The Internet was available to many teachers and students, as were "contained" local area networks, both of which allowed for the type of teaching Jennings had written about. Instead, I wanted to study teaching and learning on the Internet, specifically how people taught and learned with a technology that allowed for a collaboration that wasn't restricted by the physical constraints of the classroom.

In my proposal for the grant, entitled, "Collaborative Inquiry and Internet Technologies in Writing Theory and Instruction," I sought to secure funds to begin a research project that would study Internet technologies and current practice in teaching writing on our campus. The first part of my grant request was for the purchase of necessary hardware to connect individual workstations to the university-wide network, SONNET, that would in turn give us an Internet connection, allowing students and teachers to use bulletin board and electronic mail systems to communicate and collaborate with each other as well as with those not enrolled in the class. Also, they could use the network information system to access local, university, national, and international databases, participate in electronic discussion groups, and conduct research in the main campus library directly from the classroom.

For four years, the English faculty on the Marion Campus had been meeting their classes in a computer-supported writing classroom featuring IBM PCs—286 processors, one megabyte of memory, forty megabyte hard drives, single disk drives. After some frustration with the slow speed and continual crashes of early Microsoft Windows programs, the department began to use WordPerfect 5.1 for word processing. The only networking in place was that which allowed all of the computers to print to one of three laser printers. Even then, this networking was really nothing other than very long printer cables attached to "the black box," a terribly unstable spooler that organized print jobs so that papers were distributed to the three printers in an orderly fashion. Otherwise, the twenty-five computers were free standing, individual workstations arranged around the walls of the room with tables in the center to create a seminar classroom work area. The only "public" viewing of a single document was made possible by an overhead projector system which allowed teachers to demonstrate various uses of the computer for revision and composing processes. The computers in this classroom were used almost exclusively as word processors, the theory behind their use almost exclusively that which was concerned with revision.

Over the years, our computer-supported writing classroom had become relatively obsolete; Intel's 486 processor had just been released (word was that the Pentium chip was not far behind), and the Internet was gaining popularity. We were afraid that we were doing a disservice to our students by teaching them on such dated equipment, especially when many had access to more powerful hardware and software in the workplace and at home. But replacing the hardware was out of the question; quite simply, the funds were not available. And without new hardware, there would be no new software. As we talked to other teachers who were starting with their first computer classrooms, we learned that computer networking was quickly becoming the standard by which computer-supported writing classrooms were being designed. Adding some type of networking to our already existing computers seemed to be the next logical—and affordable—step in the development of our classroom.

The second goal of the Ameritech grant was to study invention and Internet technologies. I identified two areas of invention and the Internet that I wanted to learn more about: students' ways of working with others to find and explore topics for writing, and teachers' ways of creating writing instruction that would direct students toward these collaborative opportunities. In support of my proposal, I argued that much current composition theory contends that writing should be taught as a process of problem formulation and inquiry that should take place in social, collaborative settings. Research strongly demonstrates that a collaborative atmosphere in the writing classroom can be created by the addition of computer technology: "Computers, which were once thought to promote isolation, may in fact prove to be of greatest help in creating cooperative learning environments" (Spitzer, 1986, 58–59). Because of accessibility and the potential for extended, dynamic collaboration, techno-compositionists have directed attention toward the use of Internet technologies in the writing classroom that could extend across "large geographical areas" but still allow for users in the same geographical area (a classroom) to communicate easily (Howard, 1988, 56).

Furthermore, I argued, students who work with computer networks can create their own text bases to be shared among the members of the class. Janet M. Eldred points out that "when students find their own work becomes part of a text base, they understand more fully the notion of 'intertext': the idea that their work is integral to a network of knowledge available to augment and increase the knowledge of others" (1989, 212). Also, computer conferences available with computer networking can promote a social and conversational model of writing and allow for an easy and open exchange between students and teachers. In their research on computer conferences, Marilyn M. Cooper and Cynthia L. Selfe found that network exchanges offer to students "an opportunity . . . to learn through engaging in discourse" (1990, 867).

Our students and faculty were eager to expand their experiences with collaboration by using the Internet. As I envisioned this project, both in terms of teaching and the research that would grow from our experiences, I was acutely aware of how "place" played a role in my expectations. The OSU-Marion Campus is one of five regional campuses in the university system that offers about 1,200 placebound students the first two years of coursework toward an undergraduate degree (students majoring in psychology and English can complete their entire degrees on our campus). The campus is located in mostly rural Marion County (the city of Marion claims a population of 30,000), approximately forty-five miles north of the Columbus campus, and serves students from the surrounding seven-county area. Fifty percent of our students are over the age of twenty-five (with an average student age of thirty-eight), and eighty-five percent of our students hold full-time jobs or have full-time family responsibilities.

Our link to the university network and the Internet, we believed, could "[dissolve] the temporal and spatial boundaries of the conventional classroom" (Hawisher and Moran, 1993, 633) and allow students to use the computer as a tool for inquiry outside of the physical constraints of the classroom walls, and in many ways, outside of the physical constraints of the rural, seven-county area in which our students live. Students and teachers could use bulletin board and electronic mail systems to communicate and collaborate with each other and with those not enrolled or directly involved in the class. Also, students could access local, national, and international databases, discussion groups, and the university libraries from their classrooms. We imagined the benefits our students would experience if I were able to connect the classroom to the Internet:

- Students working in a networked computer-enhanced writing classroom could communicate and exchange texts with their peers via the network, and thus experience writing and learning in a social context.

- Students having access to computer networks could experience dynamic transactions between the often separated acts of writing, reading, and research, and as a result, would be better able to become active composers of meaning.

- Students having access to a vast array of written/multimedia texts could conduct research by accessing databases and global networks. They would be better prepared for larger research problems in their advanced-level courses and in their post-baccalaureate endeavors, and they would be able to approach these problems with the developed electronic literacy necessary to succeed in an increasingly more technological world.

I had some pretty grandiose plans for our department, with classroom expectations to match. It wasn't until I actually received the letter from the Ameritech Foundation informing me that I had been awarded the grant that I realized my own limited experience using the Internet. My office computer was connected to the network, but really all I was using was a slow, user-hostile e-mail program and a basic information program that would give me university information that actually was readily available on paper in most offices: program and departmental descriptions, computer documentation, and student and personnel information.

My limited experience teaching with the technology was also evident upon consulting our campus computer technician. After I had received the grant money, I was informed that my plans would have to change. Connecting our computers to the Internet was not going to be a problem. What we could actually do with these computers once connected, however, probably would be. The computers we were using were never built to meet my expectations, and we were warned about pushing them too far beyond their capabilities. We were adding new parts—cards and cables and translators—to very old hardware. Also, the technician assured us that we could run a simple e-mail program— NUPop—but that the university was considering dropping its license for this software, and thus its technical support of the software, because it had adopted a more widely used, more powerful application that, of course, wouldn't run on our computers.

Given these restraints, we decided to concentrate my efforts on e-mail, using the software until the license ran out and hoping that we didn't need any expert help in solving problems down the road—not exactly what we thought the Internet was going to be about at first, but new and exciting to us nonetheless.

Technology Round 1: An Invention

Because the Ameritech Fellowship program provided grant money for *research* and not just for the purchase of equipment, I was on course from the beginning to conduct some type of a study. I wanted to investigate a small group of students in the context of a course in which they were enrolled; I was interested in my own reflections on students' learning and faculty's teaching as a primary vehicle for reporting my findings; I wanted to conduct interviews with students and describe class meetings in a journal; and I wanted to work primarily with first-year writers, although opportunities arose to work with a group of basic writing students and a small group of classroom tutors.

I planned a longitudinal study, one that wasn't particularly narrow in its number of participants and its time frame. Although I selected a small group of students to observe, I also wanted to add students throughout the study who seemed to be having interesting experiences with the technology. I also wanted to follow classes over an extended period of time. I felt this was especially important because part of my research was to look at the development of instruction in the writing program; I could not effectively look at development by restricting my research to, for example, one class during the winter term. And finally, I was interested in working with an assistant; the Ameritech funds were housed in the university's graduate school, and I was encouraged to hire a graduate research assistant. He was to help observe classes, interview students, create written transcripts of interviews and class sessions, and help with day-to-day tasks.

In some ways, the research design I employed was much more elaborate than I had originally thought. For example, for some classes, I interviewed students throughout the course, asking them to answer basically the same questions every three weeks. I wanted to see if their answers to these questions changed as their experiences with the technology became increasingly more involved. The research was completely funded and I was expected to report on my findings to the research granting agency. I employed a number of people, I had a "research protocol number" for the use of human subjects, and I purchased equipment. I also adopted a somewhat haphazard approach to this project; I often "grabbed" stories and evidence as I noticed them, later connecting these to other ideas. I have found that my rather chaotic approach to gathering data mirrored the chaos that the new technology brought to my teaching and to the department, and for this study, has produced fruitful results that I might otherwise not have seen.

I first narrowed my research lens by defining the technology and its use in relationship to my research topic: invention. I expected that students would notice things while they were using e-mail, and I hoped that they would make connections and see relationships at the same time. But this technology allowed my gaze to focus on something different from my hypertext study. The purpose of this technology was to communicate. I mostly wanted to study *collaboration* as invention and the ways this *collaboration* could help students notice, connect, find and work through disorder. Similarly, I wanted to observe how the use of e-mail could help them reflect while finding content for their writing. Also, I wanted to know how collaboration using e-mail could illustrate students' learning processes for them. As with my study on hypertext, I began by asking a number of general, directive questions:

- In what ways could student writers use Internet technologies to collaborate with other writers throughout their writing processes?

- In what ways could this collaboration made possible by the technology enrich their experiences in invention throughout their composing processes?

- In what ways could writing teachers create interactive learning settings and promote collaborative invention in the classroom when they gained access to Internet technologies?

- In what ways would interactions between students and teachers change when both had access to Internet technologies?

- In what ways would writing instruction begin to change throughout the Marion Campus with the integration of Internet technologies in the writing curriculum?

The expediency with which the technology came to us did not offer us much planning time; it certainly did not give us the luxury of reconceptualizing our courses before they began. My grant award was made in November, and the money was available shortly thereafter. Our campus computer technician, with the help of student assistants, connected our classroom computers to the Internet and installed our e-mail program over the December break, approximately a two-week period after the autumn term ended. We began teaching with the technology during the winter term.

When any new technology is introduced to a writing program, there is a significant amount of preparation work involved. First of all, I needed to learn the software before I could even think of teaching it to my students. I also had to write documentation for the software—the program we were using, NUPop, did not come with any instructions for student use. All of the faculty in our writing program expressed an interest in using the Internet in their teaching and attended workshops I conducted on how to use the technology. But for the first year at least, most were content to wait while my colleague Marcia and I forged onward into unexplored territory. The two of us, faced with time pressures and fully enrolled courses, could have easily decided to wait for the next term to begin using e-mail in our classes, taking the time to discuss theory, develop assignments, and test the technology. But, much like the advice we give our students when faced with a new assignment, we decided to "figure it out," learning as we went, expecting to make many, many mistakes.

Together, Marcia and I made sure all our students applied for and were assigned e-mail addresses, and we discussed what students did and did not need to know about the technology. Although disappointed about how limited our options would be with the Internet, we saw an advantage in only having to learn and teach one new application. And even then, we saw that if we taught students only the basics of e-mail, there would be fewer chances for them to get into technological problems that we would invariably need to solve.

I was teaching first-year composition, and Marcia was teaching basic writing. My students met in the computer classroom recently connected to the Internet, while Marcia met with her students in our older lab that had no Internet connection. The difference was significant in terms of students' access to the technology. I could teach my students the technology as a part of the class, connecting my technical instruction directly to a writing assignment. I could begin (and revisit, if necessary) assignments during the class meeting time. Marcia needed to schedule a special time in the computer classroom so that she could instruct her students on NUPop and then hope that they could manage to use e-mail on their own outside of class. She then gave them assignments that they began outside the classroom. (We were certainly cognizant of the fact that the basic writers were the students who did not have immediate access to the technology, another marginalization in their educational experience. This inequity was erased in our recent upgrades where all writing students on our campus have access to the best technology available to them.) Eventually, we were able to connect ten other machines on campus to the Internet—two in the basic writing classroom and eight in our general computer lab—so that Marcia could have access, albeit limited, to the technology in her classroom and students could use e-mail when classes were scheduled in the computer classroom.

In much of what we do, Marcia and I work collaboratively. Oddly enough, however, with only a fledgling understanding of how our Internet connection worked, Marcia and I worked almost independently of each other for the first year for reasons directly tied to my study. Even though this was a project I established with plenty of questions, I had very few answers with which to lead my colleagues; the purpose of the project was to discover these answers. Also, I deliberately framed one of my research questions—In what ways could writing teachers create interactive learning settings and promote collaborative invention in the classroom with access to Internet technologies?—so that I could see how teachers, including myself, invented new pedagogies for teaching writing. It certainly would have made sense for the two of us to work more closely in order to invent collaborative teaching methods. At the same time, I wanted to see what individual teachers would create after their initial contact with the technology, and Marcia was the only teacher who was eager to jump into the technology with me. Whereas we developed what seemed to be very different assignments for our students to work on over the first year, the similarities in our goals—and our mistakes—were striking.

Marcia's basic writing students were required to meet for "labs," structured writing time beyond their regularly scheduled classes intended to provide them with extended writing experience and instruction. Typically, students met in the basic writing lab and worked on their assignments, sometimes with Marcia and sometimes with a tutor. Marcia was curious to see if these labs could be "replaced" with e-mail assignments:

English 052
Marcia Dickson

E-mail Labs

This course is structured to encourage maximum interaction among class members. Therefore, to enhance and expand our interactions, we will be using a new electronic system of communication for the ENG 193 Lab. At the beginning of the quarter, you will be assigned an e-mail address and given instructions on using NUPop. For your lab exercises, you must compose three e-mail entries a week (plan to spend about 40 minutes per entry; this will be equivalent to the two hour period you are expected to spend in the required computer lab). You may submit more than three e-mail messages, but the total time you spend should be divided between the following exercises:

1. Responses to the reading—What issues have the readings made you think about? What is your opinion about the author's position? Why do you agree or disagree with him/her? What connections do you see between

---

the current reading assignment and the previous ones? Between the reading for our class and the reading or lectures in other classes? Between the reading and current issues in the print and electronic media?

2. Free topic discussion—What's going on in your intellectual life? What has caught your interest at school, in the news, on the talk shows, or in life in general? Why does it seem interesting or important to you and to others? (Please—no personal crises unless they relate to a larger issue—and even then be careful. This is not a true confessions journal.)

3. Evaluation of yourself as a class participant and as a writer—What have you done to contribute to the class discussion this week? Do you think people understood your points? Why or why not? What have you thought about saying and held back on? Why did you hold back? What are you having a good time writing? What is giving you a severe pain? How can I help you work through the current writing project? Be specific about the days you're writing about and how your thoughts connect to the discussion. I will want a record of your entire class participation—complete with recorded absences and evidence that you have done something to keep up with your work during your absence.

E-mail computers are available in Rooms 286, 216, and the General Computer Lab. E-mail machines are not reserved; they can be used on a space-available basis, so plan ahead. At the beginning of the quarter, I will expect you to decide upon and notify me of a two-hour period (or up to three 40-minute periods) that you will be working on your lab exercises. I will record these hours and expect to receive e-mail transmissions at those times.

THIS LAB IS NOT OPTIONAL, NOR IS IT TO BE TAKEN LIGHTLY. IF YOU DO NOT COMPLETE THE E-MAIL EXERCISES IN A TIMELY AND ADEQUATE MANNER, YOU WILL RECEIVE AN UNSATISFACTORY IN YOUR FINAL GRADE REPORT.

I asked students in my first-year writing class, entitled "A Generation Constructed," to work on two assignments using e-mail. They had just finished the first section of a text that they were reading for the course, *13th Gen: Abort, Retry, Ignore*, in which the authors, Howe and Strausse, investigate what might be better recognized as the "Generation X" phenomenon. Students in the class believed that the authors did not paint a fair portrait of the 13th gen, which was based solely on the subjects interviewed for the book. My students complained that these young people's views were not "real," that they did not truly represent the struggles of today's 13th gen. I presented them with the following assignment on a Wednesday:

English 110
S. DeWitt <dewitt.18@osu.edu>

Short Writing Project #5

In order to complete today's in-class assignment, SWP #5, you need to have created a "group" that consists of everyone's e-mail address in this class. Then, respond to the following prompt:

Something pretty spectacular has just happened. An opportunity like this doesn't come around every day. You have a chance to talk to the folks in your generation, and they are interested in what you have to say. For the next 30 minutes, you have their undivided attention to talk about any issue 1) about which you feel you have something to say, and 2) about which they are interested in hearing your point of view. In other words, you have an attentive audience (the easiest kind to write to), and you have the opportunity to tell your generation what they are doing wrong, what they are doing right, how they make you angry or frustrated, how they can change the world, and/or how you wish the world would change them.

I will tell you when the 30 minutes are up. After you are finished writing to your generation, queue your message and send it. If, by chance, the network is not working, exit NUPop and try sending it at another time.

Before Monday, take the time to read your e-mail. We will use this writing to generate topics for our next paper.

On the following Monday, I e-mailed the next short writing project to the class, asking them to find common themes that emerged in their peers' writing and to describe what they found intriguing in what they had read thus far. My assignment concluded,

> I encourage you to respond directly to your peers, paying particular attention to ideas you agree with and those with which you disagree.

Students were asked to send this writing to everyone in the class, too, for a total of forty messages (twenty students x two messages each). I received copies of all students' e-mail and responded to their writing via e-mail in much the same way I would if they turned the writing in on paper: noting ideas I found interesting, pointing out where they could develop their ideas more fully, indicating where I thought they had discovered interesting content for an upcoming assignment, etc.

During the following class meeting, we discussed their e-mail texts. We bounced around some of the ideas they came up with, and I offered feedback to them as a class on how I thought they handled the assignment. As a class, we chose four general "themes" relevant to the 13th gen discussion. These themes would be the subjects of our next assignment, a collaborative annotated bibliography: social concerns and issues; multiculturalism and diversity; educational trends and learning experiences; political, civic, and community involvement. Students were assigned small groups that were given one of the themes to research; each group was assigned a common essay to read on their given subject. Finally, each group was assigned a "team leader," a student whom I felt was highly organized and extremely talented with the technology.

English 110
S. DeWitt

Writing Project 2

Create an annotated bibliography that includes the following:

1. A collaboratively written annotation that includes a summary and commentary on your research team's

"common essay." Your research team will collaborate to produce one (1) annotation of this essay. Your annotation should be 1–2 pages in length.

2. Individual annotations from each team member that include a summary and commentary. Each team member must research the team's given topic and find some type of library source that would prove to be informative to the members of this class concerning our continuing investigation into "A Generation Constructed." Each annotation should be 1–2 pages in length.

The completed Writing Project 2 will consist of the collaborative annotation and an annotation from each team member. Writing Project 2 will be evaluated as a whole, and all of the writers will receive equal credit for the work.

As much as possible, collaboration should take place using e-mail (please include me in any exchange that has to do with this writing project).

When you submit your final draft of Writing Project 2, you should send me an e-mail copy in addition to a clean hard copy of your work. Team leaders, then, are responsible for forwarding an e-mail copy of their team's Writing Project 2 to all other team leaders. Team leaders will then forward other teams' writing to their own team members.

These annotated bibliographies will serve as resources for Writing Project 3, a researched essay.

Marcia and I had paid careful attention to how our assignments connected students' reading and writing and how these assignments were sequenced within the context of our specific course designs. But did the technology really make a significant difference in our classes? in the way our students learned? in how we conceived of the instruction we were imparting? We both finished our first ten-week term less than impressed with what writing instruction on the Internet brought to our writing program. Although our assignments were, we felt, pedagogically sound, there was very little evidence that would have led us to believe that students were actually learning anything about writing by completing the e-mail assignments we had created that couldn't have been done—more easily, sometimes—with printed texts or by meeting face-to-face.

In all of our assignments using e-mail, Marcia and I shared a common agenda: Use the technology to enhance two types of interaction, that which occurs among students and that which occurs between student and teacher. After all, this was a communications technology, and it seemed obvious that we should use it to that end. However, not all communication in our assignments was created equal. I think the easiest way to look at the different opportunities for communication we created is to work backwards through the sequence of assignments as I have presented them above.

Consider how I asked students to use e-mail to distribute copies of their annotated bibliographies to their peers. This task was purposeful in that it allowed students to see the work of other students, it gave public report to student writing, and it required a great deal of collaborative effort on the part of the assigned research groups. However, for the most part, our use of e-mail for this part of the assignment was little more than a mechanism for one student to deliver a text to another student. There was basically no interaction among students using the technology once this bibliography was distributed. Catherine Smith's distinction between a technology as an information system and a technology as facilitation, originally concerned with hypertext and applied more extensively in a later chapter, is a useful way to look at what I asked students to do. When a technology works as an information system, it merely houses or manages or delivers some type of text or data or image. The system is given attention over the user—once the information has reached the user, the technology plays little or no role in how that information is used. When a technology acts in the facilitation of learning, its ability to house or deliver information is but an early stage of a more complicated act. In other words, technology as facilitation foregrounds the users and the users' experience over the system. We need to think of the technology in the context of use, in this case learning and writing. When a technology facilitates learning, it allows our students to see relationships and create meaning, and it allows teachers to illustrate these acts to their students.

I don't mean to imply that technology as an information system is not useful. Gaining information is often an integral part of learning; it is an especially important part of invention. I do, however, believe that we need to achieve a balance in how the technology can serve as both information system and facilitation. And my assignment to this point did not effectively achieve that balance. For example, each collaborative team used e-mail to put together their bibliographies, but really they only e-mailed their contributions to the assignment to each other, and one team member took the initiative to collect all of the citations. Even though I stated, "As much as possible, collaboration should take place using e-mail (please include me in any exchange that had to do with this writing project)," at no time did students in groups use the technology to share ideas or drafts of work; they only used the technology to "transport" their contributions to the team leader to be included in the final product. This was also true of the finished product; everyone received an electronic copy of each group's bibliography. To this point, the technology had only served as an information system. Students didn't really use it to create or discover, just to store and deliver.

Next, consider the two assignments that preceded the collaborative bibliography. Students were asked to "tell your generation what they are doing wrong, what they are doing right, how they make you angry or frustrated, how they can change the world, and/or how you wish the world would change them." After sending this writing to everyone in the class, they summarized and responded to the ideas found in their peers' writing and sent this to everyone in the class. These assignments come closer to the idea of a "communications technology" in that there are initial ideas posted and responses formulated to them. However, a closer reading of this assignment reveals problems, too.

On the surface, the first of my two assignments—where students initially write *about* their generation *to* their generation—carefully considers the relationship among assignment, writer, and recipient. In this particular class, all of the students enrolled could be considered a part of the same generation (an anomaly at my campus), and the writing was being sent to its intended audience. This shared relationship among assignment, writer, and audience directs student writing away from "writing for the teacher." Yet, the second assignment sent a two-part, perhaps conflicting directive to students: After they summarized common themes and noted what they found intriguing, they read, "I encourage you to respond directly to your peers, paying particular attention to ideas you agree with and those with which you disagree." On the one hand, students are asked to respond to *writers* (peers), while on the other hand, they are asked to respond to each other's *writing* (ideas). Also, they are asked to make this writing public by sending it to everyone in the class. It's not difficult to see that cognitive dissonance might grow in the students' minds: why would students respond directly to a writer, but then send this to the class, along with a summary of common themes that run throughout their peers' writing and other ideas they found intriguing. In the end, the writing produced responded to students' texts as if the students were not a part of the class or really on the receiving end of the e-mail. Also, its tone was similar to the writing the students had been producing throughout the quarter in response to reading assignments; they relied on a schema they had already developed. For example, after reading twenty e-mail texts, Karen was discouraged by what her peers had to say about and to their generation. She wrote:

> I just couldn't get over the fact that everyone seemed so interested in such su-
> perficial subjects. I have to believe there are more important things happening
> in the world than Tonya Harding and Nancy Kerrigan. Fifteen people in this
> class decided that this was the most important topic to address. I bet they were
> a bit surprised to hear what I had to say to them. I suppose the fact that so
> many people chose to write about skating scandals is an interesting subject in
> and of itself. What do young people today value?

When interviewed about this assignment, Kelly's feelings were similar:

> It . . . it was remarkable. Some of the responses were, uh, many of them were
> very shallow. So very shallow, which was frightening. But you know, I had
> the opportunity to respond to whoever, or whatever I thought was in need of
> response. So I told them that I thought they were shallow.

It is interesting that Kelly believed she directly responded to her classmates. Indeed, that is what I had instructed them to do. But instead, she described a group of people as shallow, and, along with everyone else in the class, decided to write *about* whomever instead of directly responding *to* those with whom she had taken issue.

Marcia's assignments faced similar difficulties. She asked her basic writing students to continually respond to three writing prompts throughout the quarter: responses to the reading, free topic discussion, and self-evaluation as a class participant and writer. Student writing was sent to Marcia, and she spent a significant amount of time responding to their texts, encouraging them to continue writing as much as possible. Students in this class were also asked to send the writing to everyone in the class. Although not articulated in the assignment itself, Marcia instructed the students in how to use the "reply" feature of the technology and asked them to respond to each other's writing.

Clearly, Marcia's assignments are carefully structured and require students to participate in high levels of critical thinking as well as participate in a great deal of writing—two of the most important goals for her basic writing students. All three prompts could be framed to encourage written exchanges between students, but as Marcia reported, students almost never responded to each other's writing. As is, the prompts are identical to the types of "school" writing these students were learning to compose. Also, much of the assignment leads students to not only write to Marcia, but to believe that she is the primary audience of the texts they produce. This is especially true in the third assignment: although assignments and class activities can be structured in ways that enable students to learn about their own and each other's learning, for whom else would a self-evaluation in this vein be appropriate or interesting except for the teacher? The writing they produced that responded to the assignment did not necessarily invite response from their peers. Also, students read instructions that included, "How can I help you work through the current writing project? Be specific about the days you're writing about and how your thoughts connect to the discussion. I will want a record of your entire class participation—complete with recorded absences and evidence that you have done something to keep up with your work during your absence." The assignment concluded, "I will expect you to decide upon and notify me of a two-hour period (or up to three forty-minute periods) that you will be working on your lab exercises. I will record these hours and expect to receive e-mail transmissions at those times."

The most productive communication—and possibly, by definition, the only communication—that occurred out of these assignments was between student and teacher. Students sent their writing to their teachers and were offered critical, written feedback in reply. Based on interviews with our students, I quickly realized that Marcia was far more successful than I was with this type of communication. The type of writing her students posted to the entire class did not encourage others to respond; in fact, these basic writers possibly did not have the rhetorical strategies at their disposal to respond to a text for which they did not seem to be the intended audience. Marcia, on the other hand, was the intended audience and had the rhetorical abilities to deal with texts whose audience was not clear. Marcia responded to individual students, not making her texts public to the rest of the class. At this moment, students began to see the value in a communications technology. During an interview, Jane says:

> We had to write these assignments, and . . . uh . . . they were hard, because you like have to come up with an idea and . . . the other . . . they were like short papers. And then Marcia would write back. Probably the one that stands out in my mind is when we wrote about the environment, and how they could do more things to help the environment. And we wrote back and forth about three or four times on that, about cloth diapers and not disposable ones. Aerosol cans. Once Marcia would write back, it was easy, because we were like talking about it instead of, like, me writing a paper about it.

Important to note is Jane's distinction between the first writing and the conversation that ensues. She sees her initial posts to an on-line discussion like writing a paper—probably the most difficult task that lies before basic writers, in their eyes. But once Marcia responds to the student's original post, the exchange transformed from writing to discussion.

Brad, another of Marcia's students, continues in this vein, yet as scrambled as his comments are when transcribed into writing, Brad offers us a great deal of insight into the potential for using communications technology, that which was missing from much of our first assignments:

Um . . . for school work, we've . . . uh . . . had . . . we've been . . . um . . . our assignment was to have a thoughtful . . . use a . . . how can I put this . . . um . . . we've been carrying on like a conversation. Like Marcia and I have been doing a thing on gun control, and she's anti . . . oh, I wouldn't say "anti-gun," but is not for everyone owning a gun, and I would . . . uh . . . personally like everyone to. So, we've been having this long, drawn-out argument about this. And I think . . . I think the system's neat, because it gives you more time to think. You're not sitting there trying to top each other . . . uh . . . as if you were in a conversation in class, and it's more . . . how would I put it, polite. I write about whatever I feel like writing about. I've written about . . . uh . . . racism before. All kinds of stuff like that, like stuff gets me riled on TV, I'll send something in. I think that once, I fired one that was kinda a little bit preachy, which is a little easy to do with the e-mail. You get yourself on your little soapbox and just keep on going. I like how you can look back on something. Like you said something in your previous letter . . . where in writing I'll just . . . I like being able to refer back to stuff. And like I can leave something . . . like I can leave the e-mail . . . like I can leave the e-mail, save it, and then go back to it after I do something. I don't have to finish it right now.

I want to look at Brad's comments again later in the chapter. However, now I want to take a closer look at Brad's overall experience in Marcia's class using the technology. Although I have not, as of yet, painted any personal portraits of research subjects, I think Brad's story is important to consider. Brad enrolled in my first-year composition course after finishing the two-course basic writing sequence with Marcia; together, the two of us learned a great deal about him. College was difficult for Brad. And for good reason: For a great deal of his public school education, Brad was incorrectly placed in courses for students with learning disabilities. And whereas he made great strides after returning to regular classes, he was a basic writer if ever there were one. Reading and writing, especially at the levels expected of him in the academy, were grueling. He was impulsive in his studies, easily frustrated when his first attempt to solve a problem didn't work (this was especially true when he was asked to revise his writing), and initially resisted any suggestions that he may not have gotten it right the first time. He eventually accepted, however, that at least when it came to writing, he probably wasn't going to get it right the first time, and as much as he didn't want to revise, he understood its necessity. When in a rigorous yet nurturing classroom environment, he would struggle for long periods of time before taking large steps forward in his learning. Working as closely as we did with Brad, we learned that he had strong opinions about issues that played out in his day-to-day life and did not shy away from topics with which he knew his audience would disagree. However, we also learned that he often used the opportunity to voice these opinions as an avoidance tactic; by starting an argument or debate on a controversial issue, he would appear to be engaged in school work when actually there would be no connection with the class's subject matter at hand.

Interestingly, he gravitated towards those folks—like his English teachers—who would take the time to explain difficult concepts to him as well as show an interest in his opinions. Marcia spent twenty weeks with Brad, and for the last term they were together, they carried on a number of e-mail conversations that were initiated by Marcia's "E-mail Labs" assignment. Marcia has recalled many times how difficult that assignment was for her to manage. If all fifteen students fulfilled their obligation to the assignment, she would receive forty-five texts to read. It was quite simply impossible for her to respond to every text that was sent to her, in addition to the other work of the class as well as other teaching and professional responsibilities. She needed to decide which of each student's three messages to respond to, not to mention any further messages that followed in conversation. (Also, it became apparent that the struggles Marcia was facing could very well be what hindered students from responding to each other's initial posts: a great deal of text to read, a great deal of text to manage, and a great deal of work added to their already busy lives. What typical freshman student *wouldn't* avoid such a situation?) Marcia could always guarantee that there would be further messages from Brad, usually focusing on issues about which the two of them disagreed. Brad loved the nature of these exchanges. He was eager, he was excited, and he was engaged in school work, in this case, increased writing and fluency for a basic writer.

Obviously some of our applications of this technology to our writing instruction worked. But overall, we knew that there was a great deal of work ahead of us if we expected to see this technology truly influence and enrich our teaching, and vice versa. This included a process of reevaluating our assignments, drawing out what was working, rethinking what was not. Again, a number of new questions arose:

- How do we ensure that the assignments we create are based in communication and not in just the storage and transmittal of information? Clearly, the "communication" aspect of the technology is what interested students, as indicated by all of the research subjects during interviews. The clearest distinction between defining e-mail as a communications technology and as information technology came in how two students defined the technology after using it for five weeks:

MARK: It's like the phone, only you are doing it in writing and the conversation takes place over a longer period of time. Like, instead of deciding what we are going to do, like this weekend in three minutes, it might take three days. But it's cool because I work second shift, and my friends can't usually catch me at home on the phone.

JAMES: It's like sending a wire or something to someone. It's like a fax, where you transfer documents to someone, only they see it on the screen instead of it printing out on paper.

• In what ways can "communication" define the technology as facilitation for learning? Just because students are communicating via the technology does not necessarily mean that the technology is facilitating their learning. In fact, in all of the interviews, when asked how they were using the technology, students related that they used e-mail primarily to communicate with friends, who were mostly students on our campus, about social activities or gossip. However, in two cases, distinctions were made:

ANN: My friend, Michelle, she goes to Kenyon Uni . . . College. She sent me a message about her biology. And in her message, she was talking about biology. But it sounded familiar to my psychology class. And so we . . . you know, just kinda compared 'em, and she was having a problem. And in psychology, we was talking about that, and I kinda understood it, so I wrote her back. I wrote her what I knew and . . . it helped her kinda, and we kept writing back and forth about it. I think it helped.

RICH: I actually sent a paper to a friend to read. I wanted him to tell me what he thought of it . . . how I might make it better. He didn't, he just made some joke like, "Thanks for the paper. Now I don't have to write one." But I thought it would be cool to have an e-mail partner for writing. Someone you could get help with and brainstorm with. Read each other's papers. And I guess that person could be anywhere, not just at OSU.

• In what way could the "management" of e-mail assignments enrich students' learning processes? All students who were interviewed for this project made reference to some type of management problem with the technology. Some were frustrated by the instability of the network that could, without warning, crash in the middle of assignments. But most referred to the number of messages they received and a lack of strategies for reading and responding to them.

• How do we create e-mail assignments that pique students' interest and at the same time are directly connected to the pedagogical goals of the class? During their interviews, Marcia's students spoke only of one assignment: free topic discussion. They indeed completed reading responses and self-evaluations, but these exchanges were not memorable or, in their eyes, worth talking about during their interviews. One could argue that these exchanges did have pedagogical value—writing students, especially basic writing students, need as much experience writing in a variety of forms and forums as we can possibly create for them. In content, however, the writing these students produced in response to this assignment was rarely connected to any course content.

• How do we create assignments using e-mail where the teacher is not the primary recipient of and respondent to students' texts? Whereas I do believe that Marcia was quite successful in establishing extended conversations with her students on e-mail, we both felt that all of our students missed opportunities to discuss the issues of the class with each other. Both of us use peer response extensively in our writing courses, believing that students can offer good critical feedback to their classmates, which will, in turn, help them develop good critical reading and writing skills that they can apply to their own learning experiences. This philosophy, we believed, should also direct our use of the technology in our writing instruction.

Technology's Second Round: A New (Re)Invention

Before we entered into a new phase of our educational/technological experiment, I returned to our beginnings: the Ameritech Fellowship Grant proposal that established the foundation for how we were using e-mail in our composition classes. Although I cited a great deal of research, I realized that I had very little knowledge of how to connect the technology with what I was doing with my writing students beyond what I had read. I had read *scores* about the potential for teaching composition with this technology. However, my claims in this proposal were not much different from those I had worked against in a great deal of my research on computers and composition. For example, most of the research I'd studied on hypertext was written in what I now call the "potential tense," language with lots of "could"s, "would"s, and "if"s. (For an extended example of this point in regards to hypertext, see DeWitt, "The Current Nature of Hypertext Research in Composition Studies: An Historical Perspective," 1996). My own writing about the Internet used the same language. I had read about, seen demonstrations of, and personally used the technology I was advocating. I simply "lifted" language about Internet technology and composition studies and applied it to an imagined teaching situation.

Such language, while perhaps necessary at the start of an investigative and exploratory project, could not carry me forward solidly to deeper studies. A similar problem plagues many new ventures involving technology and writing. For example, at the same moment that I was investigating the use of the Internet in composition, I was appointed to our campus's Long Distance Learning Consortium, a group of local educators, health care providers, government officials, and business leaders who were charged with bringing closed-circuit television/live video feed educational opportunities to the community. We were not really doing anything too terribly new. Distance learning and the use of technology, today a commonplace topic of discussion at any meeting of college administrators, was errupting all over the country, and universities and community colleges were leading the way. Our mission-statement included phrases such as "committed to life-long learning" and "implement change in the use of technology to enhance the quality of life." I have no doubt that the members of the consortium were committed to lifelong learning and the quality of life. However, I also cannot ignore that this educational trend, distance learning, is being driven by market forces, by economic competition, by a vision of the university as corporation. College administrators are convinced that they must offer their educational programs "on-line" or else fail to survive in the mega-mall of higher education: "Students," we are told, "will simply shop somewhere else."

Educational programs will always emerge out of "what students need and what students want." But how we operate in those programs—how we design and implement curricula—must be informed by *how students learn* in those programs. The rhetoric of distance learning, that which convincingly argues that we need to *reach* students where they are, *deliver* education, create programs that *fit* into students' lives, is only a starting place. To invent curricula based on those goals alone limits teachers and students to a very narrow portrait of learning and completely undercuts what we as compositionists know about how students learn and how they learn to write.

As part of my work with the Long Distance Learning Consortium, I was asked to attend a meeting of the Ohio Long Distance Learning Association. The purpose of the meeting was to provide a starting place for educators whose schools were beginning to explore the possibilities of distance education. Clearly, those of us who spend our time in the classroom were in the minority. Most in attendance were network administrators or "technology coordinators," specialists hired by college campuses to assist teachers in designing and implementing technology practice in their classrooms. After listening for about an hour—and after learning a great deal about video and imaging technology—I asked what I thought to be an important question: How is this organization distinguishing between the term "interactive technology" and "interactive learning"? The response

I received was shockingly simple: Any learning that takes place using interactive technology must be interactive.

I am certain that, had I engaged the organizers of the workshop in a discussion about this issue in a more intimate setting, they would have explained their answer in much more complex terms (there were about 150 in attendance, so the setting was not conducive to such discussion). It was apparent, however, that this organization had simply "lifted" ideas that used common language, such as "interactive," and connected those terms to a theory of learning. And it doesn't take long to find the holes in their theory. Just as the first round of my Ameritech project contained unproven, almost "empty" pedagogical theory—connecting composition theory with descriptions of technology operations without any solid grounding in classroom practice and research—so, too, did the work of this organization promoting technology in the university. In both, the pedagogical principles are highly speculative.

Yet, I do not want to see such speculation as entirely negative. I argue that we invent pedagogies in much the same way as we invent content for writing. We begin by bringing together—consciously or unconsciously—seemingly unrelated ideas that yield a moment of invention. As newly formed ideas connect with other pieces of information or opinion, new moments of invention are created, especially when one begins to see connections between these various moments. As ideas are superimposed and layered, they reshape and reform, they adapt and respond until the mental text, the invention, is solid, dense, sturdy.

My work with Marcia and our students started with a simple, singular connection: claims made by the published literature and the possibilities of the technology recently made available to us. The connection was singular, and the invented pedagogy that resulted was not the product of a complexly intertwined, dense fabric of ideas. However, what we learned in that first round provided us with numerous threads, laid out straight and flat, that we were eager to begin crossing, looping over and under each other. The binding threads still missing from our fabric, those that would begin to tighten our technology practice, would do two things:

1. Closely tie the use of e-mail to our writing courses and our writing program. (How did we define the goals of specific writing courses, and how were these courses sequenced within a writing program? How could e-mail help us to imagine new ways to meet these course and programmatic goals?)

2. Allow the use of e-mail to reimagine and reinvent ourselves as a writing program. (In what ways were we resisting the technology from changing not only how others perceived us as a program, but also from how we perceived ourselves as a program?)

At the same moment that we decided to critically review how we had used the technology to rather unimpressive ends, I happened to return to using *Our Times* as the textbook in my first-year writing courses (3rd edition, Robert Atwan, editor, 1995). I was quite familiar with the book; I had used it for years in other courses—all three editions—because I found that its premise, that students need to learn to negotiate and move effectively among reading, writing, and discussion, provided a supportive rhetorical foundation, eliminating the need for a separate, formal rhetorical apparatus per se. This particular reader offers thoughtful questions at the end of each selection and is one of the few readers on the market that emphasizes the role of discussion in the writing process. Its agenda has influenced much of my teaching, even when I'm not using this particular text.

Discussion, Atwan says, pushes students to work with others when they are developing topics for writing (1995). Even when we teach "audience-based" writing, sometimes students don't collaborate with others when they are trying to find subject matter about which to write. When we use discussion as an integral part of our writing instruction, students will learn that a great deal of real world writing grows from conversations with others. Also, these collaborations become important moments of invention for students who are trying to discover topics and content for their writing. But how might computer networking and e-mail help us reach this goal?

Researchers in this area of on-line interaction have adopted the term "computer-mediated communication," or CmC, to refer to any written interaction generated and transmitted with the use of computer technology. CmC encompasses a wide range of communications in many different settings: short memos and messages, ongoing arguments on specific topics, formal business letters, political petitions and letter-writing campaigns, collaborations on group projects, requests for information, announcements for social gatherings. Even a deposit slip from a banking ATM could be considered CmC. These communications take place on a multitude of computer systems, both in and out of the education arena, some relatively simple, some highly specialized.

In many ways, the term "computer-mediated communication" fails to describe the type of interaction in which we want our students to actively engage. It certainly doesn't illustrate the vision of invention I am promoting in this book. "Communication" is a general term that encompasses a wide range of activities in which some type of information is transmitted and received. We want our students to participate in *discussion*, "the free and open exploration of a specific topic by a small group of prepared people" that, at the same time, "is purposefully conducted around a given topic" (Atwan, 1995, 3). Thus, the term "computer-mediated discussion," or CmD, more accurately describes how computers can be used most effectively in our writing classrooms to meet central pedagogical goals. We are still talking about written interactions that are mediated by computer technology, but CmD refers more specifically to multiple, continual exchanges that are focused in topic and purpose between two or more people, where each exchange potentially becomes a moment of invention.

I am working with the following definition of CmD:

> Computer-mediated discussion is in the form of written text that is created, exchanged, and read with the use of a computer. The topic and purpose of the discussion as well as the specific task at hand are made clear at the onset, most often by the teacher (although, like all discussions, purpose and topic can shift throughout the course). All discussants compose written contributions to the discussion and make them available to all other discussants. All discussants carefully read these written contributions and respond to them, again making their responses available to everyone involved. This process continues until, for one reason or another, the discussion is terminated.

This definition was created with the classroom in mind where writing is used not only as an end but where students use writing to learn. The most sophisticated, high-tech computer equipment can incorporate digitized sound and graphics in CmD, but when these are used, not all of the discussion takes the form of written text. Many teachers, especially English teachers, have limited (or no) access to such state-of-the-art technology. Also, most teachers, especially English teachers, would agree that *more writing* is a high priority in their classrooms, especially the type of writing where the end goal is learning, not necessarily a polished product. Use of powerful technology that allows students to avoid writing could undermine teachers' pedagogical goals. My narrow definition is not intended to limit the possibilities of how CmD can be used in the classroom, but instead to keep attention focused on writing and, more importantly, on the relationship of discussion to writing.

The description in this definition of the teacher's role is also specific to the classroom. As with classroom discussion, effective CmD needs a sense of direction provided by teachers creating a clear context for the discussion. Participating students need to understand the discussion's starting point, usually phrased in the form of a discussion question based on readings from the text. The question clarifies the general topic and purpose of that particular discussion. Teachers manage the exchange, attempting to keep it moving forward by assigning students to read and respond to their peers' contributions to the discussion, by intervening appropriately and constructively, and often by bringing the discussion to closure.

To better understand how CmD works, it may help to consider traditional, face-to-face discussions. Classroom discussions take place with students sitting at the same time in the same room with one student's comments immediately following another student's comments. The social convention of "taking turns" gives traditional discussion a sense of order. Teachers and students alike are often caught off guard by the concepts of *time*, *place*, and *sequence* when they first imagine CmD. As in classroom discussion, all are still crucial elements of CmD, yet they are redefined by the use of the technology. CmD can take two forms. Synchronous CmD requires that discussants are "on-line" at the same time (but not necessarily at the same location) using a "real time" or "chat" conferencing system that allows their written texts to be transmitted and received as they are written. For the most part, participants are discussing a topic as they would if they were talking face-to-face, yet their contributions are created, exchanged, and read with the use of a computer. I am concerned here with CmD that uses an asynchronous—literally, "not at the same time"— mode of electronic discussion and therefore necessarily alters our traditional ideas of discussion. Participants create written contributions to a discussion, but their texts are "delivered" or "posted" to other discussants to be read and responded to at a later time, often in a different place, and rarely in a linear sequence such as occurs in a traditional discussion.

I introduce CmD to my students by first getting them into CmD teams, small groups of four to five discussants. On my campus, I am able to arrange these teams using campus-assigned listservs. In short, I program one e-mail address that serves the entire CmD team, so when any mail is sent to the team address, everyone in the group receives a copy, including the person who sent the mail. For a class of twenty-four students, then, I might configure six listservs— one address per group and four students per group. We also have our computers configured so that copies of students' e-mail are saved to their disks—they can keep a personal record of all of the CmDs they are participating in. I include myself in each of these CmD teams so that I, too, can keep a record of the class's discussions.

The CmD teams receive some simple instructions. These instructions assume that students know how use e-mail, to create a file, send "group mail" (i.e., send the same file to many different people simultaneously), and use "reply," a feature of e-mail that allows users to insert written comments directly into a text that they have already received from a team member and send both the original text and written commentary to many different people simultaneously. In most e-mail programs, when using the "reply" feature, each line of an original text is preceded with >. For example, a reply might look like this:

> >This would be a line of a message I received as part of the
> >discussion. When I select "reply," the program automatically
> >inserts these symbols at the beginning of each original
> >line.
>
> Then, when I enter my response that is not designated with
> any type of symbol, a reader can see the back and forth move-
> ment of the conversation, easily noting what is in response to
> what.

Because there are many different e-mail software packages, it does not make much sense for me to go into too much detail about program operations. Teachers will need to teach these basic operations to their students according to their classroom's software and hardware configurations while also considering how knowledgeable and comfortable everyone is with the technology. For example, on our campus, we find that we are spending very little time teaching e-mail operations. Many students come to the university with personal e-mail addresses already, and all students learn to use their university addresses in a one-hour practicum course they take as freshmen.

At the time when we were inventing CmD pedagogy, my first-year students were studying issues that had been dominating the popular press. This particular issue was "Identifying Generation X," an assignment that asked them to analyze constructs of various generations and the labels attached to them. They had completed a pretty hefty reading assignment, and they were prepared for a discussion with their peers. This assignment illustrates the basic premises of instructional CmD:

> **CmD Assignment: Unit 3—Identifying Generation X**
> **Friday, 21 April**
>
> Over the next two weeks, outside of our class meetings, your
> CmD team should respond to the following question:
>
> Question:
>
> In his article, "Profiles of Today's Youth: They Couldn't Care
> Less," Michael Oreskes cites a number of possible explanations
> for the "alienation and apathy of young people." These include
> the "lack of mobilizing issues," "the decline of the family, and

the rise of television." To what extent are these useful explanations? What do these explanations leave out or ignore?

After your initial statement, your contributions to this discussion should respond to your team members' ideas. Your contributions to this discussion should be thoughtful and purposeful, and all responses should have clear, textual references to provide your readers with a context for your comments. Do not hesitate to challenge your fellow discussants or to raise questions about which you would like their input.

Each team member should make a minimum of four contributions to the discussion before Monday, 28 April.

In this particular discussion, students are asked to keep the discussion tied to their reading assignment. From beginning to end, students are aware of the topic and purpose of the discussion. The participating students make their contributions to the discussion available to their peers. And in the case of our example, the discussion is formally constrained by an assignment that requires students to make a minimum of four contributions (although many discussions will continue beyond the boundaries of the assignment).

As we began using on-line exchanges with this newfound emphasis on "discussion," I was able to identify distinct ways in which this technology was facilitating students' learning as well as their invention processes:

Greater Participation and Depth of Participation.   The amount of writing and reading that students do in CmD is worthy of our attention. Without a doubt, students are participating in the act of writing as well as reading their peers' writing a great deal more than during in-class discussions. And, students need as much practice writing and reading as possible, especially as first-year college students. Also, the more writing students participate in, especially when this writing is collaborative and involves discussion, the more opportunities become available for students to experience moments of invention. Marcia and I learned that smaller group discussions are more manageable for students and allow them a greater depth of participation. Also, as the CmD instructions prescribe, *all* students will contribute to the initial shaping of the discussion before anyone begins to respond to each other's ideas. In classroom discussions, rarely do all students get to voice their initial opinions about a discussion topic before their peers begin responding to a point already raised. Also, as teachers intervene in CmD, offering feedback to students on both the content and structure of their writing, the length and quality of different students' contributions will begin to level. And finally, if all students meet the requirements of a CmD assignment, they all will make an equal number of contributions to a discussion—no student can be silent, along "just for the ride," in CmD. Some students, at times, go beyond the minimum number of required responses, depending on their involvement in the topic at hand.

Illustration of Learning and Difficult, Abstract Concepts in Writing.   After experimenting with CmD in my composition classrooms, I saw two ways that I could use the technology to meet important pedagogical goals. CmD could be an end in and of itself. Marcia's early e-mail lab assignment, "free topic discussion," showed us that students are eager to participate in e-mail discussions when they choose and initiate the content. Perhaps the inventions that grow from these discussions will become topics for other writing at some point. However, I don't think that these discussions necessarily need to be connected to other class projects in order to be effective. For example, I will often present small CmD groups with hypothetical/rhetorical situations that present complicated scenarios; students will sort through the many different issues included in these situations and respond to them with their CmD groups. Students not only learn from their peers' contributions to the discussion, but also they learn about their own perspectives on tough issues. They learn about what background knowledge and experiences they bring to solving problems, they learn when their opinions are grounded in evidence and when they are driven by emotion, and they learn when their approaches toward discussion—voice, tone, rhetorical strategy—are effective or not. All of this self-awareness is important in invention as they begin to understand *how* they see relationships and make connections.

Any type of self-awareness concerning invention brings our students closer to the abilities of experienced writers. One such ability that students struggle with is understanding that discussion and writing are connected experiences. Instead, they view writing and discussion as two distinct matters; writing, they believe, is a solitary, isolating activity, and discussion is a collaborative activity that has very little to do with the creation of a written text. Therefore, students need instruction that reflects the fact that "experienced writers invariably write in a climate of discussion. . . . Their ideas often originate in discussion, their writing is a response to discussion, and their papers are designed to stimulate further discussion" (Atwan, 1995, 2).

I often find it difficult to illustrate for students how discussion can feed into and enrich writing. The discussion and conferencing that writers go through as they write are almost never "visible" in a final product; "showing" students this process becomes an arduous task. Even after the most exciting, invigorating classroom discussion, I am frustrated because I lack what Atwan calls a "tangible source of ideas for individuals to pursue later in their papers" (1997, 8).

CmD offers teachers and students a record, an artifact of sorts, of not only the discussion itself, but also of the unfolding of a discussion. This unfolding becomes an important text for capturing real invention processes. Students can easily return to the beginning of the discussion and follow it through to the end by using the computer or by printing the document to be studied away from the computer. Such documentation serves as a powerful pedagogical resource:

- Students can return to the written record to pick up lost threads in a conversation that they feel are worthy of exploration.

- The written record can be used to show how students take advantage of the opportunity to revise an unclear thought or a changed opinion in writing at a later date.

- Students can do close readings of each other's contributions to the discussion and use these readings as points of departure for their own contributions—an important skill in academic writing.

- Small-group discussions can be shared with other groups in the class to compare and contrast.

- The written record can be used to illustrate invention strategies, characterize carefully developed opinions as opposed to knee-jerk reactions, and highlight the differences between written and spoken discourse.

In the end, CmD offers students a straight forward, visible illustration of the difficult-to-grasp concept that writing itself is an on going discussion.

Development of a Reflective Posture.   Reading and writing CmD *require* a reflective approach due to the chaotic nature of how CmD is presented. Even within the smaller groups, this disorder is present. Also, on any given day, there are different discussions "coming" to my computer—faculty discussions, the local volleyball league committee, student assignments. Add to the mix any "personal" mail that the students may be sending and receiving outside the context of my classes. None of this employs the traditional sense of sequence that most of us are used to in discussion. Reading and responding in this way are, at first, indeed difficult. But as one moves through the progression of texts, he or she will begin to see connections and relationships, to sense a pulling together of ideas to the point where the discussion evolves into a unified text.

One way to develop the reflective posture necessary for CmD is through understanding "context"—the relationship of audience and occasion. Establishing context in writing and identifying context in reading are difficult tasks for students. And often, our classroom discussions don't provide students with concrete examples of context that easily translate into their writing. For example, consider what we often think of as the qualities of a "good" classroom discussion: the participation of many different students with different perspectives, lively exploration, raised levels of excitement, a quick forward pace. In such a discussion, audience (the students in the classroom) and occasion (the class meeting and the discussion assignment) are clear from the onset. The teacher—or sometimes a student—begins by posing a question or prompt, and students and the teacher take turns making contributions to the discussion. The faster the conversation moves forward, the more linear its sequence—one comment is followed by a direct response which is followed by another response.

Especially when first learning the art of face-to-face, classroom discussion, students rarely "go back" to respond to a comment made ten minutes previously (and unfortunately, if students who wish to speak aren't offered the opportunity to do so immediately, all too often they put their hands down and their contributions go unspoken). On the rare occasion that students do wish to return to a point made earlier, their comments need not be contextualized much beyond, "I want to go back to what Amy said earlier." In the setting of the classroom discussion, this contextualization has served our purposes—the occasion and the audience of the discussion probably haven't changed, and no one has really forgotten what Amy said.

Time, place, and sequence make students' work a little more perplexing when establishing context in CmD; it more closely resembles what is required of them in audience-based essay writing. Just as in a classroom discussion, a carefully planned CmD begins with a clear context, a defined occasion and audience, planted by the teacher. However, students are not sitting together at the same time in the same room, nor do their contributions to the discussion follow any type of linear sequence. Stephen may be eager to respond to something Amy said about a reading assignment. However, Stephen's response probably won't immediately and directly follow Amy's text in a linear sequence. Therefore, every response made to a previous contribution must be contextualized by some type of summary; "I want to go back to what Amy said earlier" will make little sense to Stephen's discussion team. Stephen must precede his contribution with a summary or paraphrase of what Amy said that caused him to respond. Paraphrasing and summary writing in CmD are reflective activities that promote careful reading and critical thinking, a balance between what has been said and what will be said.

I want to return to an interview I cited earlier in this chapter with Brad, a student of ours who truly struggled with his writing. When asked about his experiences conversing with Marcia using e-mail, Brad relates:

> I think the system's neat, because it gives you more time to think. . . . I like
> how you can look back on something. Like you said something in your pre-

vious letter . . . where in writing I'll just . . . I like being able to refer back to stuff. And like I can leave something . . . like I can leave the e-mail . . . like I can leave the e-mail, save it, and then go back to it after I do something. I don't have to finish it right now.

As a student who requires more time to complete his work than most of his peers, Brad sees two important elements of CmD: He has more time to think about his ideas and can thus work at his own pace, and he has the opportunity to review parts of the discussion that have already taken place. These are important reflective qualities of CmD's ability to facilitate invention. It is impressive, to say the least, that Brad recognized these qualities and sees how they can influence his learning. He sees that CmD invites an exploratory approach toward discussion and requires a reflective posture; he is allowed time to process his readings of and responses to his peers' texts, thus avoiding the immediate pressure to perform in class or to produce a "correct" answer.

Integrating CmD: Sequencing Assignments

I have found great value in using CmD as an end in and of itself. At the same time, CmD can play an important role in the sequencing of larger projects, existing as a significant vehicle for students' invention. For example, consider the following assignment:

Part I: The Research Project

Research Teams

On the first day of this class, I asked for you, in small groups, to respond to the following assignment:

In your research groups, make a list of ten thematic units that you feel belong in a reading text that is arranged around topics of interest to college freshmen. Your group should make a final written copy of your list and turn it in to me at the end of class.

From those lists, I created the following list of items that appeared on almost everyone's list:

---

1. AIDS

2. Race relations/racism

3. Education/college life/curricular trends

4. Family/relationships

5. Crime and violence

Then I asked you to respond to the following SWP:

Provide a brief justification for why ONE of the above topics should be included in the textbook. What makes this topic interesting to college freshmen? Why is this topic important? What types of information and points of view could be included in a chapter about this topic?

Based on the writing that you completed, I have divided you into research teams that will investigate the following broad topics:

1. Race relations and racism: Can we really all get along?
   e-mail: englsld2@lists.acs.ohio-state.edu

2. AIDS: What progress have we made?
   e-mail: englsld3@lists.acs.ohio-state.edu

3. Family/relationships: How do they shape our lives?
   e-mail: englsld4@lists.acs.ohio-state.edu

4. Education: What are our concerns, what is our future?
   e-mail: englsld5@lists.acs.ohio-state.edu

Your group has been assigned a Computer-mediated Discussion (CmD) e-mail address. Much of your group collaboration will take place on the network. When you send mail to your group address, all members will receive a copy. Scott DeWitt and Kent Baker (class tutor) will also receive copies of your group mail.

The Assignment

Your team is responsible for putting together a collection of research resources for the members of this class. The finished collection of research resources will be a series of articles that team members have located and copied on their given topic, each preceded by a cover sheet consisting of a summary and a proper MLA bibliographic citation.

Your research team needs to complete the following tasks by the assigned dates:

Friday, 3 February 1995

- Using your CmD address, send a message to your research team in which you 1) discuss your interest in your assigned research topic and 2) discuss the types of articles/issues that you think your group should include in its collection of research resources.

- Reading assignment. Each group will be given a reading assignment that they should complete before the next class period.

Note: Your reading assignment may or may not guide the direction your research team takes in preparing its collection of research resources.

Tuesday, 7 February 1995

- Check e-mail. Find consensus in your research team concerning the types of articles/issues that you think your group should include in its collection of research resources.

- Respond to CmD assignment based on your reading assignment.

- Locate three articles for your collection of research resources.

- All articles should be "substantive."

- All articles must be signed (no AP articles, for example).

Thursday, 9 February 1995

- Write at 3–5 sentence summary of the three articles you located. Mail these summaries to your research team.

- Check e-mail. Based on the 3–5 sentence summaries written by your team members, recommend to each team member two of the three articles they located that should be included in the collection of research resources.

Thursday, 16 February 1995

- Each team member chooses two articles to include in the collection of research resources based on the team's recommendations. Team members should make a clean copy of each article and attach a cover sheet that includes proper MLA bibliographic citation and a full-length summary of the article (I will offer you a sample of this cover sheet).

- The entire collection of research resources should be turned in to me by 2:00 p.m. so that I can put it on library ` reserve.

Again, I have presented my students with a complex, detailed assignment that outlines a sequence of what they are to have completed by a certain date. This assignment also clearly describes the types of e-mail discussion students are to participate in within this sequence:

1. Personal interest in the research topic.

2. Personal interest in how to narrow the broad research question assigned to each team.

3. Consensus about how to narrow the broad research question assigned to each team.

4. CmD based on the groups' reading assignments.

5. Peer response/suggestions for which materials to include in the research resources.

CmD teams were sent the following CmD questions based on their reading assignments to begin generating ideas for their projects:

1. Race relations and racism: Can we really all get along?
   e-mail: englsld2@magnus.acs.ohio-state.edu

"Disillusioned in the Promised Land"
Trey Ellis

"The problem is that both sides need to be educated about each other. It's not only that the white kids see the blacks as illiterate athletes or affirmative-action-lottery winners. The blacks see the whites as callous and corny, garden-variety rich kids. But those polarities are seldom acknowledged publicly."

Question to consider:

Many students in this class have said that a unique quality of your generation is that you are more open-minded than generations in the past. Open-mindedness, it would seem, is predicated on open communication.

Do you feel that young people today communicate openly about racism and race relations? Describe ways in which you feel young people today do or do not communicate openly and open-mindedly about race and race relations. Also, describe ways in which this communication could improve.

2. AIDS: What progress have we made?
   e-mail: englsld3@magnus.acs.ohio-state.edu

"Magic and AIDS: Presumed Innocent"
Michael Bronski

"But when all is said and done, the problem with the press coverage on all AIDS cases is that it relies on soap-opera scenarios and flash-and-trash sound-bite journalism. After almost a decade, the press still has no idea of how to write about AIDS clearly and honestly. People living with AIDS have to be labeled as either "guilty" or "innocent" victims; the failings of the health care system to deal with the range and variety of HIV infection is seen as idiosyncratic and not part of a larger social problem, and the reporting of personal tragedy is seen as more important than consistent and useful prevention guidelines and information."

Bronski's text was written in 1992—more than ten years after the discovery of AIDS and the beginning of a health care crisis. Do you feel that his criticisms are consistent with your experiences with the media's coverage of HIV and AIDS? Describe ways in which you feel the media have done a good job reporting on the AIDS crisis and ways in which you feel they have focused on "flash-and-trash" journalism. Also, do you feel the media have provided you with "consistent and useful prevention guidelines and information," or have you had to find that information elsewhere? You may consider this in terms of your own personal need for information or in your responsibility to convey accurate information to someone else (as a parent, teacher, older sibling, church leader, etc.).

3. Family/relationships: How do they shape our lives?
    e-mail: englsld4@magnus.acs.ohio-state.edu

Karen Lindsey
"Friends as Family"

"The traditional family isn't working. This should not come as a startling revelation to anyone who picks up this book: It may be the single fact on which every American, from the Moral Majority member through the radical feminist, agrees . . . Now an even greater concept [of the family] has entered into our minds. We can choose most of our family. We can choose ALL of our family. In some ways, recognition of this possibility has begun to surface in popular culture. Recently, several magazines published articles about the need to create new, familial ways to celebrate holidays. . . . Friends, neighbors, coworkers have often lived through as many experiences together as husbands and wives and have created equally strong bonds."

Consider the statements made by Lindsey. First of all, do you think that "the traditional family isn't working"? Why or why not? Also, how do you respond to her proposal, that we need a new definition of family that extends beyond blood and marriage? What is your definition of "family?" Does it include "friends, neighbors, co-workers?" Do you think we can "choose" our family?

4. Education: What are our concerns, what is our future?
   e-mail: englsld5@magnus.acs.ohio-state.edu

Theodore R. Sizer
"What High School Is"

"[Many believe that] school is to be like a job: [Y]ou start in the morning and end in the afternoon, five days a week. School is conceived of as the children's workplace, and it takes young people off parents' hands and out of the labor market during prime-time work hours. Not surprisingly, many students see going to school as little more than a dogged necessity. They perceive the day-to-day routine . . .as one of 'boredom and lethargy.' One of the students summarizes: School is 'boring, restless, tiresome, puts ya to sleep, tedious, monotonous, pain in the neck.'"

Do you feel that most people hold the above view of today's public school system? Do most young people find school boring? If so, describe why so many students view their educational experience as boring. If not, describe ways in which the present school system is engaging students. In what ways could our current educational system be more interesting to students, and what would the effect be?

Because I am included in all of the discussions described above, I am able to intervene in instructive ways. My intervening comments can add to students' inventions, especially when they are content-based, where I share my own experiences, offer information that I've come across, or illustrate how I disagree with someone's point of view. I also play the role of facilitator, keeping the discussion focused, purposeful, and on topic, serving as a model of a

good discussant. When I ask students to gather in small groups in my classroom, I usually move from group to group, dropping in on the clusters of students. At the end of the activity, I may summarize the bits and pieces I heard
for the entire class and then ask the students to fill in what I missed, trying to
bring together the fragmented pieces of the various discussions into a "sense
of the class." I play a similar role in CmD. I learned early on that I cannot expect to read every contribution to every discussion: if each student in a class
of twenty-five makes four contributions to a computer-mediated discussion,
I end up receiving one hundred pieces of e-mail per class, for just one unit.
However, by occasionally "dropping in" on computer-mediated discussions,
I can model appropriate discussion strategies, direct students back on topic
when they stray, praise students for insightful commentary, and urge students
who are not contributing significantly to the discussion to participate more
actively. Because students' contributions to CmD must be made available to
their entire discussion team, it is only fair that my intervening comments are
made public, too:

Date: Thursday, 9 February
From: Scott Lloyd DeWitt <dewitt.18@osu.edu>
Subject: School
To: englsld5@magnus.acs.ohio-state.edu

Obviously, everyone in this class is interested in the topic
of education at some level. You are all going to college
(and I went for 10 years and plan to teach for a very long
time), so we all have something in common. But there
were some interesting threads that were common in each
of your responses. The first is that you believe that teachers need to take more responsibility in the learning
process. For example, Lori said:

>Most students feel this way because the teachers act
>like they are just doing their jobs, not helping to further
>our education. Most teachers don't do fun activities
>for students, and that is what makes school fun and
>interesting. I think that maybe teachers should be
>required to take some special seminars or classes on
>making school interesting and fun for students.

Tim said:

>The best teachers I had were ones who got students
>involved in the studies by posing interesting problems to
>us, got us to work on them in groups, and assist us in
>our brainstorming. A teacher who is entertaining and has
>a passion for what he/she teaches is outstanding.
>Finally, teachers who understand their students and can
>relate to them on their level get students enthusiastic
>about learning.

I don't know if I agree that the seminars should only focus
on "fun," but I do believe that teacher training should be
ongoing. The concept seems simple enough: As times
change, students change. And as students change,
teachers need to find new methods to reach these students and to solve the new problems that arise in the
classroom. So if one of the problems is "boredom," then
yes, I agree with Lori that we need to make school fun
again. But if the problem is that students have fallen behind or are not prepared, like Alice suggested, then we
need to find ways to catch them up.

Alice said:

> Most people I've talked to think that there is a problem
>with public schools, and that the kids aren't being
>prepared to go out and get a job, or even continue their
>education.

And now compare that to Jon's response:

>With the system the way it is today you are required to
>take certain classes whether you want to or not. Which
>can make the classes pretty boring if they're not about
>something you enjoy.

I can speak firsthand that this is a conflict that teachers really don't know how to handle—and truly are taking a lot criticism for. First of all, I guess that I don't think that school is only about "getting a job." It's about becoming a critical thinker about our world and becoming a creative citizen who has the capacity and compassion to "give back." But the reality is that people need training, and school is where they are going to get that. So teachers prepare curriculums, in turn, to prepare students for the workplace. And people tell us that a) we are not preparing our students and b) we make them take a bunch of classes that they don't "need" (the boring ones). Some-days I'm not really sure what to do.

Do you think that the problem is just about maturity? Tim said:

>Most young people find school to be boring because
>they are young and want to do so many things in a day,
>and they have different priorities than older people.

And do you think this is really a new problem? Perhaps, as Alice suggests,

>school has always been boring to kids.

I guess that the one person we haven't placed any re-sponsibility on in this conversation is—the student. If, as a teacher, I am supposed to be exciting and entertaining, prepare my students for the workforce, and continue my education to bring the best teaching practices to the classroom, what are the students going to do? What are their responsibilities?

Scott

Often, I find that this type of summary/feedback approach can "jumpstart" a conversation for students by not only reminding them of what they have said and read—a "sense of the class"—but also by raising new questions for them about their research topics. For such a long posting, I answered very few questions, and I did very little "professing," as difficul as that was.

All the work students have completed to this point, including the discussions, the research, the bibliographic citations, and the research resources—culminates in Part II of the writing project.

Part II: The Researched Essay

The Researched Essay asks you to develop a paper based on Part I: The Research Project. Although this writing task seems open-ended, I have guidelines for you to follow:

- Your essay must grow out of one of the broad topics this class chose to research:

    1. Race relations and racism: Can we really all get along?

    2. AIDS: What progress have we made?

    3. Relationships: How do they shape our lives?

    4. Education: What are our concerns, what is our future?

You may continue working on the topic you were originally assigned, or you may work with another of our class's research topics. Four copies of your research resources are available on reserve in the library. I encourage you to use these resources.

- Your paper should exhibit a clear purpose. Two general directions are available:

Critical documented response: Similar to Writing Project 2, a critical documented response allows you to present a thesis that grows out of your reading of a particular text. Your research serves as support of your thesis.

Critical documented exploration: A critical documented exploration seeks to explore conflict and controversy on a particular topic. Instead of forwarding a position, your thesis acknowledges that differing perspectives exist about your topic, and your research explores and presents multiple viewpoints.

- Your essay should be directed towards a specific, academically educated audience, one that is interested in and/or personally involved with the issue or topic you are addressing.

- Your essay should be fully developed, rich in details and examples. Your essay must be supported by strong evidence and thoughtful reasoning. You should carefully incorporate into your essay at least five research sources using correct MLA documentation.

- Your essay should be in the neighborhood of 5 double-spaced pages.

All of the different types of discussion students participated in for this project did not take place exclusively online. At times, they carried over into classroom conversations and beyond the classroom walls. However, many were initiated and truly actualized using the computer.

Concluding Discussions

CmD serves as an example of how we can advance a rich, positive integration of computer technology and sound pedagogy. Much of what I learned in developing methods for using e-mail in my writing classes directly influenced my experiences with a very different teaching technology: the World Wide Web. Yet, as with any new teaching strategy I have employed, I continually remind myself that the focus of my computer-supported classes needs to remain on the study of our subject areas—writing, reading, thinking, learning—and on embracing any new technology that might help us reach our pedagogical goals.

I have decided to include as an appendix to this chapter a computer-mediated discussion that reveals volumes about the use of this technology in the teaching of composition. This CmD occurred among three new writing tutors, their supervisor, and Marcia and myself. These tutors worked part-time in our classes and part-time in the writing center and were witnessing our early attempts at using e-mail in our classes. I stumbled upon this conversation years after it actually took place and found it to be an interesting reading of some of the stories I have told in this chapter. The tutors' perspectives are as insightful as they are entertaining.

Appendix: One Computer-Mediated Discussion on Computer-Mediated Discussion

---

Date: Tue, 14 Feb 1995 11:57:05 EST
From: Scott
To: englsld8@magnus.acs.ohio-state.edu
Subject: CmD—Cautions

In his article, "Computer-mediated Discussion," Scott Lloyd DeWitt, for the most part, discusses the benefits of using CmD in the writing classroom. Should he have issued some "cautions" for teachers who are new to his methods? What potential problems oan you foresee, both pedagogical and practical?

Write a response to the above question. You should mail your contribution to your group address.

Date: Thu, 16 Feb 1995 17:20:11 EST
From: Amanda
To: englsld8@lists.acs.ohio-state.edu
Subject: CmD response

Hi, everyone! I haven't been able to connect to the server and acquire my messages—that's one problem I can see with CmD! Anyway, one problem that I can see happening is students feeling intimidated the first few times that they do this type of a response. (I'm feeling that way right now and I usually feel pretty comfortable around everyone in the group!) I think this will lead to less productive disscussions in the first few weeks. I can also see where the extra time involved would hold students back from adding all of their thoughts. They may come up with a really great point, but not have time, or just be too lazy, to send the response to the group. Some students may also be more comfortable expressing themselves verbally than on paper (or in this case, computer screen). This could also lead to input that is not shared with the group. A few students may also choose to blame things on the computer. ("I wrote my response, but it disappeared.") I hope you guys understand my points. If we were face to face, I could ask you and make sure you knew what I meant!!!

Happy responding!!

Amanda :)

Date: Fri, 17 Feb 1995 15:50:57 EST
From: Lon
To: englsld8@lists.acs.ohio-state.edu
Subject: RE: CmD—Cautions

Discussions with nobody there is really different. This could be one problem area that I see, especially if the group is in 052 or 053. Some students in those classes are unaccustomed to discussions anyway and might be intimidated by the computer, the writing, or the audience. If a person has never used a computer they are intimidated by the "monster with the keyboard" anyway. When I was in 052 I was so scared that I was going to "hurt" or break the computer.

Face to face discussions are hard enough at times but to talk to others that the student doesn't know or can't see can scare them from "saying" what they really mean in a way that others can understand.

Another problem that I see with using e-mail discussions could be procrastination. Some such as myself would put off the assignment until they had to do it.

Date: Mon, 20 Feb 1995 09:54:31 -0600 (CST)
From: Scott

Subject: RE: CmD—Cautions
To: englsld8@lists.acs.ohio-state.edu

The problem that I am dealing with most now that I am using CmD is "basic management." I have included my e-mail address in all of my students' group discussion addresses. This means that everytime a student posts a contribution to that address, I receive a copy. Add this to another e-mail discussion group that I belong to as well as the normal, day-to-day e-mail, and I can get up to 100 messages a day. I don't have to tell you that I can't handle that much mail.

Many people are concerned that e-mail will further blur the boundaries between work and nonwork for faculty members. Especially for those of us who use e-mail at home, now students and bosses can have access to us in yet another way and be more demanding of our time. I'm not sure I actually agree with this one. It seems to me that If a student wanted to reach me to ask a question about a paper, or if my Dean wanted to assign a new project to me, he or she would pick up the phone and call me at home if they couldn't wait until they saw me at school. Also, one of the things that I love about my job is that those boundaries have always been blurred, that I don't work a 9 to 5. I don't think e-mail is truly going to further blur boundaries—I think the technology is new, it's different, and it APPEARS to blur boundaries. In reality, I don't have to check my e-mail at home. And if I do feel that I have to check it at home, I don't have to respond to a request until I want to. If I answer my phone, for the most part, I have to talk to the person on the other end of the line.

Amanda made the following point:

>Anyway, one problem that I can see happening is
>students feeling intimidated the first few times that they

>do this type of a response. (I'm feeling that way right
>now and I usually feel pretty comfortable around every
>one in the group!) I think this will lead to less productive
>disscussions in the first few weeks.

This reminds me that we often forget that students need to
"learn" to participate in good discussions—both verbal and
computer-mediated. Everyone participates in discussions
on a daily basis. But the "classroom" discussion is a very
different bird. Students need to "learn" how to participate in
discussions. This will also be true of CmD. I need to teach
them the priciples of CmD, and then they need to practice.

Lon said:

>Face to face discussions are hard enough at times but
>to talk to others that the student doesn't know or can't
>see can scare them from "saying" what they really mean
>in a way that others can understand.

I wish to continue my point above. What Lon is saying is
that we are, just like other types of writing, running into a
problem with "audience." I think what Lon is saying is that
CmD requires yet another understanding of audience,
one that we can't assume of our students. This, of course,
falls back on the instructors to "teach" this sense of audience necessary for CmD.

I hear myself saying that if any boundaries are blurring,
they are "writing" and "discussion"—I wonder if this is
good or bad for our students? I wonder if this helps some
students and confuses others?

      Scott

Date: Mon, 20 Feb 1995 11:50:54 EST
From: Amanda
To: englsld8@lists.acs.ohio-state.edu
Subject: Another reply

Scott was questioning whether the "blurring" of writing and discussion was good or bad for students. In my own personal experiences, it has proven to be beneficial. Writing as a way of discussing has helped me to become a more active participant in "actual" oral discussions. Writing responses has enabled me to develop my ideas more quickly than I used to. I feel like I can jump in on a discussion without sounding stupid or finally coming up with a point after we have moved on to another topic.

Discussion through writing has also helped me to be more concrete in my writing. It helped me to realize that audience is important in writing. When you are not talking face to face, the reader is not given a chance to question something that they don't understand. As a writer, you have to make sure that everything is clear.

After spending time in the 053 class, however, I can see where some of the students would have a problem with putting writing and discussion together. They are still not willing to open up in discussions and many of them are not comfortable with their writing which would hinder the progress of CmD groups.

> See you Tuesday.
> Amanda :)

From: Lynda
Subject: Re: Another reply
To: englsld8@lists.acs.ohio-state.edu
Date: Tue, 21 Feb 1995 08:58:20 -0500 (EST)

Dear Amanda et al.,

As usual, your (Amanda) response shows sensitivity not only to the context in which you work, but also awareness of others' styles. Because you are such a good observer, can you think of anything we can do to meet the needs of students who are inhibited by writing? Would making the initial prompts shorter make any difference? Do you think that it makes a difference that in the beginning, they are only writing to the members of their group? Would deleting the instructor's name from the groups in the beginning help them to be freer in their responses? Are there other ways we can make writing more like speech? Is that even a valid way to encourage response? I'm thinking that even the most reticent of formal text writers write notes back and forth to each other during class; can we structure the initial computer discussions to be more like little letters? Do we want to?

So many questions, so little time :—> Lynda

Date: Mon, 20 Feb 1995 23:01:33 EST
From: Kent
To: englsld8@lists.acs.ohio-state.edu
Subject: cmd response

I see the problems that are pointed out by Lon and Amanda in terms of hesitation to use the computers, and the questions raised of being nervous about the audience, and not knowing exactly how to write to an audience in this forum. I can also see a problem in terms of procrastination, but over all, I do not see this type of communication as an obstacle or a problem that has to be overcome. I think that the cmd is a wonderful tool that can be used in the classroom, and also have a great outcome. I feel that the fact of being afraid of the computer is cured simply by time on the computer, this is evident in the English 110 class that I am tutoring at the present time. Many students were terrified of the computers when they first arrived in the class, and after about two weeks, they seemed to be very comfortable with the whole idea. The same thing occured when we started the cmd in that same class, but after they sent a couple of messages to their peers, and recieved some, they seemed to loosen up quite a bit.

Another area that was discussed was "audience." I myself, have never been nervous when talking to a group. I have found the cmd to be a way that I can get more of my ideas out into a discussion, and also I have greater control over what I am saying. If I am in a very large group, I have problems in terms of getting a chance to speak. This really bothers me, and often causes me to forget what I am about to say, or it causes me to get extremely upset when I can not interject my opinions into a conversation, even though not everyone may want to hear what I have to say. The other way in which I think the cmd is beneficial, is that I have greater control over what I am saying, especially when discussing a heated topic. In a live, in class discussion, I can get excited, and often stick my foot in my mouth. This still happens, but in the forum of a cmd, it happens less frequently.

Procrastination, this is one of my trademarks, in fact it is a way of life for me. I think that if one wanted to, they could find a way to put anything off. In my case, I think that one of the easiest ways to communicate is by cmd. I personally find it a pain in the neck to sit down and write to someone on paper. With the cmd, it is possible to talk to someone anytime, especially when I am around computers everyday. This also makes it possible to talk to someone whenever an idea pops into mind.

Over all, I like computer-mediated discussions. I did however forget to mention one very important downfall of the whole system. When the computers go down, like they so often do, I get the sudden urge to fix them with a large hammer, as do the rest of you, I'm sure.

Tuesday sounds good! Where are we meeting?
    Kent

Date: Mon, 20 Feb 1995 23:56:13 EST
From: Kent
To: englsld8@lists.acs.ohio-state.edu
Subject: cmd...Another response from Kent.

First let me apologize on behalf of my friend, Mr. Computer, for neglecting to send any of my e-mail on Monday. This would explain my lateness in sending all of you some response writing.

I would like to respond to Amanda's second response. She mentioned how writing helps to establish a very firm sense of audience, and also helps to form solid points of view. My own experience has taught me that my own comments and thoughts are much more developed when I have time to write them out first. This does not happen often in a face-to-face conversation because there is obviously no time to think things out to the extent that there is when they are written out. And as far as audience goes, you usually know exactly who you are talking to. Amanda also points out that she can now jump into a discussion and feel more confident about her views. I agree completely. Not only do I feel more confident about my opinions in a well thought out cmd, but my thought process has improved to the point that I can speak in a face-to-face conversation more effectively.

> That's all for now!!
> Kent

Date: Mon, 27 Feb 1995 12:49:03 EST
From: Lon
To: englsld8@lists.acs.ohio-state.edu

The discussion that we had Wed. about the paper that Scott brought in started me to thinking. I thought about why I chose to focus in on developing paragraphs and not on the thesis and developing the paper from there. Scott and Lynda both said that they would suggest that the student start with the thesis and clarify it. Then write the paper from there. As I was helping a student Thurs. I decided to really think about the process that I go through in trying to help someone with their paper. The student brought in his paper and I did the following.

1) I read the paper without saying anything to the student or without marking the paper.

2) I then talked to the student and asked him what he was trying to say or prove in the paper.

3) I then went through and discussed with him what it seemed to me he was saying in the paper.

4) We then went through and decided that what his thesis statement was saying and what the paper were saying were two different things.

I guess this was the reason that when we were discussing what we would suggest about Scott's student's paper that I honed in on developing the paragraphs and not the thesis. I was looking for what the student was saying because I feel that the thesis can be written to go along with what the student really thinks and is trying to say in the paper.

Date: Mon, 27 Feb 1995 20:12:10 EST
From: Amanda
To: englsld8@lists.acs.ohio-state.edu
Subject: response

I tend to look at papers in the same way that Lon does. I read the paper the whole way through and ask the student what their thesis was. Then, I tell them what I saw as being the main idea of the paper. Most of the time, they realize that what they wrote wasn't exactly what they wanted to say. We talk about it and (usually) they have a better idea of how to clarify their thesis and make it fit the rest of the paper. Personally, I have to sit down and write a paper and then write my thesis to (hopefully) tie everything together. What method does everyone else use?

From: Scott
Subject: Re: response
To: englsld8@lists.acs.ohio-state.edu
Date: Tue, 28 Feb 1995 08:35:27 -0500 (EST)

I think that Amanda and Lon are onto something here, and it's not necessarily their methods, but instead their philosophy—USE WHATEVER WORKS! I remember when I was on the job market and would be asked about my philosophy of teaching writing. I always wanted to say, "Whatever it takes, know what I mean?" The funny thing is—I could have said that here at Marion and Marcia and Lynda would have nodded and said, "Yes, we know what you mean."

Your methods are good. Basically you are putting yourself in the position of a reader who summarizes the writers' papers. Keep in mind that the writer SHOULD have a summary of his/her own paper in mind. And when your summary doesn't match the writer's summary, you've got something to work with. At the same time, you have to keep in mind that the writer often DOESN'T have a summary in mind. Then you have to take a different approach, because telling them what you think the main point is defeats the purpose. Students will say, "Ya, I guess you're right. That's the main point." And you have done the work, not the student.

Yesterday I worked with a student who came to my office and asked me to read a paper. She said, "I think that when I finish this, it will be five times as long as everyone else's." Her problem was that her thesis was perfect—right on the money. The problem was the next three pages. She wanted to define terms, yet she didn't begin to address her thesis until page four. Here asking her to write a thesis to "fit" the paper would not have worked. The thesis became a good tool to get her back on track.

So where are the rest of you? I think there is something wrong with my computer—it tends to delete all mail from Marcia. I haven't received a thing yet. ;-p""

Scott

From: Lynda
Subject: Lon's methods
To: englsld8@lists.acs.ohio-state.edu
Date: Tue, 28 Feb 1995 08:52:12 -0500 (EST)

Dear Englsld.8's,

I found Lon's summary of his methods interesting because it seems as if he DOES the thesis stuff when he's working with a student, but when confronted by a "studentless" paper, he does what many of us teachers do—he hones in on the (for want of a better term) little stuff like paragraphs. It takes conscious effort on my part to hold off paying attention to surface level errors, syntax problems, and paragraph incoherence until the student has stated his/her thesis and explained how she/he intends to develop it. I have this problem much more when I have the paper without the student. When the student is in front of me, it's easier. We had sort of set up an artificial situation last week by just looking at a paper and saying, "What would you say to this student?"

I will not be at the meeting today because I am going to hear Ann Townsend and David Baker read. See ya, Lynda

Date: Sun, 5 Mar 1995 19:41:14 CST
From: Marcia
To: englsld8@lists.acs.ohio-state.edu
Subject: Everyone's response to everything

Okay, okay . . . I checked my computer and discovered that all my e-mail to englsld8 had been wiped out by a conversation virus (not the computer's, mine). So I guess I could either reproduce what I *might* have said or continue with the conversation in this last week. I chose the latter, but it seems to me that the Bartholomae article brings up a great many of the issues from the responses of last week.

In nearly all cases, the question seems to be—"Where do I start?" I agree with Lynda that when faced with a paper that is a mire of problems—both surface- and content-level problems—the easiest thing to do is attack the surface- and language-level problems. It also may be the least helpful. Here this writer is, struggling to figure out what it means to "write an essay" (it's not, remember, a natural act), and the source of help (the teacher/tutor) starts talking about noun/pronoun agreement or about topic sentences. How can you know what a topic sentence would be if you don't know what you're supposed to do with one much less how a topic sentence differs from a thesis sentence?

That "not knowing what to do" aspect of teaching writing is the most interesting to me. Surely, I didn't know how to write an academic essay when I was first in school. I wrote something that fell somewhere between a creative writing assignment (I always made up hypothetical examples that proved my case) and tirades against the author, the system (any system) and whatever else seemed fair game. I see that in the basic writers and early freshmen also—the basic writers, however, don't have a sense of writing as a conversation. Thus the audience part that's come up several times. I find my basic writing students have a much easier time writing on e-mail than writing in class (it's easier for them to make journal entries, too). Their mistakes often disappear (exception—spelling) and their tone starts to sound like one person writing to another. So . . . my question is this: How do we convince basic writers and other students to abandon the discourse they don't know and use the discourse they *do* know? They've got to reach that point where they are explaining what they want the audience to know before we can show them the "right" or academic way.

I guess I ramble—but it all seems tied in with everything else. Bartholomae wants to make students write like their professors. I think most of their professors are pretty dull and unimaginative writers. What he really means is that he wants students to *think* like their professors . . . and that's a danger of an entirely different sort.

See you in class on Tuesday—Bartholomae is up for conversational analysis. Do we really want to think and write like this man?

Marcia

3

Inventing Hypertext Reading

I run into Michael regularly, even now, eight years after he left a second-year composition class I was teaching. We have friends as well as social hangouts in common, so, much to my enjoyment, our paths cross often. Always, within the first few minutes of seeing him, he manages to say, "hypertextuality," with a big grin on his face: "So, how are things going with *hypertextuality?*" or "Just the other week, I was thinking about *hypertextuality.*" Michael had seen a copy of my doctoral dissertation sitting on my desk one day as I was revising a section of it for publication. I explained hypertext to him and offered a few real world examples he recognized that helped ground my definition for him. During the time he had been enrolled in my class, we didn't have access to computers that supported any hypertext programs, so he was obviously more interested in the word itself than he possibly could have been in the technological application. Today, I don't think he knows what "hypertextuality" means, but the word rolls off his tongue like it came from his own dissertation.

Interestingly, Michael may be one of the few people I know who still speaks the term, "hypertext."

Although many people do not know the term "hypertext," they do know its concept, especially with the popularity and accessibility of the World Wide Web, a computer environment where users design or navigate among chunks of information or data with the use of electronic links. I imagine that "hypertext" sounds too academic or too scholarly to be a part of a popular lexicon; in fact, aside from a few computer hackers, academics and scholars are the only folks I know who still use this term. Maybe it's just the "—text" in the term that pushes people away from it, associating "text" with "textbook" which, again, brings us back to the academic. One of the first widely accessible hypertext applications, HyperCard, that came with every new Macintosh computer, didn't even use the term "hypertext" in its documentation. Most who know that Web pages are written in "HTML" see the acronym as a word in and of itself and don't consciously think (if they ever knew) that it stands for "hypertext markup language." After a number of years' experience on the Web, I had to turn to the discussants on a LISTSERV to find that "http," the beginning of all Web addresses, actually stands for "hypertext transfer protocol." So for as much as hypertext is used today on the Web alone, the word itself is somewhat invisible.

Usually, if a word or term doesn't work for people, I figure, "Let it go." And I'd be more than happy to let go of "hypertext," except that it so perfectly represents how compositionists can think about this technological application and how I am going to describe the union of technology and invention in this book. Ted Nelson, who in the 1960s coined the term, used "extended" and "multidimensional" to define the prefix, "hyper-" ("Replacing," 1980). "Dynamic" also comes to mind, as in "always evolving and ever-changing," as does "beyond," as in "to push a superficial boundary." The Latin, *texere*, meant "weave," and its past participle, *textus*, was often used in a noun form to mean "woven material" (the English "text" actually has its origins in the Old French "texte") (Ayto, 1988, 526). This vision of text as woven material is appealing to me as a metaphor for the type of thinking I want students to do as they invent content for their writing. I want students to see invention as a series of moments that occur when they notice and see relationships and make connections. The more numerous and diverse these moments of invention, the more elaborate the cognitive fabric that begins to form. This fabric, a mental text made up of students' thinking, is, in this case, their invention. The instruction that I create pushes students to become deeply engaged in invention so that they create a cognitive fabric that is dense in weave and rich in pattern. "*Hyper*" and "*text*" work together, then, to refer to a woven fabric of created and discovered knowledge, ideas, and information that is extendable and alterable with the use of computer technology. When we begin to combine metaphors of computer texts and mental texts, we begin to see students' thinking as a technology represented to a certain extent in hypertext technology. Even more so, we can see how the technology can heighten students' awareness of their learning processes.

Still, the etymology of the word keeps its definition rather vague and nebulous, especially for someone new to the technology. When I first heard the term "hypertext" in 1989, I was directed numerous times to Jeff Conklin's 1987 article, "Hypertext: An Introduction and Survey." For a number of reasons, this piece is still cited as a definitive research base for those needing background and historical information on hypertext. Besides offering simple definitions, examples of hypertext applications, and a history of the technology, Conklin argues for the importance of "hypertext as experience," emphasizing or highlighting the "user." For example, Conklin asserts that no matter how clear the definition of hypertext, a reader will probably still never gain a clear understanding of the concepts of hierarchical and nonlinear organization, linking, and associative branching that are key to hypertext systems without the experience of working with hypertext or without some knowledge of certain literary or rhetorical theory (even with my descriptive scenario above, many readers unfamiliar with hypertext may find themselves in the very place Conklin identifies). Conklin stresses, "The reader who has not used hypertext should expect that at best he [or she] will gain a perception of hypertext as a collection of interesting features. . . . In fact, one must *work* in current hypertext environments for a while for the collection of features to coalesce into a useful tool" (emphasis mine) (1987, 17–18).

Almost every hypertext survey published, including Conklin's, directs its readers to the year 1945 while trying to define hypertext. No one can claim that 1945 was lacking in historical moments. World War II ended after a year that saw the succession of Harry S. Truman as President of the United States after the death of Franklin D. Roosevelt, the dropping of atomic bombs on Hiroshima and Nagasaki by the United States, the birth of the United Nations, and the death of both Mussolini and Hitler. George Orwell wrote *Animal Farm*, while Rodgers and Hammerstein's *Carousel* opened on Broadway. Woman's suffrage became law in France. The Nobel Prize for Medicine was awarded for the discovery of penicillin.

One can also pinpoint in 1945 the birth of the concept of hypertext.

The concept began as a vision in 1945 when Vannevar Bush, science advisor to President Roosevelt, wrote of the "memex" in an article, "As We May Think," for *Atlantic Monthly*. At the time, Bush was using the microfilm reader as a point of departure for his ideas, a machine considered by many to be the most sophisticated technology of the time (Bevilacqua, 1989, 159). Bush wrote, "A memex is a device in which an individual stores all his [or her] books, records, and communications, and which is mechanized so that it may be consulted with exceeding speed and flexibility. It is an enlarged intimate supplement to his [or her] memory" (1945, 106–07).

Bush's imaginative concept was a response to a moment in history when visions of technology were beginning to erupt because of the "information explosion." However, it is clear that when Vannevar Bush wrote "As We May Think," he was not thinking only of two separate entities: vast amounts of data and developments in technology. Instead, he bridged the gap between the information explosion and the machine he called the "memex" with what was known about the human mind and its processes:

The human mind . . . operates by association. With one item in its grasp, it snaps instantly to the next that is suggested by the association of thoughts, in accordance with some intricate web of trails carried by the cells of the brain. It has other characteristics, of course; trails that are not frequently followed are prone to fade, items are not fully permanent, memory is transitory. Yet the speed of action, the intricacy of trails, the detail of mental pictures, is awe-inspiring beyond all else in nature.

[We] cannot hope fully to duplicate this mental process artificially, but [we] certainly ought to be able to learn from it. In minor ways, [we] may even improve, for [our] records have relative permanency. The first idea, however, to be drawn from the analogy concerns selection. Selection by association, rather than by indexing, may yet be mechanized. One cannot hope thus to equal the speed and flexibility with which the mind follows an associative trail, but it should be possible to beat the mind decisively in regard to the permanence and clarity of the items resurrected from storage. (1945, 106)

Vannevar Bush was certainly not the first to think of the human mind in relationship to association. The concept of associationism can be traced back to Plato (*Phaedrus*) and Aristotle (*On Memory and Reminiscence*), both of whom believed that we recall or relate ideas because they are "either similar or dissimilar to one in our present thought, or because the two objects were originally perceived . . . closely in time and space" (Wesley, 1972, 87). Also according to the classical rhetors, "Association implied that thoughts are environmentally determined and not 'God-given'" (Wesley, 1972, 86–87). However, Vannevar Bush's visionary memex was the first record that bridged associationism with a "thinking" machine, a personal technology that privileged the accessibility and organization by association of large bodies of information with speed in the processing of this information.

Soon following Conklin's introduction were numerous published texts that attempted to create nutshell definitions of hypertext. Ben Shneiderman and Greg Kearsley say hypertext is a "non-linear viewing of information" (1998, xix). Clay Carr, a specialist in personnel training, states that "hypertext is a specific form of data retrieval—one that's significantly different from other data retrieval methods. . . . A fully developed hypertext system allows a user to access information in an associative, intuitive way—without regard for its actual location or for any visible database structure" (1988, 7, 8). Karen E. Smith, a specialist in research and information, defines hypertext as "non-sequential reading and writing" (1988, 32).

One feature that is true to all hypertext environments, though, is the capability of linking. Although hypertext draws on a vast amount of information stored in some form of a database, what is key to hypertext is the way in which this information is linked since "it is this linking capability which allows a non-linear organization of text" (Conklin, 1987, 18). The essence of hypertext, then, is focused on linking capabilities, bringing the user into prominent view. Hypertext links allow a user personal choice in accessing information. Patricia Baird writes, "In a non-linear document, there is no preordained 'right way' to go through the data. Certain stacks of information and subsets of the network of subjects can be structured along hierarchical lines, offering an easy-to-follow, recognisable structure. But for a system to warrant hypertext status, the links between and within stacks must allow multiple paths through the data" (347). Also, hypertext linking allows for the intertextual experience of the user to be dynamic and interactive (Bevilacqua, 1989, 158). In turn, hypertext systems "present the user with an added-value information system by repackaging and restructuring the data and producing a new learning environment" (Baird 346).

The potential of this new learning environment led hypertext to quickly become an exciting area of inquiry for scholars in computers and composition studies. On the surface, the connections between hypertext and composition studies in general were clear. The qualities that different researchers ascribed to hypertext closely mirrored some of the basic theories and practices of composition: constructing knowledge and making meaning, like writing, are complex, nonlinear processes that take place in collaborative, social settings; inquiry requires hierarchical cognitive processes; there is a need for individualized instruction that is not bound by rigid rules; students need to make connections between multiple texts while creating their own texts. As researchers tried to make sense of this technological concept and bring it into composition studies, they developed models and paradigms to better understand how hypertext "fit" in the scheme of what we already knew about teaching writing. Two studies proved most influential in how compositionists think about hypertext today.

Michael Joyce characterizes two types of hypertext, a distinction he asserts must be identified before hypertext can facilitate pedagogically sound reading and writing instruction. The first type, *exploratory* hypertext, is used for the conveyance of information : "Exploratory hypertexts encourage and enable an audience . . . to control the transformation of a body of information to meet its needs and interests" (1988, 11). The audience of an exploratory hypertext navigates through a preexisting network of linked material while creating a knowledge structure. The second type, *constructive* hypertext, moves beyond hypertext as "delivery or presentational technology" (1988, 11) as the user is given scripting and authoring responsibilities:

> Scriptors use constructive hypertexts to develop a body of information which they map according to their needs, their interests, and the transformations they discover as they invent, gather, and act upon that information. . . . Constructive hypertexts require a capability to act: to create, to change, and to recover particular encounters within the developing body of knowledge. (1988, 11)

Hypertexts, both exploratory and constructive, enable users to draw upon vast amounts of information stored in some database form; what is key to hypertext is the way in which this information is linked. Exploratory hypertexts— prepackaged databases that provide access to information intuitively and associatively—do not allow the user to add to the information in terms of constructing text or links. Constructive hypertexts, while retaining exploratory features, allow the user to add to and reconfigure a nonfixed structure.

The most useful view of hypertext for composition teachers, in my opinion, is Catherine Smith's distinction between hypertext as information system and hypertext as facilitation. Although her terminology hasn't necessarily caught on as well as Joyce's "exploratory/constructive," her terms truly address the concerns that many compositionists have about learning technologies. Hypertext as *information system* exists as a body of text to be searched, restructured, and reconfigured. Its purpose is to be explored so that the users can gain a wealth of knowledge from the texts they will encounter. Hypertext as information system, then, positions the application as exploratory in nature, a place where text is managed and retrieved. Although users can access information associatively, intuitively, and hierarchically according to their needs, hypertext as information system foregrounds the system over the user (1991, 225–26). Hypertext as *facilitation*, on the other hand, foregrounds the users and the users' experience over the system. Conceptualizing hypertext as facilitation encourages us to view it in the context of use, as a space where students make relationships and construct meaning, activities that feed into and enrich other processes. Hypertext as facilitation, then, positions itself as exploratory in nature, but more importantly, it positions itself as constructive as its application adds to and enhances learning experiences (1991, 225–26).

Positioning the Web

It doesn't take long to realize just how big the World Wide Web is. I don't mean "big" as in its collective size. True, there is a lot of the Web, but really, the Web in that sense doesn't have measurable size, nor is there really anything to compare its size to. Instead, when I say that the Web is "big," I'm talking more in terms of its collective impact, as in, "This is going to be BIG." Aside from the obvious character of this technology—the vast amount of information accessible to an astronomical number of people—other of its qualities are impossible to discount.

Its mere existence has brought about many significant changes in a very short time. For one, the Web changed the Internet. (Contrary to popular opinion, the Web is not the Internet. It *uses* the Internet, it's a *part* of the Internet, or it's *on* the Internet. But it itself is not the Internet.) Except for difficult-to-use databases, for years the Internet was about communication—getting in touch with people, making requests, exchanging knowledge. We had to create the communication through written texts that were e-mailed, or through written texts that we used to "chat" with one another. We *had* to communicate, and we had to do so in writing. This was, quite simply, how the Internet worked. The advent of the Web, though, changed all that. First, the Web is not necessarily about exchange. It involves presentation that comes into view screen by screen. One can access through the Web e-mail accounts, bulletin boards, and various chat rooms. But when one thinks of a Web page or a Web site, he or she is typically imagining a static medium. In many ways, it is television. One can talk back to the screen, but in the end, what's there is there, quite distinct from the earlier dynamic conversation of the Internet.

Certainly the industry has boomed as people tuned into the Web. Whereas many quickly learned how to find specific information important to their personal lives, its popularity and its potential to bring a new kind of play into their lives sent thousands of people to electronic superstores to purchase their first home computers. In fact, systems, like WebTV, have been designed for Web use only. Surfing the Web has become a hobby to many, and whereas there have been no landmark studies to prove it, one can't help but think that screen time on the Web has replaced a chunk of screen time normally spent with the tube. The Web is a place to celebrate already established hobbies, with sites dedicated to Star Trek, women in rock music, Corvair enthusiasts, and tattoos, to name a few. Of course, someone has to create these Web sites, a meta-hobby of sorts, as most exist because of an individual's adoration and commitment toward the site's subject at hand. Because of the ease with which people can create Web pages, the personal home page, an exercise in identity creation and self-promotion, gives anyone who longs for it his or her five minutes of fame.

The vastness of the Web has spawned new "professions in creativity," such as Web writer, Web designer, Web artist, increasing the range of the Web as not only a functional entity, but also an art form. Publication is no longer limited to the offer of a contract from a press; on the Web, one can find anything from full length academic book manuscripts to poetry chapbooks, from political manifestos to rant and rave letters to the mayor. At times, one will find the writing spectacular, at others, anything from dull to disorderly. A quick survey of Web pages reveals spectacular designs created with the sensibilities of brilliant artistic intention. At the same time, what a friend of mine used to call "Mac Abuse" in the early days of desktop publishing is alive and well on the Web—disasters in design that proliferate when tools of the trade are not coupled with the art of the trade. As with any art form, the creation of convention and custom comes into play (What makes writing on the Web effective? What makes a Web page good in design?) which lends itself to Web criticism and the Web critic.

Anyone doing work on the Web has been a pioneer in the true sense of the word, a trailblazer, forging new territory with every step. This has never been more true than with those who are using the Web in their classrooms. And the very reasons the Web is so "big" are the same reasons this technology has such appeal to compositionists. At a recent conference, I overheard a breakfast conversation where one woman, I assume with many years' teaching experience, confessed that no technology embraced by the field since the introduction of word processing had excited her more with its potential to reach students than had the World Wide Web. "It's really going to change our teaching and how our students write," she assured her companions. I share her enthusiasm, tempered only by a few pressing questions: How is the World Wide Web going to reach our students? How should the World Wide Web reach our students? And most important, how should our students reach the World Wide Web?

Web Workings

I want to take a moment at this point to describe how this technology works, not because I think teachers, at this moment in the book, need to understand the intricate workings of computers, but because the way the technology functions is directly tied to how we might answer the questions above. For anyone who has designed a Web page, this short description will be rudimentary. Others who may have years of experience using the Web but who have never designed a page may find themselves exclaiming, "So *that's* how it works." Regardless, I want to reiterate that I'm not offering a short lesson on Web site development. Instead, I want to begin an examination of how users are *reading* this technology.

The Web, like e-mail systems, uses the Internet; that is, computers (and thus their users) are able to communicate primarily through the use of "lines"—phone lines or cable—and some type of server that provides users with an Internet address. The Web is a hypertext system in that users navigate through it by clicking on links that bring them from one text to the next. They use a Web browser, software like Netscape or Internet Explorer, to find and read Web texts. The Web uses the term "page" to designate a unified, continuous text, a collection of graphics and/or writing that one can scroll through from beginning to end on one screen, and "site" to designate a collection of two or more pages connected by links, usually by design, and by theme or topic. A "home page" is a single page that exists on its own and is not a part of a site, or is used to describe the first page of a site.

To create a Web page or site, one uses what is called hypertext markup language, or HTML, a computer language that allows different Web browsers to read the same file. To manually type HTML to create a Web page at first may seem tedious, having to begin and end text with commands that will give it specific appearance when read with a browser. To create a Web page title that would look like:

Orbit Design

I would type in HTML:

```
<TITLE><B><I><CENTER>Orbit Design</TITLE></B></I></CENTER>
```

to signal where I wanted my title formatting to begin and end. Although Web designers claim that HTML actually comes quite easily with a little practice, software companies are marketing Web design programs that are WYSIWYG, or "what you see is what you get." These programs allow creators of pages to use a system with features that function like word processing software, where text attributes can be achieved with simple commands or mouse clicks and where the attributes are represented on the page. Using scanned images and clip art, Web designers can also incorporate graphics in their pages.

A created Web page needs to be stored on a server, a rather powerful, fast computer with a high capacity hard drive, that has an Internet address of some kind called an IP (Internet Protocol). These addresses usually begin with "http://" (hypertext transfer protocol) and include the name and/or location of the server and the name of the Web page file. For example, an imaginary address where one might find Orbit Design's homepage could be:

http://www.colnet.orbitdesign.com

Because each page is saved as a separate file on the server, each page has a different address. Usually, though, only the home page address is made public; paths to other pages collected in a site are accessed through links. Links are either graphics or text; text links are printed in a different color than the other text (usually blue) and often have some other type of attribute (usually an underline). Web page files stay on the server, and the server's power is left on at all times.

When users want to access a Web page, they simply type the address of the page in their Web browser. In very little time, the page appears on their computer. Many users believe that when they are looking at a Web page, they are connected to the server that houses the page. However, by the time they are looking at a page, they have already disconnected from the server. The Web browser actually contacted the server, requested a *copy* of the page, delivered this copy back to the users' computer, and dropped its connection from the server—a process called downloading. The speed of this process depends not only on the speed of the users' computer and their internet connection, but often on the complexity of the page being downloaded—pages with high resolution graphics take considerably longer to download than pages with only text.

The downloaded page more than likely contains links that when clicked will take users to another Web page. Clicking a link automatically signals the browser to make a connection to the designated server; this was programmed into the link by the Web page designer. That link may lead to another page within the Web site, or it may lead to another site altogether, perhaps on a different server altogether. Web designers can create links to any Web page on the World Wide Web by simply knowing the address of the page. (Web browsers usually have navigational tools, too, that allow users to go back through the pages they have visited with relative ease.) Whereas Web designers can create links to any page they have an address for, someone surfing the Web using a browser does not have access to create such links or alter another's page.

Many people surf the Web with very little knowledge of this process, especially when they are new to the Web, perhaps a bit awestruck by the vast amount of information that is so readily available. With more experience, however, they soon learn about this clear-cut division between Web designer and Web surfer, a split that isn't necessarily as defined in other hypertext systems. While more and more people are creating Web sites, a majority of people surf the Web without ever having had the experience of creating a Web page. Even those who design Web pages spend a significant amount of time surfing the Web.

I make this point because I want to revisit the two terms created by Catherine Smith that are of particular interest to teaching with this technology: hypertext as *information system*, and hypertext as *facilitation* (1991, 225–26). As it exists, the World Wide Web has been positioned as an *information system*, a collection of texts of various sorts that presents facts, statistics, narratives, schedules, pictures, translations, plans, and the like. Whereas one may learn a great deal from and about this information, the World Wide Web typically has not been positioned as a *facilitator for learning*. In most cases, as currently designed and made available to users, the Web itself does not account for instruction or learning. This, of course, is where we come in, those of us who may be directing our students toward use of the Web, or those of us who realize that our students are turning to the Web on their own while they search for content in their writing. It becomes our task to push this technology beyond its information system nature. Only through careful guidance can we help students perceive and use the Web to facilitate their learning.

Upgrades and Upshots

I had been using the Web myself for some time before the opportunity to use it with my students ever arose, and I remember being struck by the possibilities for teaching composition with this technology. In the summer of 1996, I received official word that the administration on my campus had committed to purchasing enough new computers to equip two English Department classrooms—twenty-five computers each. After years of teaching with dated and failing equipment, the news was indeed encouraging. Not only would we teach writing on up-to-date equipment that would, subsequently, provide our students with up-to-date computer literacy, but the possibilities for new teaching approaches and student assignments would energize a faculty who had pushed its old technology—and perhaps its techno-instruction—to the limits.

Our new computers came with large hard drives capable of storing a great deal of software and CD-ROM drives with Microsoft Bookshelf, an integrated reference package consisting of a dictionary, thesaurus, almanac, time line, abridged encyclopedia, atlas, and a book of famous quotations. The Windows operating system would allow users to run numerous software programs simultaneously and to switch between them with a simple click of the mouse, a process called multi-tasking. The computers were installed with enough memory to allow for this task switching with little to no strain on the speed of the machine. The department chose to use software that was made available through the purchase of the hardware and that the university had purchased licenses for: Microsoft Office, including Word for word processing; Eudora for e-mail; Netscape for the World Wide Web; and Microsoft FrontPage for Web site design. Each computer connected directly to the university network, offering users easy, fast connections to the Internet. And finally, with money remaining from my Ameritech Fellowship, I purchased a powerful server, which, among other things, could be used to launch an English program Web site.

A significant amount of work and responsibility came with the new technology. Teachers in the department needed to familiarize themselves with the technology before they could expect to use it with their students (although in certain situations I have learned more about the workings of our new system from my students than from anyone else). We needed to learn new software that we had never used before, and the upgrades in the hardware meant upgrades in software, almost always a move from simple DOS to more complicated Windows programs. And once again, just like when we added our first Internet connection in order to use e-mail with our students, we were under incredible time pressures. Not only were we getting new technology, but our classrooms were moving to a new, state-of-the-art library/classroom building. The university "took possession" of the building from the architects and construction company two weeks before the school year began. Before we could learn how to use the computers in order to teach our students how to use the computers, they had to be literally taken out of their boxes, set up, connected, and configured. Such a large-scale and sudden change in our technology, along with the time constraints, meant that we were once again faced with a high probability of technocentrism (Hawisher, 1989, 44–45). Although we were preoccupied with computer configurations and operations, we needed to ensure that we didn't lose sight of sound teaching practice.

The World Wide Web was the only technology made available to us in our new classrooms that was completely new to my teaching. I had used word processing and e-mail and desktop publishing in my courses before, so I was really only learning changes in the specific software, not learning something completely new, as I prepared for teaching in our new classrooms. The Web, however, was completely new, and that meant that I needed to develop a theory and a practice for its use; it was certainly going to require an inventing of the wheel. I recognized a number of hurdles. First, no one else in my Department had any more experience teaching with the Web than I had, which in all cases amounted to "none." Next, we had little time for preparation. As the "technology person" in the department, I accepted some responsibility in our new venture. I would instruct the faculty in the technology itself. Yet, how I instructed them and how I modeled its use in my own teaching would set the tone for how my colleagues would begin to define teaching with the Web. I surveyed, in the short time I had, published literature on using the Web for writing. I found that almost every handbook now includes a section on the Web and writing, mostly covering "here's how to look for a topic on the Web" and styles for citing electronic sources in a research paper. A new swell of textbooks and readers that focus on technology or that include Web assignments have hit the market, riding the wave of Web-mania. And I could find countless commercial books on how to write a Web page. But I found myself, a teacher/researcher with many years' experience in techno-composition, in the position I described in the introduction to this volume: Very little was available to the teacher new to a particular technology that coupled sound teaching theory (that wasn't watered down) with teaching practice that could be applied in a variety of learning settings.

Although I knew a great deal about hypertext, I was using a hypertext *system* that I had very little experience with: an *exploratory* hypertext, a preexisting collection of linked texts that the user cannot reconfigure or manipulate. I believed that while exploratory hypertexts could facilitate learning in our students as a dynamic reading experience different from what they might experience with a traditionally organized print text, the act of constructing a hypertext could be a dynamic, meaning-making act that would push them to make connections, both mental and electronic, between seemingly unlike ideas. I still believe this. However, I also understand the pervasiveness of Web technology and how, in the late twentieth century, it demands to be a part of students' experiences looking for content for their writing. In many cases, asking students to write for the Web is not only appropriate, but doing so can teach them a type of writing that they very well might be asked to do some day. But for the time being, I am still concerned here with writing courses where writing print texts is the dominant activity to be practiced and studied and with how technology is best used in these classroom settings. With this type of writing course in mind, the question then becomes, how can we use the Web in ways that push its boundaries as an information system, ensuring hypertext as facilitation, and how might we make students' experiences with the technology more constructive than exploratory?

Inventing Instructional Web Sites

This was the question I attempted to answer as I set out to design my first Web site. I was eager to try my hand at Web site design, yet the learning curve I perceived was intimidating. Surprisingly, I discovered that creating this technological application did not necessitate painstaking hours of sitting in front of a computer, or at least as much as I expected. I made a few sketches on paper of what I wanted individual pages to look like and where I wanted links to lead. I used a program called Microsoft FrontPage, Web writing software that is both WYSIWYG as well as packaged with templates and preprogrammed features that significantly simplified the technical task at hand.

Creating my Web site did, however, demand a level of thinking more abstract than I had expected. How did I want this site to reflect my overall theories of teaching writing? How did I want the site to work with specific assignments I had already planned to use in specific courses, and how might the site help me imagine new assignments for the courses I taught? Would I be able to easily provide information resources to my students? How might the site help students sort through the chaotic nature of the World Wide Web? Could students take part in creating the site, or would the site be fixed by my creative control? Could I communicate with my students in this space? As I had with other technologies used in my composition courses, could I set up this system in ways that would illustrate student learning, both to students and to me?

Soon, these questions translated into defining features as I began to conceptualize what I now call **instructional Web sites**. Teachers across the disciplines with a variety of pedagogical goals can use instructional Web sites to make their students' Web experiences more constructive than exploratory and more concentrated on facilitation than on mere information. As I define them, instructional Web sites must meet each of the following criteria:

- their purpose is teaching a particular subject;
- they facilitate specific pedagogical goals of a course;
- they act as an information resource;
- they serve as a virtual meeting space for students and teachers;
- they provide a space for students and teachers to make sense of their experiences with virtual worlds;
- they allow students to contribute to the overall makeup of the site itself;
- and they give teachers a glimpse into students' learning processes and students a glimpse into their own and their peers' learning processes.

At first, one may find creating a Web site a formidable task, especially creating one that includes these seven qualities. Those newly introduced to the Web might find its inclusion in teaching an especially overwhelming thought. Yet, *marion.comp: An Instructional Web Site for Composition*, was really quite modest in design. After three years of loyal service to our program, *marion.comp* was put to rest. As our program expanded, we found that our site needed to meet the needs of courses other than composition—literature, film, and professional writing—and an expanding major. We now have *MCSET, The Marion Campus Studies in English and Technology*. By many Web designers' standards, this site is still modest in appearance and function, although I have exercised much more artistic freedom than I did in the past.

I planned an overall organizing structure that would allow individual faculty members in the department to build off a single site. Students who logged into the site were greeted by a few initial screens. From this point forward through the Web site, instructors pick up creative control of their own sites, and links are organized according to instructors' names.

I teach two different composition courses using *MCSET*. English 110, our first-year writing course, is required of all freshmen at the university. This course only meets for ten weeks, and I feel pressured to cover a great deal in the short time I have with my students. Currently, I emphasize texts directed toward public and academic intellectual communities both in what students read and write, which means that much of my instruction centers on occasions for writing, audience and forums, synthesis and summary writing, acceptable types of evidence, and appropriate forms and structures. Students complete a number of short writing projects (SWPs) that are intended to feed into the three major writing projects (WPs) for the course. The sequence of these three writing projects pushes students toward an increasingly sophisticated involvement with texts of various types. They begin the quarter by formulating a critical response to one text of their choice and move toward juggling multiple texts by the end. Whereas their first assignment includes a directive for why they are writing, the sequence of assignments requires students to continually take more responsibility for developing occasions for writing toward the end of the course. Students in this class were examining the potential or actual outcomes of a specific education reform, examining it "In the Context of Community," where they wrote about a "problem" specific to a defined community.

Students are also required to take a second writing course intended for their sophomore year. This course is offered across the disciplines at the university and is numbered 367. English 367, subtitled "The American Experience," offers writing instruction in a seminar format, focusing on one topic of the instructor's choice throughout the term. This seminar approach is key to the philosophy of the course: Students learn to write in the context of college courses where one narrow topic is the focus (History of the Civil War, Contemporary Film: 1965–Present, Animal Behavior, Abnormal Psychology). These are courses where, according to John A. Reither and Douglas Vipond, "students collaboratively investigate a more or less original scholarly question or field. The teacher sets a long-range research project or question for the class, casting the students as members of a research group" (qtd. in Mitchell, 1992,

393). The course I taught using the Web was on learning theory as a subject of inquiry for noneducation majors entitled, "Learning '97: A Conference Course for and about Students." My premise was that students will become better learners if, while studying the theory of learning, they are made aware of their own learning processes. The course began by posing the following questions:

- What are the various theories of learning that exist in our educational systems?

- What assumptions about students and learning underlie these theories?

- How do perceptions of learning vary among academic disciplines?

- How are various emerging technologies altering how and what students learn?

- How does a metacognitive awareness of learning feed into and enrich students' learning abilities and experiences?

Following a similar sequence of assignments as the first writing course, where students become increasingly more involved with texts as the course progresses, the class completed two writing projects and an elaborate research project that included a class presentation, an annotated bibliography, and a final paper on their research project.

I provided both the first- and second-year classes with "Business" pages, where I posted anything that I typically would give them in a handout: syllabi, assignments, schedules. It quickly became evident that I had to carefully consider my student population when relying on the Web to post these documents. My students, for example, do not live on campus, and many travel up to fifty miles to get to school. Among nontraditional students who care for families and work full-time, many arrange their courses so they only have to come to campus three days a week. Many of these same students do not have access to computers with Internet connections off campus. They rely on being able to pull an assignment out of their folder during a break from work, or when they finally get their young children to sleep late at night. Also, my Web pages are printable, and students informed me that if I didn't provide them with a paper copy of assignments, they would simply print the documents from the Web on the classroom laser printer. The only time that it seemed appropriate to post an assignment to the Web and *not* provide a handout was when students would begin and complete the assignment in a given class session.

Posting assignments on the Web, however, even if students had paper copies, had its benefits. First, it provided students with a backup copy of handouts for those occasions where they might be near a computer but not near their class notebook. More importantly, though, I was able to electronically connect a copy of an assignment with students' writing. When students are working on a draft of a paper, they often lose track of the assignment and what is being asked of them. Especially during the first few weeks of a freshman course, I am always asking students, as a revision strategy, to "return to the assignment—often." I use this as an exercise in strategic backtracking to move student writers forward. The computer's multi-tasking abilities allow students to open the assignment on the Web while they are working on their writing; they can easily move back and forth between the two with a simple click of the mouse. This strategy of returning to the assignment soon becomes habit as students grow accustomed to using the computer's multi-tasking.

Inventing Method

One term that has been attached to the Web is "surf," as in "to surf the Web," which basically means to ride the wave, to hop on and journey the links to wherever, usually with no particular destination. I have used it already in this chapter, although I find that "surf" is actually a rather careless metaphor that really doesn't describe very well what one does on the Web. Surfing—the ocean activity—requires that one paddle to a certain destination, against the force, only to be returned on a one-directional course to his or her starting point. Surfing—the Web activity—allows one to easily leave the starting place and travel numerous courses with endless possibilities, almost never returning to the starting place. I've been looking for a better term to describe this latter activity, and after finding a problem with every catchy metaphor that I could come up with, I've come to describe this activity simply as "riding the Web."

Eventually, I want my students to be able to ride the Web as invention. In other words, as they are given assignments in English composition or in other courses, or as they pursue writing for work or personal pleasure, I hope that they can move from site to site and from page to page on the Web, participating in those rich invention processes I outlined in the first chapter of this book. I want students to learn to notice what's on the Web, to let their guard down and take in the connections, the idiosyncrasies, the oddities, and the parallels that exist in this virtual world. I want them to gain from the disorder that becomes a part of the Web experience, and I want them to prosper as they make sense of and bring order to the disarray. I want them to create a reflective sense of the task, slowing their pace and looking back while moving forward. And I want them to read the texts of the Web, learning from and questioning what is there and not there, developing schemata for summarizing, analyzing, and evaluating this technology. Although I am asking students to ride the Web, I feel there needs to be some method in the instruction that gets them to these destinations, a method that keeps them both open to possibilities and focused on their learning.

Multi-tasking, having two or more software applications running simultaneously, plays a significant role in the method I introduce to students using the Web in my classes mostly because it brings a writing space to the Web. In other words, it allows students to create text on the screen at the same time that they are moving back and forth between other programs. Many computer platforms allow for this operation, but I find that I've grown partial to current Windows platforms. At the bottom of the screen is the task bar that always shows a "Start" button. Clicking this button allows the user to "start" applications, one after the other, if necessary. For each application opened, Windows creates a button next to the "Start" button along the bottom of the screen that remains accessible until the user closes the application.

The method I ask students to use requires a word processing program (Microsoft Word) and a Web browser (Netscape). With both programs open, they would see two buttons (in addition to the "Start" button) on the bottom of their screen. A simple click of these buttons takes them from one program to the other. This multi-tasking has very practical uses. For example, it allows students to use "copy/paste" commands to easily copy text and citation information from a Web file and paste it into an open Word document. This convenience saves students time in retyping and encourages them to incorporate quoted material from electronic sources into their papers. They can also copy a Web address from Netscape and paste it into a Word document, which not only saves time, but also prevents errors.

But multi-tasking here does more than facilitate simple copying and pasting. It adds a writing and thinking segment to the Web that is otherwise not present in an exploratory hypertext, a segment that is an integral part of instructing students to use the Web as a writing invention. Students can take notes, raise questions, and challenge texts—writing that becomes moments of invention—in their open Word documents in response to what they are seeing on the Web. Thus, multi-tasking allows students to experience and instructors to meet two important qualities of instructional Web sites: "They provide a space for students and teachers to make sense of their experiences with virtual worlds," and "They give teachers a glimpse into students' learning processes and students a glimpse into their own . . . learning processes." Multi-tasking makes students' Web experiences constructive by allowing them to create a written text that is connected to the Web.

The graphic presentation of Web pages plus the browser software—what a Web screen looks like and how its graphic design allows the user to interact with it—allowed me to first imagine how multi-tasking enables students' Web experiences to be constructive. One gets from place to place on the Web mostly by clicking on links that have been programmed by the Web page's designer. But one also moves around the Web by accessing pull-down menus and clicking on buttons that are a part of the Web browser software. These menus and buttons remain constant on the screen, no matter what Web site the user is observing. They are a part of the "graphic user interface" of the browser. Buttons and menus often used are "navigational." For example, Netscape uses "Back" and "Forward" buttons to allow a user to move backwards and forwards through sites they have already visited. The "Go" pull-down menu keeps a running record of visited sites, allowing users to directly return to a selected site.

The multi-tasking system of Windows mimics Netscape's navigational buttons by adding buttons to the graphic user interface of any program that is open, thus bringing a writing space to the Web with the simple click of a button that looks and works much like any other button in Netscape. In other words, the "Word" and "Netscape" buttons are both present on the screen regardless of which of the two programs the student is using, and a simple "point and click" will take users back and forth between them.

Admittedly, while adding this inventive dimension to working on the Web, multi-tasking, unfortunately, still does not make the Web truly constructive. It does not allow the user to permanently alter the Web by adding text to it—a truly constructive hypertext system. It is not possible to write on the Web in this way using a browser; in reality, the students' writing remains basically word processing. Also, no other Web user has access to the students' writing, and after the student leaves the computer, the written text is no longer electronically attached to the Web. But we are less concerned here with hypertext as a system than with how it might facilitate learning for the user. Therefore, we need to shift our attention from the system to the complete experience the student is having with the Web at a given moment. The students' written text, during multi-tasking, is a part of the Web because of a simple button that allows students and their writing to be momentarily attached to any Web page. The students' writing becomes a temporary Web document that allows their experience to become constructive rather than merely exploratory.

Multi-Tasking Applied

As with all of my teaching, I think of multi-tasking as a constructive, facilitating activity that needs to be carefully sequenced within the context of real writing assignments. My first-year writing students were introduced to a writing project that asked them to analyze the effectiveness of a particular educational reform. This assignment was difficult for students because it forced them to write against their immediate inclination toward this assignment, which was to propose their own reform for a problem they had identified. Instead, they were to find a reform that someone else had implemented or proposed already and critically examine how this reform addressed or would address a problem. This type of assignment teaches first-year students to move beyond a simple, two-step cause/effect, problem/solution mode of invention and learn critical reading and critical response as an ongoing process. In addition, it helps them see that solutions themselves often become new problems.

I encouraged students at this point in the term to use the Web for invention. Before students were given this assignment, however, I wanted them to get a sense of how the Web is used as a resource to find information on education in general: What's there, who put it there, how can it be used, and by whom? I wrote an in-class writing assignment that introduced students to searching the Web for research, multi-tasking, and making their Web experiences constructive. I asked students to open an empty word processing file and use it to complete a Short Writing Project found on the class Web site:

SWP #7 (due at the end of class)

Find three WWW sites that present a particular vision of education. At this time, avoid sites that only present statistical data or list information. Instead, find sites that forward an agenda or a view of how education should or could be implemented.

Use the following outline for each WWW site you find:

Title of WWW site:

Sponsored/created by:

URL/WWW address:

Summary: (Write a four- to five-sentence summary of the WWW site)

In addition to teaching students how they might begin to look at the Web for research, this assignment also introduces students to Web conventions: Who is the author? Who is the sponsor? Are these the same people? Is this a single Web page, or a Web site? How does one tell where he or she is within a site or if he or she has seen the entire site?

In Netscape, I instruct students to begin using a search engine using key words and topics. (I shall not go into detail at this point about conducting meaningful and efficient Web searches. Almost any current English handbook now has a section about conducting effective searches on the Web.) From the opening screen in Yahoo!, my search engine of preference, students can type in a subject and click on "Search." However, they can also narrow their search by selecting from a short list of subjects: arts, business, entertainment, health, science, society, sports, travel, etc. One of these subjects is "education," and I encourage students to narrow their searches using Yahoo!'s suggestions whenever possible. Once they are taken to the "education" search page, they are offered another list from which to choose subjects (the number following each heading refers to the number of sites available):

Academic Competitions (48)	Journals (19)
	K-12 (808)
Adult and Continuing Education (258)	Language Education (163)
	Lectures (5)
Art@	Literacy (31)
Career and Vocational (227)	Magazines (27)
Companies@	Math and Science Education (172)
Conferences (74)	
Distance Learning (268)	Music@
Educational Standards and Testing (41)	News (16)
	Online Forums (29)
Educational Theory and Methods (282)	Organizations (827)
	Products@
Employment (117)	Programs (185)
Financial Aid (312)	Reform (20)
Government Agencies (38)	Religious Education (17)
Guidance (171)	Resources (9)
Higher Education (770)	Special Education (86)
Instructional Technology (246)	Teaching (59)
	Usenet (13)

At this point, I encourage students to "see what's out there" with two goals in mind: Take in as much as they can on the Web while keeping in mind that there is an assignment to finish. In other words, experience and enjoy the disorder, noticing what's out there to explore while using the assignment to bring method to the search. They are encouraged to return to the assignment often.

A number of things struck me as I observed my students working on this initial assignment. First, with no instruction from me, a majority of students copied the outline headings from the assignment on the class Web site (Title of WWW site, Sponsored/created by, URL/WWW address, Summary) and pasted them three times into their word processing document. They were well aware of how copy and paste worked in Word, and recognized that the pull-down menus in Netscape operated in the same way; recognizing the similarities in the software configuration, they experimented with this computer operation before I chose to instruct the class as a whole. This is a relatively small point to make about my students' use of the technology, but their already existing or developed knowledge about this operation lays a foundation for getting students to make their Web experiences constructive rather than merely exploratory. By the time we were into the assignment, students recognized the potential for multitasking to bridge independent computer platforms and operations, the first step necessary before more meaningful, more constructive use of the Web can take place.

Students raised important questions about reading the Web during this class session, questions that might not have arisen if their Web search had not been contextualized by the assignment. Their questions and my answers to them would not have received public report had I not created this assignment to be completed in class, I realized later. The first two headings in the assignment, "Title of WWW site" and "Sponsored/created by," were intended to get students to look for information that is sometimes difficult to locate on the Web but is necessary not only to understand the site completely, but also to document the site if they choose to cite it in a paper. Web conventions for documentation are not as clear-cut as in print publications, especially with regard to the sites' authors. Sometimes there is a specific author listed, but it's impossible to know the person's qualifications and sense of authority on the subject. Sometimes there is no author listed, sometimes the author is an organization, and sometimes this organization and the title of the site are the same, as with the *International Center for Leadership in Education*. Locating a site's home page and its connecting pages is also important. Often, as students are traveling through a webbed environment, a link will land them in the middle of a large site. For example, a student might be reading a page on computers and mathematics education that includes a link to another page of related material. This new page, however, is part of the Ohio Education Association's rather large site, part of which focuses on mathematics education and technology. The student needs to find not only the address of the page where she is, but she may need to backtrack through the site in order to find the title and the author of the site—Web designers don't always include this information on every page within the sites they create.

I also recognized that students were struggling with the "summary" portion of the assignment. By this time in the quarter, I had hit students hard with summary writing assignments. By no means do I look at summary writing as "busy work," nor do I assign such work because I think it's "good for our students." I see summary writing as an incredibly difficult task that connects reading and writing by forcing students to read content critically, understand formal structure and convention, and separate general from specific and main from supporting examples. It also pushes them to examine and negotiate the differences between descriptive and evaluative rhetoric; we spend a great deal of time in class repeating that the goal in summary writing is to represent the gist of a primary text without explicit commentary.

I suspected that students were a bit conflicted by differences in what I had taught them about summary writing to date and what this assignment asked of them. First, I had taught them to begin their summaries with what I call a "model opening sentence." My instruction on summary writing states:

> Your summary needs to begin with a clear statement that reveals: author, type of work, title of work, and a general, all-encompassing statement that conveys the main point of what you read. Use this sentence as a model, mimicking its structure:
>
> > In the introduction to their book, *Multicultural Literacy*, Rick Simonson and Scott Walker discuss the controversial issues surrounding cultural literacy and the complex knowledge bases that such a literacy includes.

This opening sentence serves many purposes. First, it teaches students a straightforward approach to introducing source material in their writing, one that allows them to establish a minimal amount of context. Also, this structure helps them avoid the repeated subject so common to their texts: "In Eric Cromley's book, *Tuned Out*, he states that . . . ." Students learn how to keep summaries centered on the author, which, subsequently, helps them to avoid inserting explicit opinions; if they are consistently recalling what an author said, there is little room to add what they have to say in response. In addition to already understanding the basic form of a summary, my students also knew the "purpose" of writing a summary, and that the length of the summary was determined by the length of the original text.

Some students were able to carry over what they had learned about summary writing to this assignment:

> Title: Computers as Tutors: Solving the Crisis in Education
> Sponsored/created by: Frederick Bennett, Ph.D.
> URL/Web address: http://www.cris.com/~Faben1/
> Summary: In his article, "Computers as Tutors: Solving the Crisis in Education," Frederick Bennett, a psychologist and computer programmer, writes that education could be greatly improved through the use of computers. He states that computers would help conquer illiteracy, allowing ordinary students to make massive gains, and they would dissolve restraints on

> bright students. On a downside, Bennett states that parents fear that their children would become engulfed in their computers and what they could find. Lastly, teachers oppose bringing computers into schools for fear that the computers would take away from their jobs, and that they don't know how to teach with them.
> (Kent)

Unfortunately, others' memories of our summary instructions seemed to fail them:

> Title: "The Center on Education Reform"
> Sponsored/created by: The Center on Education Reform
> URL/Web address: http://edreform.com/
> Summary: This site has many different articles on education reform. It includes surveys that have been done by the Center on Education Reform showing different responses by the public on this topic. There is a letter from the president explaining things on education reform and the purpose of the Web site. The site also includes editorials about different topics involving education reform.
> (Ed)

These two examples are striking to me not only because of the differences in the texts, but also because of the similarities in the writers. Both students, I had discovered throughout the course, were good writers who came to college with strong abilities, who concentrated on their studies, and who improved with each writing assignment. One would think as much after reading Kent's text but would probably think otherwise after reading Ed's. I do not think, however, that we can completely fault Ed for his apparent weakness nor blindly praise Kent for his success. Instead, we need to examine what type of Web documents these two students discovered and how that affected this assignment.

First of all, Kent's discovery was an essay that appeared as a complete text on the Web just as it might in a newspaper, a magazine, or an academic journal. Whereas its length would have normally called for a more substantial summary, Kent is still successful at capturing the essay's gist in four sentences (the sophistication of his sentences allows him to do this). However, while he addressed an important element of the assignment,

> At this time, avoid sites that only present statistical data or list information. Instead, find sites that forward an agenda or a view of how education should or could be implemented,

he did choose a simplistically structured Web document, a "print" essay that existed as a single, cohesive, linear text with no Web links. Ed, on the other hand, attempted to summarize an entire Web site, one that contained multiple links to information within the Center on Education Reform's collection and to sites not produced by the organization. The task at hand, summarizing a substantial hypertext in only four to five sentences, perhaps caused Ed's otherwise strong writing to break down, both as a successful summary and at the sentence level. Furthermore, he faced difficulty taking a skill he had mastered using one type of source—the printed essay or article—and applying it to a source that he had virtually no experience with—a Web site. His opening sentence reveals his inexperience with the Web as a text form: "This site *has* many different articles on education reform" (emphasis mine). Ed usually would have better control over word choice than to state that the site "has" something. But the text structure (hypertext/Web), as well as the fact that the author and title are the same, is so new to him that he is unsure of how to use language to describe it in an opening sentence: Does the site really *have*? Does the site *contain*? Does the site *connect to*? Does the site *include* (which he uses twice later)? This new form obscures word choices common to the writing he was accustomed to producing: This site *suggests*; this site *presents*; this site *argues*; this site *articulates*.

Constructing Web Experiences

The goal of this assignment was to introduce a method of sorts to the chaotic, disorderly text world students were entering. I find a delicate balance must be achieved, but how can I ensure that students will experience the whimsicality of the Web, which mirrors the dynamic vision of invention that I articulated in the first chapter of this book while offering them instruction that guides them to a sense of order without squelching their creativity? And how can this method be presented to them so that they internalize it, making it an automatic part of their reading and writing the Web, thus rendering the method less intrusive on their Web experiences? Later in this chapter, I will explore the theory behind this method, but for now, I want to illustrate how the assignment I described above can be expanded to meet another qualifier of instructional Web sites: "They allow students to contribute to the overall makeup of the site itself."

Web sites constructed by teachers run the risk of eliminating the opportunity for students to have a voice and a hand in the construction of an on-line classroom space. Mostly, the nature of computer systems we use with the Web is to blame for this as are the basic ways in which the Web works. At many universities, teachers scramble for limited server space from which to launch their sites. If they are given space, the server itself is usually operated by network administrators who are reluctant to let teachers into the workings of the computer, let alone students. Usually, teachers who venture into Web writing deliver their collection of pages on disk to a network administrator who, in most cases, is happy to install and activate the site. Then, every time the teacher makes a change to the site, he or she simply updates the file on disk and gives it to the network administrator. I am fortunate that my department has its own server where I create and house my instructional Web site. More and more, departments have their own dedicated server, and some instructors who have powerful workstations in their offices are able to purchase the necessary software that will allow their machines to work as a server.

Of course, the goals of a course also dictate the extent to which students are involved in constructing sites for the Web. For many courses, teaching students to write for the Web is most appropriate. In fact, more and more courses are appearing in departmental offerings that are focused entirely on the creating of on-line texts. But for many of the courses I teach, I do not have the luxury of teaching Web writing to my students; I am pressed to devote an increasing amount of instruction in what I already feel is an insufficient amount of time to required, general education courses. However, it is possible to have students take some of the responsibility for creating our class Web site. I regularly ask them for feedback on the site's appearance and operation, and for the most part, incorporate their suggestions. My revision of the Web site based on their comments does not reflect any visible contribution by the students; I may add a link to a site on suggestion, but afterward, there is no evidence that the change was suggested by the students. I desire a more discernible presence of students' work on the class Web site that, in turn, could meet three other goals of instructional Web sites: "They act as an information resource," "They provide a space for students and teachers to make sense of their experiences with virtual worlds," and "They give teachers a glimpse into students' learning processes and students a glimpse into their own and their peers' learning processes."

In an effort to engage students with Web construction, I direct them to a page within our class site called "The Links." As students are searching the Web as invention, or as they search the Web for research, they invariably come across sites that other students (as well as teachers) would find not only helpful, but also interesting. I want them to use space on the class Web site to give these encounters public report. Those who visit "The Links" are greeted with the following instructions:

The Links
class linking space for students and teachers
English 110C
First-Year English Composition
Dr. Scott Lloyd DeWitt

links (lingks) n. Torches formerly used for lighting one's way in the streets. [Possibly from Medieval Latin *linchinus*, candle, from Greek *lukhnos*, lamp.]

The Links is a Web space where students and teachers can direct visitors to important Web sites they have encountered in their research. All postings to *The Links* must be directed through Dr. Scott Lloyd DeWitt: dewitt.18@osu.edu. Simply send e-mail to Dr. DeWitt with the Web site's title, its address/URL, and a three- to five-sentence description of the site and why you feel it deserves attention. For example:

Title—*Marion Campus Studies in English and Technology*

Address/URL—http://mrspock.marion.ohio-state.edu/mcset/

Description—*MCSET* provides students and teachers at Marion's English Studies program with resources they can use for writing. The site is organized by instructor and includes links to research resources, individual class assignments and policies, as well as numerous discussion spaces. Students will especially like the direct connection to OSU's Homepage and Libraries.

Any posting that does not include these three elements will be returned to the sender.

My e-mail address in the description of the site provides a direct "mailto" link, where users can use an e-mail program built into the Web browser to post "Links" to me. Ideally, for students to truly take a part in constructing the Web site, they would be able to post directly to "The Links" without going through me. Not only would students gain a sense of ownership and authority in being able to add to the site without "help" from the teacher, but they would also learn about the responsibility and accountability that go hand in hand with creating a public Web site. This site represents them, me, the class, and the University; honesty, accuracy, and a high level of thinking is just as important on the Web as it is with any publication.

Unfortunately, the system does not allow for students to post directly to the site. Whereas this does mean an added task for me in my teaching, the structure I have imposed on students makes the busy work minimal. Once a week, I collect the e-mail files with the students' links and usually cut and paste them into one file, often converting this file into a word processing file that is easily compatible with the Web writing program I use, Microsoft FrontPage. I then copy and paste the entire file into "The Links" page using FrontPage. Because students are required to include the Web address in the link, I can simply copy this address to create the electronic link that will lead their peers to a site of interest. I check the link after I have added it to "The Links" to make sure it works properly. This is also where I check the site for its appropriateness for the class (I have yet to refuse posting a link because I felt the content was not appropriate for our class Web site.) I, too, have posted to this site along with my students:

- Vote Smart Election '96
  http://www.vote-smart.org/campaign_96/
     presidential/index.html

  This site contains topics such as the candidates, campaign finances, the election process, the job of the president, candidates' stance on issues, the campaign trail, and citizen participation. It also contains links to other Campaign '96 sites. This site may prove to be helpful to the students in this class and pertains to our recent discussion on education and the election. (Craig)

- The Center on Education Reform
  http://edreform.com/index.html

  The CER is a nationwide program that gives support to people who are trying to reform their schools. The CER helps support communities that want change. They promote academic excellence. They try to get rid of expensive "guidelines" of federal government. They encourage chartered and private schools to broaden their curriculum. The CER promotes reform through news articles, interviews, t.v. and radio shows. The CER's president keeps people updated on important reform issues. In 1995, CER helped make the ELC-Education Leaders Council. The ELC is an organization of officials who believe that the communities should control education reform. The CER's president,

Jeanne Allen, wrote a book called "School Reform Handbook: How to Improve Your Schools." This handbook has sold over 12,000 copies. The handbook is very useful. The Center plans to make instructional video tapes informing parents and school officials how to achieve a local school reform. The center also intends to expand their information to other people who are interested in reform. (Carrie)

• School Sucks
  http://www.schoolsucks.com/

Those who visit this site will find a diverse catalogue of college and high school papers. The author of this site, Kenny Sahr, claims that School Sucks can help students by giving them the opportunity to see how other students have approached various topics in their college papers. Ya, right. DON'T BELIEVE IT! Actually, this site is equipped so students can easily download papers that they can then turn in as their own work. Of course, this is plagiarism. DON'T DO IT! Besides, you won't find anything that will help you with our class assignments, and the writing is pretty bad (I think the site should be called, "This Writing Sucks"). Regardless, you should know that these sites exist and that those who wish to undermine the value of education are alive and well on the Web. Perhaps we'll use this site to practice generating peer feedback— I'm always looking for samples of student writing we can work with in class. (Scott DeWitt)

• The Dalton School: New Laboratory
    for Teaching and Learning
  http://www.nltl.columbia.edu/groups/NLTL

The Dalton School established the Dalton Technology Plan, created in 1990 to bring the community into the age of computers. The New Laboratory for Teaching and Learning explores how the use of computers can make a school better for the future. They are trying to pioneer prototypes so educational reform can begin by letting the people know about the capabilities of the computer globally. Finally, they are trying to change the routine of the stereotypical school. (Andy)

Participation in the building of this site is voluntary, but all of my courses include a significant class participation grade that can be enhanced by posting to "The Links." Students take great pride not only in creating our class site but also in becoming an authority on a particular Web site. They had to have studied the site closely in order to summarize it effectively, and they quickly find that their description and analysis of the site provides guidance to others in the class doing research.

Connecting the Disconnected Snapshots

After I taught my students the method for summarizing Web sites as a reading strategy, Jonatha turned in the following assignment:

Title: National Alliance for Safe Schools
Sponsored/created by: WestLake Solutions, Inc.
URL/Web address: http://www.safeschools.org/
Summary: National Alliance for Safe Schools was founded in 1977 by a group of school security directors. NASS is a non-profit and tax exempt program. Located in Washington, D.C., this program helped design educational programs for troubled youth. This is a program for those who are close to being separated from a normal school setting.

Title: United in Our Diversity
Sponsored/created by: Division of Violence and Prevention, Centers for Disease Control and Prevention
URL/Web address: http://www.cde.psu.edu/C&I/OurDiversity
Summary: This is a Web site set up for a conference on violence against women. The conference was promoted by Multicultural Dialogue on Family and Intimate Violence. They wanted to explore the need for multicultural issues of family and intimate violence. The site then goes on and gives the agenda of the conference held Oct. 22–23 of 1996.

Title: Engines for Education
Created/sponsored by: Roger Schank and Chip Leary/The Institute for the Learning Sciences
URL/WWW address: http://www.ils.nwu.edu/~e_for_e/
Summary: This is a "hyper-book" set up as a Web site, written by Roger Schank and Chip Leary. It is set up on an ASK system which was developed to help users access large amounts of

knowledge. There are many pages of good ideas on education and how to reform it. This is a Web site that should give anyone good information on education. (Jonatha)

The assignment that students were working on asked them to "find . . . WWW sites that present a particular vision of education . . . [, sites] that forward an agenda or a view of how education should or could be implemented." Although it was not explicitly stated in the instructions, students knew that I encouraged creative interpretation of my assignments, especially when considering a term like "education." I hoped that students felt free to interpret "education" beyond traditional school. That Jonatha included a site, her second of three, describing a "conference" was not too surprising, especially since it was hosted by Penn State, an educational institution. But I was intrigued by her path getting to this site, and its connection to the sites preceding and following it. Just how did she get from here to there? Could this path representing the whimsical nature of a Web search reveal something about how students might use this technology as a writing invention?

Most Web browsers, Netscape included, include navigational tools that keep a running record of "visited sites," a record that is usually erased as the user exits from the program. Before exiting, however, simply clicking the "back" and "forward" buttons will take a user through the visited sites. Also, the "Go" menu keeps a running record of sites visited. One could even go to the trouble of making a "bookmark" at each visited site, an electronic place keeper used to easily return to a favorite page even after exiting the program. (On our campus, we have disabled the bookmark feature because computers are used by multiple students; there is no guarantee that students can work on the same computer each time they visit a classroom or lab, and bookmarks can clutter up a computer.)

All of these tools could be used by researchers who were trying to keep track of where students went on the Web in a given period of time. The thought of conducting such research was appealing—I didn't know what I would look for, but this could be simple data collection that might lead to findings about the technology I am very interested in. Then I spoke with Jonatha about her assignment, approximately one week after she turned it in. I asked Jonatha if she could recall how she got from here to there on her assignment. She didn't remember. (No surprise. To be perfectly fair, sometimes I don't remember how I get to work each day.) Not only had time passed, but "it happens so fast," the "it" being a Web search in general. A simple click of the mouse, and she had left one site and moved to another, resulting in a series of disconnected snapshots. I had given them about an hour to do this assignment in class, so chances are she visited a number of sites. Did she return to Yahoo!, the search engine, after visiting the Safe School site? She didn't remember, but she didn't think so. The Web was fairly new to her, so she didn't think about returning to Yahoo!, even though I had suggested it as a strategy for the assignment. Did she remember a link that connected her from the National Alliance for Safe Schools directly to the conference site? She didn't remember that, either, but she certainly saw the connection I was inquiring about when she took a second look at her assignment: violence at school and violence at home.

The more we talked, the more certain she became that there was no direct link from the Safe Schools site to the conference site. The connection in content was evidenced to her only after I asked her to take a second look at the writing she had completed. Later that day, as I was thinking about our discussion, I decided to visit the two sites; I could find no direct link. I did note the structure of the conference site. The conference site for multicultural issues of family and intimate violence was deeply embedded within Penn State's elaborate State "Continuing and Distance Education Conferences and Institutes" site. I then had one last question for Jonatha: Did she search the Penn State "Continuing and Distance Education Conferences and Institutes" site, or was she taken, by a link, directly to the conference site for multicultural issues of family and intimate violence? She was most certain that she did *not* search the entire Penn State site, that in fact, she didn't realize there was a large Penn State site (this was made even more certain as she followed her answer with a self-realization that she was supposed to understand the Web site's structure as part of the assignment, something she had missed).

I could only surmise that somewhere in her search that departed from the Safe Schools site she met a link that took her directly to the site on intimate violence, perhaps a site presenting research on the effects of domestic violence on children's lives in school. I'll never know at this point. I continued to wonder if a history of visited sites would have provided me with more concrete answers to some of my questions. Yet, Jonatha's response to one of my questions was still perplexing to me: Why didn't she see the connection in content between the Safe Schools and the domestic violence sites—that was so clear to me—until after I asked her to take a more critical look at her assignment? Her citation on the conference was, in content, strikingly different from the two more traditional education citations. Didn't this difference catch her eye and direct her toward asking questions that could have led to the connection I saw?

The answer to my question could be quite simple. The students were working on this assignment under a time constraint that may have prevented them from noticing connections they were actually making themselves. Perhaps, because of the time constraints, they hadn't reread their writing before turning it in, preventing them from reflecting on their work. Without the context of an assignment beyond "find three WWW sites," there was little need to even think about invention. In addition, because the Web was new, they had probably dedicated much of their cognitive energy toward using the technology itself rather than using the technology to another end.

I was led to believe that the answer to my question was a little more complicated, however, by a question Jonatha asked: Could the conference on domestic and intimate violence be considered an education reform so that she could use it as the topic for her major writing project? I asked her to talk through the assignment with this question in mind, and we both agreed that a conference was one way that someone could try to bring about change in the way people are educated. She thought that she would explore the connection between violence at home and violence in school made visible in her short writing assignment and, equally important, revealed to her slowly in the discussion we had about this assignment. All of this activity consisted of moments of invention that were connected to make deeper, richer moments of invention.

How did this experience with Jonatha differ from what I would have found from merely following the sites she visited? Whereas a history of visited links would prove interesting to look at, in the end, I thought, it might prove to be nothing more than a breadcrumb trail. It wouldn't show me how the student was interpreting the site, it wouldn't show me if the student read parts or the whole of the site, it wouldn't show me how much time was spent on the site. Mostly, though, a breadcrumb trail wouldn't show me how the student was experiencing the Web: what the student had noticed, how the student was dealing with the chaotic, fragmented nature of the Web, how the student had or had not reflected on his or her experience, how the student's cognitive processes may have been in conflict or in harmony with the structure of the technology. What was a series of disconnected snapshots for the student would have been the same for me, also.

My close reading of Jonatha's Web experience and my exchange with her about this experience led me to map how I think students initially approach reading the Web. I'm drawing on a variety of current reading theories that were developed from research using traditional print texts because what we know about reading derives from research with conventional sources—we know very little about Web reading—and students bring with them to the Web the reading strategies they have developed from processing traditional print texts. Most influential in this mapping is research reported by June Cannell Birnbaum on reflective thinking in reading and writing processes, research that I used in chapter 1 to articulate a theory of invention. Proficient readers and writers pause and deliberate as a necessary strategy in their thinking processes. They not only consider where they have been in relationship to where they are when processing texts, but they also imagine where they will go next, using reflection as a means of moving forward throughout a given task. Less proficient readers and writers, however, fail to see (or do not know *why* they should see) the value in reflection and are almost completely consumed with finishing, ending, and bringing a given task to closure, often prematurely.

As illustrated by the first diagram below, students' typical Web reading strategies, what I call "The Impulsive Model" (figure 3.1), involve four actions that result in the creation of what I call a "simple text," a mental text of sorts that, when left alone, never manifests beyond the moment it is created:

1. Students begin their reading experience on a screen. This is most often a predetermined screen like a class site where an assignment has been posted, a search engine, or a "home" site that has been programmed into a specific work station. At this screen, students create their first simple text, a process rooted deeply in automaticity. Here, simple texts involve two levels that are often intertwined:

   • a plan, driven by the purpose for reading the Web and an intended goal or outcome (I need to find a source for a research paper; I wonder what the weather will be when I'm in Portland next week; I'm bored and want to ride the Web).

   • an interpretation of what appears on the screen, the actual process of coming to understand text, graphics, sound, design.

2. At some point, students will choose to leave the site because they have come into contact with a hypertext link they wish to explore. With this choice to leave the site comes an expectation about where the students think they will be taken by selecting the link. This expectation is constructed through an interpretation of the link and its surrounding text and becomes another simple text. For example,

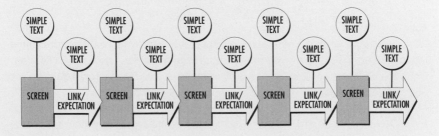

Figure 3.1 The Impulsive Model

imagine that a community college student is looking for a liberal arts college to transfer to. Reading a school's site, she comes upon a link labeled, "Bachelor of Arts in English," and would expect a description of the major, an outline of course requirements, perhaps a list of faculty in the department and short biographies of recent graduates. Sometimes, links are more ambiguous, such as graphic links, providing less certainty in a user's expectation and perhaps a more confused or vague simple text created around this expectation.

3. After the execution of a link, students are presented with a downloaded page on their screen. Again, they begin to create a simple text, yet this one differs from the one they began with. This text still includes both an interpretation of what appears on the screen—the actual process of coming to understand text, graphics, sound, and design—and also, in most cases, a continuance of the plan, although this plan may be revised according to what students discover in their search (I was originally riding the Web for fun, but I stumbled upon a site that I can use for my history paper). One additional process occurs at this point:

   • a *decentering*, or a letting go of what *was* and readjusting to what *is*.

   Landow describes this process as integral to reading the Web: "As readers move through a Web or network of texts, they continually shift the center—and hence the focus or organizing principle—of their investigation and experience. Hypertext, in other words, provides an infinitely re-centerable system whose provisional point of focus depends upon the reader, who becomes a truly active reader in yet another sense." (*Hypertext: The Convergence*, 1992, 11). Decentering is the process of having one's view realign when leaving one site and landing upon another. This occurs usually when one is engrossed in what has just been found, often resulting in the forgetting of something just viewed.

4. Again, students will choose to leave the site when they are presented with a link, the opportunity to move to something new. As before, another expectation, along with another simple text, is formed, and they leave the site, continuing the process outlined.

As described here, this process appears to be rather intricate, involving complex reading and thinking operations. Many might be surprised by my choice of "simple" to describe the mental procedures involved in creating these texts; reading and interpretation are indeed complex. (I'm not going to spend a great deal of time here describing these procedures. Many researchers before me have described these in models of reading and cognitive processing, and I think any of these models would "fit" as an example of creating a simple text in the overall framework I am describing here.) However, I would argue that the process diagrammed here of what happens as students move from one Web site to the next indicates that our students are failing to reach a place where the true complexities of learning can be realized. Their approach to reading the Web represents an ineffective invention strategy.

Consider again how this technology works. Techno-lore, if you will, leads us to think about hypertext as *anything but* linear. The nutshell definitions that were so much an early part of our understanding of technology said that hypertext was a "nonlinear, hierarchical, dynamic" text made possible with computer technology. However, some dispel this view by arguing that the Web, which is a hypertext, is a linear medium because of its dependency on written text to convey meaning. Although there are many options for how one might move through this text, in the end, the text—the words on the screen—represents a linear language structure. In fact, when I am looking at a Web page in my browser, I can select "print" to get a hard copy of the text that looks very much like a word-processed document.

I argue that the Web is linear in another way. Web technology abets a rapid, feed-forward motion. Even though one might be experiencing a variety of texts stored on several different servers from all over the world, the read texts can be laid out in a continuous, contiguous fashion. Most Web browsers do this in "history" form, where a list of visited sites is made available with a simple click of the mouse. And because it's a "history," the sites are presented in the order that they were visited. Move forward, move back. Even where one can choose to "go to" a site in that history, the choice is made from a contiguous, continuous list.

The rapid succession of the Web is important in understanding students' reading of it, also. Depending on the complexity of the Web page being downloaded, texts can appear and disappear quickly. Students are, for many reasons, inclined to literally race through a series of Web texts. (As a quick test of this point, I set out to ride, to wander, to find something interesting on the Web. In a five-minute period, during a fairly busy time on the Internet, and using my home computer with minimal to average speed, I visited twenty-three documents, only four of which I returned "back" to so I could pick up a link I thought would be interesting.) In much the same way that we read a newspaper or a magazine, students don't always read an entire Web page before they come upon a link that provokes them to move to the next text. In her research on Web page design, Kim Tresselt-Wharton found that readers were less inclined to scroll beyond an initial "screen-full" of the first page of a Web site, but more inclined to do so with subsequent pages within that site (1995). In other words, based on Web readers' habits, the first page of a site might be more effective if it is no more than a screen-full, offering little other than links to get to other pages; important text below the initial screen of a site's first page might go unread. If this is a habit students bring to reading the Web (an ineffective one, at that), then chances are they will make a decision to move forward before they have taken in all of their options, one of which is to finish reading the text. Although Tresselt-Wharton's research showed that readers were willing to move beyond the initial screen-full after the first page, many of our students process text in a rapid, feed-forward manner to begin with; their unwillingness to pause and deliberate coupled with the rapid, feed-forward nature of the technology might encourage the ineffective reading model diagrammed above.

The rapid downloading of Web pages also plays a role in the decentering process, which I describe as "a letting go of what was and readjusting to what is." Whereas a quickly downloaded page encourages students to forget what they were looking at and focus on what has appeared on the screen, decentering can be prevalent in students' reading of the Web even when the technology is not working quickly, and perhaps even just as prevalent as when they are taken rapidly from site to site. I asked students to ride the Web during peak hours when connections were busy and downloading was slow. Not surprisingly, students did not remain fixed on their computer screens while the computer slowly delivered new pages to them. Instead, they rummaged through their book bags, they talked to their neighbors, or they left the room to get a drink. My favorite image is of waiting students spinning in their chairs (adjustable office-type chairs that will make numerous rotations with one good push), probably the ultimate physical and mental decentering I can imagine.

My early desire for a history of visited sites resulted in nothing but a breadcrumb trail because what I was seeing in students was nothing but a breadcrumb approach to reading the Web. Indeed, our model illustrates the creation of many simple texts that are necessary to learning, but all too often, these simple texts remain independent of each other. I think of students' learning experiences as a cognitive fabric; the material product—knowledge—I hope is dense in weave and rich in pattern. This patterned fabric is achieved when our simple texts become interlaced and braided, when it becomes difficult, if not impossible, to follow and separate individual threads.

I'm afraid that the typical approach for reading the Web leaves holes in our students' cognitive fabric. I won't argue that each simple text created in each step diagrammed above is not a moment of invention; the creation of a simple text is an act of invention, albeit a minimal one. Unfortunately, the model for reading the Web depicts a "live for the moment" approach to invention; these moments are rarely sustained or connected to other moments. As our students move from one node to the next, the combination of speed, "out of sight, out of mind" vision, and decentering, leaves their simple texts either depthless or forgotten altogether.

I want to return to my conversation with Jonatha concerning her writing assignment. At the end of our conversation, when Jonatha began to see a connection between the site on Safe Schools and the site on domestic violence, her reading of the Web far surpassed the impulsive model that typifies students' initial approach to the technology. I want to note that much of the tightening of the weave of her cognitive fabric, where threads in her thinking were added and pulled closer together, occurred one week *after* she left the computer. With Jonatha, two additional "actions" occurred that are otherwise not present in our impulsive model of reading the Web:

- a writing assignment that asked her to compose a written text while she was reading the Web;

- an intervening conversation that forced her to reflect upon and think critically about her reading the Web and that pushed her to articulate a representation of her learning process.

Each of these is important to examine in order to outline a reflective model for reading the Web. As Jonatha worked on the assignment that asked her to summarize Web sites, she was making basic reading and writing connections. One connection, summarizing, forces a written representation of a simple text. In other words, as Jonatha read the text of a site, she created a simple text (interpretation), yet she moved beyond the simple text by creating a written text out of her simple text. Of course, this is the very reason we ask students to learn summary writing—it forces them to pay closer attention to, and thus better understand, what they are reading. An important "by-product" of summary writing is that it gives teachers a glimpse into students' reading processes, for this window into how students are reading and writing offers rich opportunities to intervene and converse with them about learning. The conversations are reflective as they almost always get students to articulate "this is how and why I did X," and this, in turn, allows teachers to suggest, to question, to guide. Again, these conversations move beyond students' simple texts.

The two actions described here—writing and conversing— begin to contribute to what I call "super texts," texts that are made up of anything that moves students' experiences with the Web beyond the creating of disconnected simple texts. Once again, calling upon research cited by Birnbaum, super texts are created in what I refer to as "The Reflective Model" (figure 3.2).

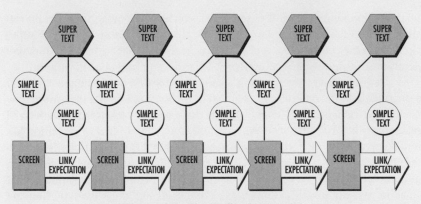

Figure 3.2 The Reflective Model

This model, with the addition of super texts, is rooted in reflectiveness as opposed to impulsiveness. I see super texts as quite different from simple texts;
what makes them "super" is a layering of a variety of experiences and
processes. Super texts are those which include connections made between simple texts, interpretations of screens and links and of link expectations. They include noticing, the realization that a simple text is similar to or different from
something already known or from something encountered. They include the
understanding of the mental processes used to work through chaos. They include collaborations that help solve problems or help find problems. They include writing that sometimes reveals connections between simple texts. They
include the revisiting and revisioning of simple texts. And finally, they include,
in their richest state, the extension of one super text to another super text.

When I originally contracted with graphic artist Jeffrey Cox to design
these diagrams, I did not include the top layer of super texts in the final reflective model, what I call, "The Reflective Model Extended" (figure 3.3).
After briefly explaining the theory I was building here (he is not a compositionist), I asked that he find a shape different from the others in the first two
diagrams to represent this high-level super text. Interestingly, he chose the triangle, he explained, as a shape that represents strength in design, architecture,
and construction. He described, for example, how his father made this point to
him when he was a boy. Three squares of wood attached to make a triangle result in a strong structure with little room to move and bend. Four squares of
wood attached to make a four-sided box result in a weak structure that bends
and wobbles with minimum pressure. That same structure, however, is made
stronger when a cross beam is placed diagonally across the box, in effect making two triangles. Based on my brief description of the impulsive/reflective
models, he felt that the upper level of super texts represented the strong,
steady, secure thinking that has moved beyond the sometimes unstable, fluid

thought characteristic of early invention. His theory of the strength of the triangle works nicely with my metaphor of a cognitive fabric. With each super text—including the multitude of connections attached to them—comes a tightening of the cognitive fabric's weave and an enriching of its pattern.

Of course, one new question now comes into view: If students typically employ an impulsive model to read the Web, one that inhibits invention, how do we move them toward a reflective model, one that encourages invention? I argued in chapter 1 that for experienced writers, the process of invention has become, for whatever reasons, automatic, and that this automaticity is considered by many learning theorists a signifier of proficiency. I countered, however, that this is not the only signifier of proficiency; we can teach invention so that students learn to be aware of inventive processes and they learn to articulate specific acts of invention to develop proficiency.

I teach a great deal of learning theory in my composition classes with much success. Of course, my pedagogy is grounded in learning theory; each activity and assignment serves to advance students' writing abilities through sound theory in learning practice. But I also teach *the theory itself* to my students because I believe that they can better understand assignments and become more cognizant of their own abilities and improvement of these abilities if they understand how they learn. Students who are aware of their learning processes and can articulate these processes are less likely to fall victim to inert knowledge. Instead, they will be able to carry abilities and practices from one learning experience to the next.

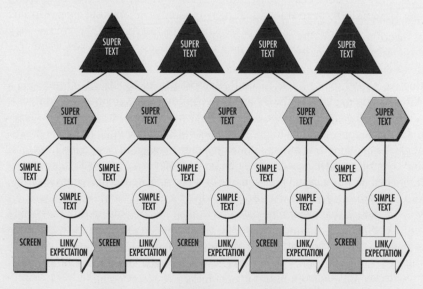

Figure 3.3 The Reflective Model Extended

I now teach the impulsive/reflective models of reading the Web to my students. I feel that teaching them this theory early in their Web experience pushes them to begin thinking about their own learning in a narrow, specific context—in my case, using the Web for invention. Learning the theory allows them to articulate what they do—or think they do—currently and to strengthen processes that are effective and revise or abandon processes that are ineffective. Asking them to articulate what they do gives me a glimpse into their learning.

The technology can offer us an opportunity to move students toward understanding research as a process that requires invention, not just one of locating evidence and backup information. It is, therefore, important to initiate a number of assignments and to teach a variety of computer skills that emphasize the reflective model over the impulsive model with the goal of having students create super texts as opposed to simple texts as they invent with the Web. I think it's important early in the process of learning how to invent with the Web to include multi-tasking with word processing as much as possible. Not all super texts include written texts, but creating written texts pushes students to be more cognitively engaged with their learning. Also, the more layers a super text has, the more "super"—beyond simple—the text will be.

Assignments that set a foundation for the reflective model as an automatic approach might include variations on the following directives:

- Students should be encouraged to do some type of writing while they are riding the Web, even if that writing is simple note taking. This includes both descriptive and evaluative writing. Methods employing writing to keep students actively reading *print* texts seem appropriate here. Because students can't write in the margins of the Web as they can in their textbooks, an open writing space affords them this opportunity.

- Ask students to keep a "running expectation log." Before they select a link, they should describe, in writing, where they think that link will take them and the reasons for their predictions. Variations might include having them record what information they think the site will provide, how it will be organized and designed, and what other types of links it will suggest. Also, students could describe why they feel the author named the link as he or she did. Once they arrive at the new site, they should describe what they find, comparing it to their original expectations. Continuing this assignment for n number of sites will help students develop schemata for reading the Web as well as teach them to be actively engaged in selecting links instead of being passively "dragged" from site to site. Dissonance between expectation and realization can often reveal interesting topics for writing.

- Ask students to set out on a course of riding the Web with a general sense of direction (look for sites about education, look for sites that might appeal to high school students, look for sites that represent nonprofit organizations). At each site, ask them to copy the address and compose a one- to two-sentence description of the site and a one- to two-sentence evaluation of the site: what they found interesting, how the site was designed or written, etc. After they have done this for *n* number of sites, ask them to note differences and similarities in the sites.

- This assignment could be continued a number of times with different general topics guiding students' searches. Once students have completed a series of searches, they could be asked to note differences and similarities among their assignments. Also, once students begin drawing these comparisons, they might notice topics for writing assignments. They could also be given an assignment whose purpose is to note similarities and differences in different search outcomes.

- Students can be asked to develop "forced" paper topics, an approach certain to yield a number of humorous results along with some interesting subjects for writing. Students can visit and summarize *n* number of sites that should, on the surface, have nothing to do with one another. They can use a search engine's directory to do this. Once they have a list of site summaries, ask them to create paper topics that combine two or more of the topics they searched. In many cases, even the more far-fetched ideas could prove to be viable research topics that would force students to create connections and relationships instead of simply inserting found material as support into a predetermined paper topic.

I want to emphasize that with these assignments, *variation* is key, and that variation should grow from the specific pedagogical goals of the course.

Conversing the Web

I want to conclude this chapter with a point I raised briefly at its beginning. The Web is presentational, positioned as an exploratory hypertext, an information system. There are far more who ride the Web than who write the Web. As I have said throughout this book, most of the courses I teach at the university require such important foundational work in such a short period of time that I'm unable to include the substantial amount of time necessary to teach Web writing. However, I have found a way to ask students to write *on* the Web in the form of discussion, applying the theory I developed using e-mail to my students' work on my instructional Web site.

I want to consider again how my student, Jonatha, came to find her paper topic. An important part of her super text—the recognition that there might be a connection between violence in the schools and violence in the home—was a discussion between the two of us. Although I spoke to Jonatha with a teacher/researcher's agenda, intervening in a directive way rather than really discussing, our conversation led her to recall a path she searched on the Web, to resee writing she had completed about the Web, and to see connections between two seemingly unlike ideas that could potentially become a fruitful topic for writing. She had already begun constructing a super text with the writing assignment that had asked her to summarize Web sites. The conversation, however, laid layer on top of layer to create and add depth to the super text.

My conversation with Jonatha occurred face-to-face. Computer technology offers us, however, other means of communicating with one another. In the previous chapter, I described how students used network technologies to conduct CmD, or computer-mediated discussions, and argued that these discussions facilitate invention by providing another moment when discoveries can be made and collaboration can take place. I also described how CmD can promote reflective thought, another important element of invention. I outlined a number of benefits of students' exchanges on-line that included:

1. *Increased writing and discussion participation.* Because CmD, as I have defined it, requires the production of written text, students are participating in a classroom activity that asks them to write more than they otherwise do. An increase in writing, even the conversational style of writing of CmD, increases fluidity and increases the possibility of discovering topics for writing. Also, because CmD is asynchronous—they are not conversing face-to-face, "at the same time"—participants are not competing for shared time in which to speak. CmD creates a leveling of participation, allowing more students more opportunities to contribute to the discussion.

2. *Discussion and writing as shared experiences.* Making connections between discussion and writing presents a real Catch-22 for teachers. Composition teachers often find that their students "write like they talk," and have a hard time separating the two types of discourse for their students. These teachers are usually trying to show the differences between *speech* and writing. But CmD allows us to see connections between certain elements of *discussion* and writing—audience, tone, familiarity with a discussion's history and tenor. Furthermore, CmD leaves a written record of a discussion that can be used to pick up lost threads of interesting topics and to characterize carefully developed opinions as opposed to knee-jerk reactions.

3. *Contextualized writing*. CmD has the potential to teach students the difficult-to-understand concept of context—the relationship between audience and occasion. CmD alters the sequence of contributions to a discussion, and often there are multiple topics being discussed simultaneously. Before students can add an effective contribution to the discussion, they must contextualize their writing so that their audience fully understands the point they are making. Context is one quality often missing from students' writing.

CmD has the added benefit of providing students an on-line space where they participate in conversations that can add textured layers to their invention super texts. These spaces are shared by other students—their classroom peers, usually—and teachers, where students are the primary players in the discussions and where teachers usually intervene with instructional intent.

Our instructional Web site, *MCSET*, includes a number of CmD spaces designed to serve a variety of pedagogical goals. These discussion spaces are created with the use of Microsoft FrontPage features called "Discussion Web Wizards," programs that ask a series of questions and take the information supplied to create a bulletin board system where students read and post contributions to a discussion. The bulletin board is a "framed" system, where the screen is split in two for two different operations. The top screen is reserved for the "Contents," a listing of all contributions posted to the discussion. The bottom screen is reserved for reading contributions or composing contributions that will be posted.

It's important to note how posting works in this CmD space and how each posting is represented in the "Contents" frame. In order to post to a discussion, students enter their name and a "subject" in the appropriate blanks. The computer is preprogrammed to "send to" the server where the site is located and to enter the date and time of the post. There is also a place to type a "comment," the text of the contribution to the discussion. Below the comment box is a button to "Post comment" that sends the contribution, when completed, to the server. Once the posting has been received by the server (a matter of seconds, in most cases), the lower frame instructs students to return to the Contents to see a complete list of items posted.

Each contribution is listed in the Contents, organized hierarchically first by subject and then by chronology. Each item in the list is a hypertext link that, when selected, displays the posted contribution for reading in the lower frame. For example, imagine that four students are participating in a discussion, prompted by a "question," posted by me, that asks them to reflect on the use of computers in the writing classroom. After the initial round of postings, where each student has posted once, the contents might look something like this:

CONTENTS

Question *Scott Lloyd DeWitt* 25 Oct 1996
Computers and my writing *Meegan* 26 Oct 1996
The Re-Write *Donna* 26 Oct 1996
Technology in the classroom *Kristie* 26 Oct 1996
Access to technology *Carl* 26 Oct 1996

Students read a posted contribution by clicking on one of the hyperlinked subjects, the text that is blue in color and underlined. They read the contribution, and when they decide that they want to respond to a peer's posting, they select "reply" from the screen where they are reading. The subject is automatically provided as "Re:__," and the response is listed under the original contents listing, indented to denote a "level of response." Responses to responses are indented again after that. After a week, the hierarchically organized Contents might look like this:

CONTENTS

Question *Scott Lloyd DeWitt* 25 Oct 1996
Computers and my writing *Meegan* 26 Oct 1996
  Re: Computers and my writing *Carl* 26 Oct 1996
    Re: Computers and my writing *Meegan* 28 Oct 1996
    Re: Computers and my writing *Donna* 31 Oct 1996
  Re: Computers and my writing *Donna* 27 Oct 1996
  Re: Computers and my writing *Kristie* 27 Oct 1996
The Re-Write *Donna* 26 Oct 1996
  Re: The Re-Write *Carl* 28 Oct 1996
  Re: The Re-Write *Kristie* 28 Oct 1996
  Re: The Re-Write *Meegan* 29 Oct 1996
    Re: The Re-Write *Donna* 29 Oct 1996
  Re: The Re-Write *Kristie* 30 Oct 1996
    Re: The Re-Write *Meegan* 31 Oct 1996
    Re: The Re-Write *Carl* 31 Oct 1996
Technology in the classroom *Kristie* 26 Oct 1996
Access to technology *Carl* 26 Oct 1996
  Re: Access to technology *Donna* 28 Oct 1996
    Re: Access to technology *Carl* 1 Nov 1996

I have found that the hierarchically organized contents provides a "structural context" for its users. Because responses are literally located under an original text, students find that they do not have to contextualize their writing in order for readers to understand their meaning. This is not true of CmD conducted with e-mail. Because e-mail contributions to a conversation arrive with little to no linear pathway and are often interspersed with other e-mail (letters from friends, memos from supervisors, announcements of social events, etc.), e-mail CmD participants contextualize their contributions by summarizing the post they are responding to: "In her last message, Maria pointed out that. . . ." We lose the sense of disorder of e-mail CmD in the bulletin board format used on the Web because of the preordered arrangement of the contents. It is clear what is in response to what because of the hierarchical and chronological organization. When surveyed, 100 percent of my students preferred the bulletin board CmD over an e-mail CmD for these very reasons. Students quickly assume that because of the hierarchical and chronological ordering of the contents page, the structural context will take the place of the written context that they needed to provide in e-mail discussions.

To a certain extent, this is true. Indeed, one is clear about what is in response to what, and all a person needs to do is click on the previous posting in the hierarchy to understand the context of any subsequent posting. This reliance on a structural context, however, forces participants to reread previous posts in order to understand context because introductory statements at the beginning of posts are absent. Imagine that I had read to the end of an available discussion on a Friday afternoon. I had been reading many different threads to many different discussions—all of which dealt with education—when I decided to call it a day. When I logged in on Monday, I noticed that a discussion had been continued, and I selected the latest post:

Re: Are we leaving students out?

From: Craig
Date: 17 Feb 1997
Time: 14:29:55
Remote name: 205.212.150.51

Comments

What if teachers who were facing this dilemma would just simply video tape the labs they are going over. I know a lot of teachers who do this. . . .

As a reader of this contribution, I would have to stop at this point and return to the original post in order to understand the context of "this dilemma," which in this case is having to repeat lectures for Advanced Placement students who can't make it to important classes because of the rigidity of their schedules.

I'm concerned about losing the valuable teaching of context as I find myself using e-mail CmD less and less and the bulletin board CmD more and more. I encourage students to situate their postings so that contextualized writing becomes more intuitive to their composing. But the structure that the technology imposes in the students' eyes (and probably in those who use bulletin boards outside of the writing classroom) renders contextualizing a post in writing "redundant" when it is so easy to both locate and reread a previous post.

Sometimes when something is lost, however, something else is gained. I do find that the Web posting's hierarchical, chronological organization promotes a reading and writing connection that I believe integral to invention, especially in the creation of a super text. Although I have stated that Web technology employs a rapid feed-forward approach to reading, I find that the structural context of the bulletin board counters this by promoting reflection, a strategic backtracking and rereading in order to feed forward—in this case, rereading in order to formulate a written response. And I would be remiss in failing to mention that as with CmD conducted with e-mail, Web-posted CmD does promote an increase in student writing and participation. Additionally, the threaded discussion offers me a concrete artifact that I can use to illustrate writing and discussion as shared experiences. And finally, the hierarchical organization of the Contents gives me a visual representation of the depth of the discussion that is not easily discernible in e-mail. Of course, the quality of a contribution is of utmost importance when considering the depth of a discussion, but CmD, like most discussions, gets its depth from the layering of response on top of response. Four students can each post a well-written, thoughtful statement that would be considered by most to have "depth," but until those statements are questioned, challenged, added to, and agreed with, they lack the true complexity necessary to benefit invention.

Four students participated in the following Web CmD over the course of seven days. Whereas I would normally hope for increased numbers of posts to this thread, the hierarchy alone illustrates a certain depth in the discussion:

CONTENTS

Are we leaving students out? *Craig & Rob* 14 Feb 1997
  Re: Are we leaving students out? *Craig* 14 Feb 1997
    Re: Are we leaving students out? *Donna* 14 Feb 1997
    Re: Are we leaving students out? *Rob* 14 Feb 1997

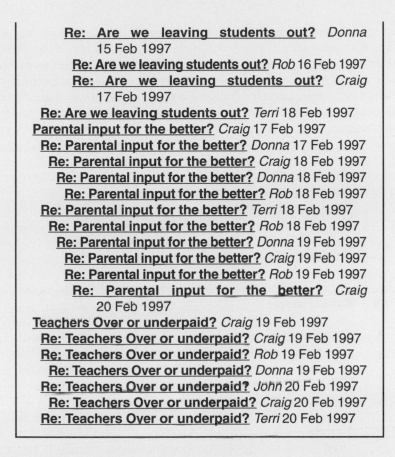

Re: Are we leaving students out? *Donna* 15 Feb 1997
Re: Are we leaving students out? *Rob* 16 Feb 1997
Re: Are we leaving students out? *Craig* 17 Feb 1997
Re: Are we leaving students out? *Terri* 18 Feb 1997
Parental input for the better? *Craig* 17 Feb 1997
Re: Parental input for the better? *Donna* 17 Feb 1997
Re: Parental input for the better? *Craig* 18 Feb 1997
Re: Parental input for the better? *Donna* 18 Feb 1997
Re: Parental input for the better? *Rob* 18 Feb 1997
Re: Parental input for the better? *Terri* 18 Feb 1997
Re: Parental input for the better? *Rob* 18 Feb 1997
Re: Parental input for the better? *Donna* 19 Feb 1997
Re: Parental input for the better? *Craig* 19 Feb 1997
Re: Parental input for the better? *Rob* 19 Feb 1997
Re: Parental input for the better? *Craig* 20 Feb 1997
Teachers Over or underpaid? *Craig* 19 Feb 1997
Re: Teachers Over or underpaid? *Craig* 19 Feb 1997
Re: Teachers Over or underpaid? *Rob* 19 Feb 1997
Re: Teachers Over or underpaid? *Donna* 19 Feb 1997
Re: Teachers Over or underpaid? *John* 20 Feb 1997
Re: Teachers Over or underpaid? *Craig* 20 Feb 1997
Re: Teachers Over or underpaid? *Terri* 20 Feb 1997

In much the same way that the super text tightens the weave and enriches the pattern of the cognitive fabric in the reflective model of reading the Web, so does the hierarchical ordering of the Contents in a bulletin board CmD.

I use these threaded discussions in two ways. *On the Table Café* is a broad-based, issues-driven, discussion "café" based on the 1990s reemergence of the coffee house as a space where people drop in and out of conversations that begin and end over time. I have created some "open" threads where students can discuss issues unmediated by me. However, while most discussions in the *Café* directly and indirectly feed into the major writing projects that students are working on, these discussion are rarely specific to any one student's paper topic. Instead, I introduce general topics that might promote discussions that will lay a foundation for students' thinking about their specific topics. These discussions have the potential for elevating students' invention beyond a simple text, adding layers in the creation of a super text. For example, students in my first-year writing course were working on an assignment that asked them to critically examine technology and its role in a variety of contexts. In one assignment, students were asked to analyze a focused on-line discussion forum in order to answer the question, "Can community exist on-line?" Early in the class, I exposed them to some general questions to help them begin thinking critically about the technology I was going to ask them to use in my class. In order to introduce these issues to them, I had assigned a number of texts for them to read. Then, I asked them to visit *On the Table Café* and respond to the following question:

From: Scott Lloyd DeWitt
Date: 5/2/00
Time: 12:02:40 PM
Remote Name: 128.146.255.83

Comments

In his essay, "Welcome to Cyberspace," Philip Elmer-DeWitt writes:

"[Cyberspace] has unleashed a great rush of direct, person-to-person communications, organized not in the top-down, one-to-many structure of traditional media but in a many-to-many model that may—just may—be a vehicle for revolutionary change."

Elmer-DeWitt wrote this passage in 1995. Technology guarantees rapid change, so it's not unreasonable to ask, "Has this prediction come true in the year 2000?"

Argue ways in which communications technology has become a vehicle of revolutionary change, or argue that his claims are inflated, hardly revolutionary in nature. Of course, any argument you pose should include examples. And personal experience is highly valued, if you wish to share.

The discussion that ensued familiarized students with some of the broader issues of the assignment and allowed me the opportunity to illustrate for them how to situate their narrow paper topics within this context. It also allowed students the freedom to "sound off" and challenge their peers as well as bring other reading assignments they had completed to the table:

Re: what I mean...

From: deanne
Date: 5/9/00
Time: 12:18:23 PM
Remote Name: 128.146.255.217

Comments

Do we want to "exceed the truth"? Is it a good thing? What do you mean by this statement? Are you saying exceeding the truth is like vacationing from reality, being something we'll never be? Doesn't the rest of mass media already burden us with that load of crap? Don't get me wrong. I know that I have given the impression in other replies that I am opposed to technology, but as John Perry Barlow mentions on page 8 of "Is There a There in Cyberspace," "Like so many true things, this one doesn't resolve itself to a black or a white. Nor is it gray. It is, along with the rest of life, black/white. Both/neither." I am not disregarding the Internet or Technology in general as bad or evil, It has helped many people and can be very convenient in many ways. But I wouldn't swear by it either. Just like anything we create, it is bound to be faulty. It seems to have taken the place of so much "reality" in our everyday life. Especially in children. I have heard that technology is just getting started. How far will we let it go? Like Dr. Frankenstein, will we create a monster that we might not be able to control or understand someday?

The second use of CmD on the *MCSET* is *Friday Forum*, a true virtual classroom that takes the place of regularly scheduled Friday class meetings. Our composition courses meet five hours a week, two hours on Mondays and Wednesdays or on Tuesdays and Thursdays, and one hour on Fridays. I find that sometimes, the one-hour class meeting doesn't serve the writing workshop format of my classes well; I usually make the class meeting optional, ensuring that students can set up conference times with me during that time and that they have access to the computer classroom to finish work. In place of this class meeting, though, students are required to participate in on-line discussions of

the week's reading assignment. I assigned my second-year composition course
Mike Rose's *Possible Lives* and asked them to discuss the book in *Friday
Forums*. In collaboration with my colleague Marcia, we created the following
guidelines:

You will have two roles in these forums: discussion **facilitator/
leader** and individual **reader/respondent**:

As a **facilitator/leader**, you will be assigned to a *Friday Forum*
Group that will be responsible for initiating an on-line discussion concerning some aspect of the reading we're doing for
class. Your group will also be responsible for keeping the discussion moving until the next group takes over. Each new
Friday Forum topic needs to be posted and available to the
class by Friday at noon. As a facilitator/leader, you will write
two (2) questions inspired by the reading that could be used to
initiate a discussion. These questions should have two parts:

1. A statement or passage that sets the context for the
   question. This could include a paraphrase of or a direct quote from the reading. "In the introduction to
   Testing Testing, Alan Hanson argues that. . . ."

2. A question or a directive that guides our thinking on a
   particular point. "Consider how your own experiences
   may or may not reflect Hanson's argument. . . ."

As a **reader/respondent**, you will do exactly what the name
implies—read the questions for discussion, respond to them,
and discuss with your classmates any observations they may
make about the topics. In other words, have an on-line discussion much like any discussion you would have face-to-face. A
one-time, Friday remark will not fulfill your obligation; you
should check the responses and continue to comment during
the week.

This is NOT an optional activity; it is part of your class participation grade, and neglecting *Friday Forum* can significantly
reduce your overall grade in the course.

I am choosing a second-year writing course I taught to illustrate *Friday Forum*. For reasons having to do with awkward scheduling, the class was under-enrolled; there were only six students participating. I think, however, viewing the discussions of such a small group illustrates the potential of this technology as an invention space. Again, none of the discussions necessarily pertained specifically to students' paper topics. The course was a seminar in writing that focused on theories of learning in various academic and nonacademic settings. When I taught the course previously, students suggested that I balance the learning theory we were reading with a text that explored the social settings where learning took place. Mike Rose's book was a collection of ethnographic narratives/creative essays describing educational systems that he felt transcended the negative rhetoric of failing schools and "why Johnny can't read." The writing assignments I asked students to complete were concerned mostly with cognitive theories of learning; the *Friday Forum* discussions, however, encouraged students to contextualize the theory they were studying in social learning environments.

I spend more time "training" students to participate in *Friday Forum* than in *On The Table Café* because it takes the place of regularly scheduled class time and the students are facilitators; they are really on their own, so I intervene only occasionally. The first assignment that I give them in *Friday Forum*, then, is to learn to ask questions according to the guidelines that will set the discussion on a contextualized course. This assignment teaches them to begin a discussion connected to their reading assignment (although, I have found, discussions quickly drift off the text but, for the most part, stay on the broader issues discussed in the reading) while introducing them to the technology.

I want to conclude this chapter with an example of these discussions, the first that my students participated in. Over the course of a week, six discussion questions/threads were introduced to the forum, and a total of forty-two contributions were posted by seven participants. Whereas the numbers were impressive enough, I was thrilled with the level of engagement with which my students approached the *Friday Forums* segment of the our class Web site. At times, I couldn't resist participating in the discussion and found myself drawn in much more as a participant who desired to contribute than as a teacher who felt a need to intervene.

I have chosen three discussion threads within this one-week forum to illustrate our work. This overall discussion illustrates how CmD can enrich students' invention in writing. First, quite simply, they are covering content that they probably otherwise would not have discovered. This content derives from reading a text, posing questions about that text, reading other students' ideas, and responding to those ideas, all of which is invented as a result of noticing, making connections and seeing relationships, and reflecting upon the discussion as it is taking place. Much of this developed content becomes supporting material for students as they complete writing assignments in the class, material that both supports their thinking about the topic at hand and material that supports the texts they are producing. Students also are able to see *how* their classmates process the ensuing discussion, thus learning about their peers' learning processes. The body of on-line thinking that is archived in the *Friday Forums* becomes a representation of students' learning and invention processes.

Appendix: Possible Lives, Chapter 1—Los Angeles and the LA Basin
Facilitators, Craig, Jenny, and John

CONTENTS

Do we take pride in the Honor roll *Craig, John, Jenny*
   16 Jan 1997
   Re: Do we take pride in the Honor roll *Donna*
      16 Jan 1997
   Re: Do we take pride in the Honor roll *Terri*
      16 Jan 1997
      Re: Do we take pride in the Honor roll *Rob*
         17 Jan 1997
      Re: Do we take pride in the Honor roll *Scott DeWitt* 22 Jan 1997
         Re: Do we take pride in the Honor roll *Scott DeWitt* 22 Jan 1997
   Re: Do we take pride in the Honor roll *Craig*
      16 Jan 1997
      Re: Do we take pride in the Honor roll *John*
         22 Jan 1997
   Re: Do we take pride in the Honor roll *Rob*
      17 Jan 1997

Replacing The National Honor Society *Jenny, Craig, and John* 21 Jan 1997
   Re: Replacing The National Honor Society *Donna*
      22 Jan 1997

Re: Replacing The National Honor Society
Craig 23 Jan 1997
Re: Replacing The National Honor Society *Scott DeWitt* 22 Jan 1997
Re: Replacing The National Honor Society *Craig* 23 Jan 1997
   Re: Replacing The National Honor Society
Donna 23 Jan 1997
Required courses *Scott DeWitt* 22 Jan 1997
 Re: Required courses *Craig* 23 Jan 1997
  Re: Required courses *John* 23 Jan 1997
   Re: Required courses *Jenny* 23 Jan 1997
    Re: Required courses *Scott DeWitt* 23 Jan 1997
    Re: Required courses *Scott-again* 23 Jan 1997
   Re: Required courses *John* 24 Jan 1997
  Re: Required courses *Donna* 23 Jan 1997
  Re: Required courses *John* 23 Jan 1997
 Re: Required courses *Craig* 23 Jan 1997

Do we take pride in the Honor roll
From: Craig, John, Jenny
Date: 16 Jan 1997
Time: 11:33:35
Remote Name: 128.146.189.99

Comments

In chapter 1 of Possible Lives, Mike Rose briefly talks about students taking pride in making the honor roll. Do you think students today take as much pride in making the honor roll as students in the past did? Do you think that the two girls on page (14) who noticed a name of a friend on the honor roll really care if someone makes it? Would someone who makes the honor roll be looked down upon by his or her peers?

Re: Do we take pride in the Honor roll
From: Donna
Date: 16 Jan 1997
Time: 13:00:23
Remote Name: 128.146.189.97

Comments

I think that most people take pride in an accomplishment no matter its source. High school students may be reticent to state their feelings about the honor roll in the presence of their peers, but I believe that, in general they do possess a certain amount of pride in seeing their names posted to the honor roll. As it concerns these two girls, yes, I do believe that the honor roll matters as demonstrated by their calling attention to the list.

Re: Do we take pride in the Honor roll
From: Terri
Date: 16 Jan 1997
Time: 15:00:45
Remote Name: 128.146.189.127

Comments

I think that in the United States or at least at my high school that it was a big deal if you made the honor role or not. I know that it was a big deal in my household to get good grades. My parents are both educators and my dad was my elementary school principal and now is the superintendant, so he was always really big on the idea of good grades. I think that the two girls who rode by on the bikes were kind of envious of their friend that had made it because everyone loves to get recognized for something good that they do. I often wondered if the emphasis put on the honor roll was as big of a deal in other households as it was in mine or if it was simply the fact that I had a principal for a parent.

Re: Do we take pride in the Honor roll
From: Rob
Date: 17 Jan 1997
Time: 18:45:47
Remote Name: 205.212.150.34

Comments

I can tell you that in my house being on the honor roll was not a concern, my parents were happy if we passed a course with a C. Perhaps I would have been better driven to succeed had I been given higher expectations in school.

Re: Do we take pride in the Honor roll
From: Scott DeWitt
Date: 22 Jan 1997
Time: 13:29:18
Remote Name: 140.254.112.42

Comments

I think Terri has used a key word in her post here: "recognized." Yes, everybody loves to get recognzied for something. And recognition is important to learning. It's an imporant part of "feedback." I believe that feedback plays one of the most important roles in learning. But that feedback needs to be meaningful, and I'm not sure that I believe that grades are the most meaningful way to offer feedback.

So I guess that I want to throw this question out: How can we recognize students in such a way that we are assessing learning, but that we do so with feedback that is more meaningful than a letter grade or a gpa?

I guess it's also important that a gpa is an "average." It doesn't really account for anything specific—the shining moments or the struggles, nor does it account for "process," just "product."

Re: Do we take pride in the Honor roll
From: Scott DeWitt
Date: 22 Jan 1997
Time: 13:31:58
Remote Name: 140.254.112.42

Comments

Take a look at the top of page 45 for an example of what I'm thinking about here.

Re: Do we take pride in the Honor roll
From: Craig
Date: 16 Jan 1997
Time: 21:44:51
Remote Name: 206.230.54.161

Comments

I think that most kids do take pride in making the honor roll but there are always the ones who are bashing it. Many of the students who bash this are just doing it because they didn't do it. But then I also feel that there is a group of students who really don't want to make the honor roll, they are simply just in school to socialize. We had a mix of everything in our school, but genuinely most students took pride in seeing their names posted.

Re: Do we take pride in the Honor roll
From: John
Date: 22 Jan 1997
Time: 11:06:59
Remote Name: 128.146.189.187

Comments

I agree. There are some students in just about every school who are there strictly to socialize with their friends. But, there are also those who bash the Honor Role and those who are on it until no one wants to really be on it anymore. Is this fair to the student who really wants to succeed and is expected to succeed by his/her parents? Children should not have to be afraid to excel in school because of a few people who make them feel ashamed of their talent and gifts.

Re: Do we take pride in the Honor roll
From: Rob
Date: 17 Jan 1997
Time: 18:37:01
Remote Name: 128.146.189.186

Comments

I believe any student who sets the goal of making the honor roll is likely to be proud of fulfilling that goal. I don't think that this is any different today than in the past. What may be different is the general attitude toward the importance of being on the honor roll, of having on your record a glowing mark of excellence for future employers or college administrators to see.

Concerning the two girls, who knows what they feel. It's possible they both have been honor students who have worked hard with their friend and are happy for her to have finally made it on. Just as likely is that the girl who made the roll is the first of the three to achieve this commonly set goal.

Peer groups, for the most part, are made up of people with common interests and goals. No doubt there has always been animosity between certain groups and others.

Replacing The National Honor Society
From: Jenny, Craig, and John
Date: 21 Jan 1997
Time: 14:05:30
Remote Name: 128.146.189.162

Comments
Is it logical to replace an organization that supports strictly academic achievements with organizations that do not rely solely on academic standards?

Re: Replacing The National Honor Society
From: Donna
Date: 22 Jan 1997
Time: 10:27:05
Remote Name: 131.187.101.102

Comments

If we are to assume that a functional and thinking individual is the end result of a high school education, then yes, it is logical to replace the strictly grade-based organizations with others that account for the various facets of daily life. In the case of the National Honor Society, nomination is supposed to acknowledge athletics and other extracurriculars. However, in practice, it is primarily based on superior academic achievement alone.

Those students who excel in art or music, for example, may not perform in an outstanding capacity in the "measurable" fields of mathematics or science. Conversely, students who score near 30 on the ACT, may never attain a deep appreciation for art or be able to compose a song.

If high schools are going to place a strong emphasis on membership to the National Honour Society, then an organization devoted to the artistically gifted should be recognized with similar zeal.

Re: Replacing The National Honor Society
From: Craig
Date: 23 Jan 1997
Time: 11:55:59
Remote Name: 128.146.189.251

Comments
At least in my school, I'm not familiar with other schools.
Our national honor society was based on the overall picture. We had many students who were straight A students
but because all they did was spend time studying, they
didn't make it into the organization. So I don't think that
they are not following standards they have set for it.

Re: Replacing The National Honor Society
From: Scott DeWitt
Date: 22 Jan 1997
Time: 13:21:03
Remote Name: 140.254.112.42

Comments

I have to admit that I have a deep "distrust," if you will, of
anything that resembles an "honor" society. First of all, let
me list a student profile here:

*Attends a small rural high school
*Active in music and theatre
*Freshman high school GPA=1.75
*Graduates in lower half of class with GPA=2.1
*Wants to attend college, but scores 14 on ACT
*Accepted to college on conditional basis
*Makes Dean's List freshman year with GPA=3.86

Maybe you have figured it out. That's MY profile. Why
was that my profile? I will accept a large part of the responsibility here. I didn't work very hard in high school.
However, there weren't many teachers outside of the
music department who really tried to engage me. And
many of my teachers wanted to work with the "best and

brightest," and that meant "those with the best grades" who were "honors" students. If you didn't make the grade—literally make the grade—there was very little attention paid to you.

I remember how life changed for me in college when I first started to get good grades. Sure, I was a better student. I worked harder. But things really changed not because I was so much a different person, but because the number that followed my name was deemed "outstanding." Most teachers, given the choice, would want to work with 3.86 any day over 1.75. But in my case, the ability was the same no matter what the numbers were.

Re: Replacing The National Honor Society
From: Craig
Date: 23 Jan 1997
Time: 11:48:47
Remote Name: 128.146.189.251

Comments

I think that Scott has valid points for his argument. But I think that we still need to have some sort of a system set up to honor students who do well. I personally didn't make the national honor society, and I don't really care if I did or not. True it is probably a great thing to be a part of. But don't put too much weight in these groups because how does one honor determine who you are? It can't, you are who you are. I didn't excel in high school either but now I find my self wanting to do better in school because the teachers are more willing to take the time to work with me.

Re: Replacing The National Honor Society
From: Donna
Date: 23 Jan 1997
Time: 12:26:01
Remote Name: 152.163.233.61

Comments

I do not see the need to heap additional "honors" upon students who are already rewarded with excellent marks. Rather, shouldn't we reward the students who truly apply themselves? Why should the end result count more than the attempt? My brothers and sisters had a very easy time of making superior grades, all were accepted into top-notch schools, which is really reward enough in and by itself, but I don't think that any of them had to ever put forth any real effort toward learning. I would rather reward the student who actually tries.

Required courses
From: Scott DeWitt
Date: 22 Jan 1997
Time: 13:34:58
Remote Name: 140.254.112.42

Comments

I teach "required" courses—almost exclusively. At OSU, these are courses that fulfill GECs. On page 48, Rick says that students would rather not take required courses. Why is this? I don't believe that there is anything inherent in these courses that necessarily makes them "boring." Is it reputation that kills these courses—who wants to take English 101? Is it youth—young people don't want to be told what to do?

Re: Required courses
From: Craig
Date: 23 Jan 1997
Time: 11:07:48
Remote Name: 128.146.189.238

Comments

I think that most students are somewhat scared to take required courses because they hear horror stories from students who took the course previously. Most of these courses that I have taken I have not had too many bad experiences with. I would say take them and form you own opinon. Approach them with an open mind. It will make them more fun and interesting.

Re: Required courses
From: John
Date: 23 Jan 1997
Time: 12:17:52
Remote Name: 128.146.189.135

Comments

I agree with the idea that many students shy away from "required" courses because of the horror stories told them by their peers. I had many experiences in my first year here with this same thing and I think that a lot of it comes down to students who get mad because they didn't get an "A" from a certain professor so that professor is too hard or not fair. This is, pardon my language, B.S.!!! Just because a student doesn't get the grade that they expect from an instructor doesn't necessarily mean that the instructor is bad. Some people do better in some subjects than others. I believe that is why the university requires students to take classes in a wide range of fields, to make them a more well-rounded individual. If it was meant to be a cake walk, there would be a lot of idiots graduating with honors and a lot of good businesses and schools would go down the tubes because they would think they were getting a person who excelled in school when all they are really getting is a person with a degree in a too easy subject!

Re: Required courses
From: Jenny
Date: 23 Jan 1997
Time: 12:34:09
Remote Name: 128.146.189.249

Comments

I agree with John that college courses should not be watered down just so we can graduate a large portion of society from college. I do think however that some required courses are a waste of time. In order to get my Bachelor of Science in Business from Ashland, I will be required to take two religion classes. I have done my time in CCD and I do not wish to learn more about Buddhism. How many times have you wondered how you will use this material when you get out. I imagine it comes in handy when you play Trivial Pursuit, but when you are paying this much money to learn, I think that you should be learning material that will serve you well in the "real world," serve its purpose in the real world.

Re: Required courses
From: Scott DeWitt
Date: 23 Jan 1997
Time: 15:22:35
Remote Name: 128.146.189.101

Comments

I understand Jenny's frustration—having to take a list of courses because "it's good for you" doesn't add much incentive to learning. But in this specific case, I think I need to take issue with your criticism.

So you are a business major. Seems to me that you may be doing business with companies who are not only from other countries, but also with individuals who practice any variety of religions. In many cultures, religion is so closely tied to the way people look at the world and approach problems that it could be quite helpful to have an understanding of their perspective. At the same time, I don't think that you'll be so lucky as to do business with someone who practices the very same religion you studied your sophomore year—that would be too easy. But think about how centric some folks are about religion. If everyone in college learned about two religions other than their own, then I can't help but think that our sensitivity and understanding of "difference" would increase.

Re: Required courses
From: Scott-again
Date: 23 Jan 1997
Time: 15:24:13
Remote Name: 128.146.189.101

Comments

I just thought of one more argument about taking religion courses when you are a business major. Different disciplines approach problem solving in different ways. I think that it would only help you learn to be a better problem solver in general if you learn as many different approaches as possible.

Re: Required courses
From: John
Date: 24 Jan 1997
Time: 10:18:28
Remote Name: 128.146.189.187

Comments

I agree with Scott. We, not only as students but also as aspiring business professionals, must be able to understand many different cultures, and this includes religions. Take myself for example; I didn't really understand some of the different rituals involved with some of the Middle Eastern religions until I met a few of the faculty members on our campus. After talking with them I came to a much better understanding of their religion and their culture. Many things about different cultures can be learned from understanding their religions.

Re: Required courses
From: Donna
Date: 23 Jan 1997
Time: 12:40:52
Remote Name: 128.146.189.97

Comments
Perhaps it is just as simple as not having control over your own education. It seems to me that after twelve or thirteen years of being told what to learn, then viewing the variety of choices available in the OSU catalogue, and STILL being told which classes to take must be very depressing. Nobody likes being FORCED to do anything.

Re: Required courses
From: John
Date: 23 Jan 1997
Time: 12:52:37
Remote Name: 128.146.189.130

Comments

I don't think that the university is forcing anyone to take any classes that do not help in making a well-rounded student. How can an English major who plans on writing books write his or her book without, in some cases, having some extended knowledge in history, or in the case of an author like Michael Crichton have a background in sciences that goes beyond what is taught in high school. Furthermore, there is ample opportunity for a student to change his or her course of major study if they are having difficulty or simply do not like the subject matter of their current major.

Re: Required courses
From: Craig
Date: 23 Jan 1997
Time: 12:53:36
Remote Name: 128.146.189.251

Comments

I guess I don't feel that anyone is forcing me to do anything. If I don't want to be in school then I don't have to be
here. But the university is just trying to uphold high standards by giving us a well-rounded education. If you don't
like certain classes, there is nothing you can do about
them. Just play the game. Once I get a job I'm sure that
my boss or company CEO will want me to do things I
think are stupid. They may be very useful to me but when
I took the job I knew I would have to do certain things that
I may view as a waste.

4

Inventing Hypertext Writing

Tim Berners-Lee, in an interview with *Time*, made it clear that the World Wide Web didn't end up as planned. He should know; as named by *Time* writer Robert Wright (1997), he's "The Man Who Invented the Web." Unimaginative as Wright's title may be, I like the fact that he used the term "invented." As the story illustrates, Berners-Lee really did "invent" the Web, the creation of the technological application and the creation of a concept, both of which seem to illustrate my own vision of invention. The Web came to be after a lifetime of noticing, seeing relationships and making connections, along with reflecting on what has been and what could be.

It's not that Berners-Lee thinks the Web, as it has evolved, is necessarily "bad." Yet, one key element is missing in today's World Wide Web from what he imagined: "It was an accident of fate that all the first [commercially successful] programs were browsers and not editors" (qtd. in Wright, 1997, 68). In other words, when Berners-Lee imagined the Web for the masses, he saw it as a writing space just as much as a reading space: "The original goal was working together with others. The Web was supposed to be a creative tool, an expressive tool" (66). The original software that Berners-Lee wrote was indeed an integrated browser for reading and editor for writing. Unfortunately, the

---

This chapter is adopted from my dissertation, "Hypertextualizing Composition Instruction: A Research Study" (1992). Two of my other publications draw heavily from this work: "The Current Nature of Hypertext Research in Composition Studies: An Historical Perspective" (*Computers and Composition*, April 1996); and "Defining Links" (*Contexts, Intertexts, and Hypertexts*, 1999, Hampton Press). Although these publications present different areas of a single research project, they share common features: cited literature, description of a research design, working definitions, etc. Readers may notice overlap among the publications that grew from the original research project.

very design of the software—a browser—that was packaged and marketed after corporate America stepped in turned the Web into a space to "take it in," to consume and ingest, not to conceive and create.

My first experience writing hypertext came well before the possibility of writing for the Web was even a reality. I had enrolled in a series of courses in the art department in computer graphics as a way to enhance my work with technical and professional document design. One of the sequences was in the use of HyperCard, a simple hypertext program that came packaged with all new Macintosh computers. The course's instructor seemed less than enthused by the prospect of teaching mostly nonmajors (especially during the summer), and simply went through the motions of teaching us some simple database applications for the program: interactive records of music collections, addresses, student records. We designed a basic template called a "card," entered data, and created links. The finished product was called a "stack." My first stack—a linked record of my graduate coursework that I hoped would eventually serve as a digital vitae—seemed hardly like the hypertexts I had been reading so much about in my research. The final product was actually pretty dull, both in design and content. I wasn't sure that anyone would want to read it, let alone be able to make sense of the connections I was trying to make between my graduate coursework and my vision for my future professional endeavors.

Perhaps the text itself was not "dynamic," the one term that kept occurring to me as I reviewed what I had created. But the experience was. I immediately described it as "inventive." For the first time, I was finally able to see the potential for bringing constructive hypertext technologies that could facilitate learning to my students. I was linking. I was seeing and creating connections. I was joining two seemingly unlike ideas with the use of computer technology. Jeff Conklin's words returned to me: "One must *work* in current hypertext environments for a while for the collection of features to coalesce into a useful tool" (emphasis mine) (1987, 17–18).

While we currently have an important general foundation for anyone doing work with hypertext in teaching writing, the groundwork for hypertext applications in specific domains of composition instruction—invention, for example—is far from complete. The parallels between hypertext and invention are not particularly difficult to see. One of the promises of hypertext for teaching is that students will better be able to see connections and associations among seemingly unlike ideas. Hypertext links are the key to this recognition and are responsible for the possibilities of hypertextual moments of invention. In exploratory hypertexts, links can take students from one text to another, following a path that they might otherwise not have seen. And in constructive hypertexts, students can create links between texts, representing a connection they have discovered. However, what needs to be stressed is that hypertext applications more often than not describe learning *opportunities*; they do not always explain *actual learning processes*. For years, claims made about the technology appeared to emphasize how students learn using hypertext, but these claims never really focused on the learning opportunities that may lend themselves to actual student learning. In other words, many of the promises made about hypertext facilitating student learning are in reality technocentric projections of hypertext as an information system that provides opportunities that *could* facilitate student learning. Carefully designed research studies and classroom instruction can situate invention instruction away from hypertext as information system toward hypertext as facilitation—from the technology as it exists to the technology as it is used. Although there are many important educational applications for powerful information systems, hypertext will mean little to us as we teach invention until it is clear how it can facilitate the learning processes of students. And as I have argued up to this point, one way to ascertain that hypertext is facilitating students' learning is to find ways that the technology itself can illustrate and heighten their awareness of their own learning processes.

This chapter presents an important precursor to my current work with teaching Web writing. In fact, I see this work as an introduction of sorts for the next and last chapter where students create elaborate Web sites in place of traditional academic texts. The research presented here uses technology that is antiquated by today's standards, although I know of many programs that still operate on similar platforms. Most importantly, it serves as a foundation for invention instruction and hypertext writing.

One Hypertext Application

In 1991, I was teaching a first-year college writing course, preparing to implement a research design that would provide me with data for my doctoral dissertation. Before that, I did a lot of floundering, looking for a project that would meet my department's expectations of a suitable topic, that would yield the *type* of results I wanted to work with in the dissertation, and that would utilize the variety of coursework I had completed in my graduate studies. Amidst the uncertainty at this stage of the process, I did know a few things:

- My work would have something to do with computers. Whereas I began graduate school with no personal computer experience whatsoever, a complete technophobe, I left after serving as the coordinator of computers for the department, a complete technophile. Over the years, computers played an increasingly important role not only in my teaching, but also in my own writing. I selected "computer technology" as a cognate area of study to my degree in composition, taking coursework in technical writing, the creative arts, and education.

- I was interested in creating a research project that was qualitative, not quantitative, in design. Qualitative studies require a "rhetoric of dialectics and (ethnographic) interpretation [which] deals with uncertainty, that is, offers arguments that display rather than obviate doubt" (Brodkey, 1987, 27). My desire was to devalue the hierarchy of research findings and to begin to value the dialogue of first-hand knowledge that occurs within sites of investigation, in this case, my classroom (Newkirk, 1991, 132).

- I was interested in conducting research where I could work with a small group of students, studying their work within the context of a specific class. In her 1991 *Written Communication* article, "Dialogues of Deliberation: Conversation in the Teacher-Student Writing Confer-. ence," Melanie Sperling organized her research findings according to "Case Portraits," where she worked with three students and described their experiences with teacher/student conferences about writing (1991). Clearly, these students' approaches to the conference were different and enlightening, and deserved individualized attention in their presentation. They are presented separately, their "stories" receiving equal significance and weight. Brodkey, in her research on ethnographic narratives, uses the term "stories" to describe the work of composition researchers (1987, 26). Newkirk argues that the use of the term "story" is significant in that the work of composition researchers "is not at the bottom of a positivistic enterprise that privileges the 'objective' research report. . . . The model for Brodkey is not a hierarchy but a conversation" (1991, 131–32).

- I wanted my subjects to be first-year college writers enrolled in an intensive, developmental composition course. This was the population of students with whom I was most familiar in the classroom and in the literature I had read. It was also a population of students to whom I had grown quite committed. These students were blindly criticized for what they didn't know when they came to college, all too often written off from day one. They were enrolled in a course that many university professionals call "the most important class in a student's college career." Yet few of these professionals wanted to teach a class that, when it came down to it, they viewed as a "service" course. Besides, I learned early in my teaching experience that I thrive on witnessing change in my students, and I know of no other course where such significant, visible change has the potential to take place. The opportunity seemed perfect for my research, whatever that was going to be.

I began to think of individual graduate classes I had taken, hoping that an area of inquiry would grow out of a peculiar or unlikely grouping, courses that on the surface had very little to do with each other but that together would set me on a course of research. I was enrolled in a classical rhetoric seminar when I first heard of hypertext, interestingly enough. The professor had suggested one day during class that I do some reading on hypertext—apparently there was quite a "buzz" about this technology at a conference she had just attended. She knew very little about the technological application, and she wasn't necessarily suggesting that there was a connection, at least that she knew of, between hypertext and classical rhetoric. Her suggestion was more of an aside, a mentoring comment from professor to student. In her course, we spent a significant amount of time studying invention, especially in early classical work: the Sophists, Plato, Aristotle, Cicero, Quintilian. My take at the time was that invention as defined by classical rhetors, while important for the modern student to study, lacked a context of writing in the late twentieth century. Could hypertext allow me to imagine a context for teaching invention, one that might be influenced by classical rhetorics but that was truly situated in a modern classroom?

One other course came to mind as I began asking the questions I hoped would eventually lead to a research project. Taught by a cognitive psychologist, "Applied Theories of Learning" sought to train teachers across the disciplines in various approaches to looking at human learning patterns and processes. One such area was information processing, often viewed as an integration of behavioral learning theory and traditional cognitive psychology. Instead of seeing learning and behavior stemming from the mind or the environment, information-processing theory "holds that learning and behavior emerge from an interaction of the environment and the previous experience and knowledge of the learner" (Andre and Phye, 1986, 3). Information-processing theory is like traditional cognitive theory in that it views the mind as a structure that processes information and like behavioral learning theory in that it sees learning occurring partially by forming associations. More specifically, though, to the information-processing view is that "knowledge is represented in mental structure in a hierarchically organized network of associations among schemata" (Andre and Phye, 1986, 3). Whereas this course covered many schools of learning theory, from a study of memory procedures to knowledge monitoring and management, its underlying premise argued that students learn best when instruction is grounded in metacognition, a knowledge of and control over thought and learning processes. Instruction influenced by metacognition includes a thick description of learning processes, a rationale for why particular learning processes are appropriate in certain settings, and an application of the learning processes in multiple situations. Could hypertext reflexively represent students' invention, helping them to identify, define, and apply their learning processes, thus heightening a metacognitive awareness?

As I started to peruse the published literature on hypertext, I considered many of the claims that researchers make about how learners can benefit from classroom hypertext applications: Hypertext provides students with a new, powerful tool for accessing and creating knowledge, helps students make connections between seemingly unrelated ideas, promotes organized and integrative thought, encourages collaborative learning, and gives students easier access to their own writing. These are the very areas that first-year college writing students, particularly those enrolled in intensive or developmental programs, have difficulties with. I began to construct a study that sought to examine how students employ strategies of inquiry and problem formulation for writing while using a hypertext application. While constructing this study within the context of a course that I had designed, I drew on what I knew, from research and from my own teaching, about readers and writers, both novice and experienced. I operated from a premise that experienced and successful writers observe and respond to the worlds around them, using not only a wealth of information available to them, but also the connections and relationships they see among and within this information as a means of inventing continuously throughout the writing process.

I knew that hypertexts, both exploratory and constructive, enable users to draw on vast amounts of information stored in some form of a database, and what is key to hypertext is the way in which this information is linked. But mostly, the literature described these linking capabilities in classroom situations in terms of exploratory hypertexts—prepackaged databases that, while still allowing a user to access information intuitively and associatively, do not allow a user to add to the information in terms of constructing text or links. I could see how constructive hypertexts truly bring together the acts of reading and writing, an important element of invention instruction: constructive hypertexts are exploratory in nature (reading), but allow the user to add to (writing) a nonfixed structure. Composition students using constructive hypertexts can read text, respond to it in writing, design links between chunks of text, thus truly configuring a hypertext according to their personal needs. Whereas students were once restricted to structuring and presenting knowledge linearly in print, now they could connect ideas and knowledge hierarchically and associatively.

With little hypertext experience myself, I imagined that students would see the advantages of working in constructive hypertextual environments over working in exploratory hypertextual environments. Reading and writing would begin to take place in the same space. Students could access a variety of available texts, following links associatively to other texts. Furthermore, students could create texts that include links so that their own writing would become a part of the hypertextual space in which they were working.

I was primarily interested in the prospects of students creating a hypertext completely of their own writing. This hypertext could stand alone as an elaborate piece of student writing in and of itself. But I saw a two-fold application of the technology in my classroom. Creating links could be integral to invention and hypertext. Students must make meaningful, associative connections between the concepts and ideas when they are creating electronic links. Creating a hypertext link between two chunks of writing forces students to construct a representation—usually a linguistic one—of the connection. The very creation of these links becomes a meaning-making act connecting reading and writing. I also wanted students to complete more "traditional" academic papers. I was teaching a first-year composition course, where students were introduced to the practices and conventions of public and academic written discourse. Could students' work with hypertext feed into and enrich this type of writing? I would ask students to create a hypertext and use the experience as invention for the academic essays I assigned them. In addition to the experience of creating the hypertext, students would use their hypertext as an information source they could search as invention.

I designed a hypertext component for a unit of a freshman writing course, then analyzed that section of the class as teacher/researcher. The unit included short inventive and exploratory readings and writings, class discussions, in-class writings, in-depth reading assignments, and summary writing, all of which led to a major writing assignment—a documented essay. Students created a hypertext of their inventive writing that later served as a database that they explored to find topics and discover relationships. As teacher/researcher, I recorded daily occurrences in the classroom. Also, I analyzed the students' hypertexts, their writing, and carefully examined the transcripts from interviews I conducted with students near the completion of the project.

In the end, the overall project drew conclusions about hypertext and invention in two general areas. The first examined how students defined "hypertext" for themselves after their experiences with it. Specifically, that study, summarized throughout this chapter, concentrated on associations between how students define hypertext *links* and the role these links play in their self-constructed definitions of hypertext itself. A detailed discussion of this part of the study can be found in *Contexts, Intertexts, and Hypertexts* (edited by De-Witt and Strasma). The second area of the study, presented in its entirety here, looked closely at how students used a hypertext application to facilitate invention in writing.

The class I was teaching at the time was an "intensive" section of first-year composition. My department at the time offered a special writing track for those who are identified by placement exams and ACT scores as students who may have difficulty in a first-year writing course. Although students who are enrolled in an intensive section complete the same program requirements and receive the same credit hours as those enrolled in a regular section, intensive students attended class five hours a week instead of only three. The department did not offer a specific basic writing course. It developed this course after recognizing that many students needed more contact hours of individualized writing instruction to foster their written language abilities within the university setting.

I was teaching in a networked classroom of Apple Macintosh SE 20 computers. The core software in the classroom, which consisted of Microsoft Word 4.00D, HyperCard 2.0, and PageMaker 3.01, was driven by Macintosh System Software v6.0.7. Each workstation was networked to the other workstations via a high-capacity classroom server/storage hard disk using AppleShare Network Software. (I should note that this computer-enhanced classroom was considered "state of the art" at the time I conducted this study. Whereas the technology has changed greatly over the years, many are teaching today—with great success—using similar configurations.) Students were expected to complete all of their writing assignments using the computer. For the most part, students turned in their writing on-line via the classroom network, and it was returned to them with written comments in the same way. Also, most handouts were distributed through the network instead of in paper form. By the end of the first complete unit of study, students were familiar with most of the computer classroom's capabilities and features.

The course I designed was organized thematically around the broad topic, "Current Issues." Topics for units included, "Taking a Closer Look at the University," "Defining Family," "The Chaos of the AIDS Pandemic," and "Representations in Popular Culture." The course held rigorous expectations for students in terms of developing their critical reading and writing skills. All units included many short invention reading and writing assignments that led to a major writing assignment. This study was conducted while students were working on the unit entitled, "Freedom of Expression and the University Community," which covered issues of free speech specifically on college campuses. The topic was pressing and timely as a current social issue. Much of the dialogue in the popular press and media paralleled volatile situations on campus, and the unit placed much emphasis on strategies of problem formulation and invention. The topic of freedom of expression and First Amendment rights is one of many topics that students often approach simplistically and superficially: Students are unsure of how to problematize the issue and think critically about it. At the heart of this composition course is a theoretical framework that posits that exploring a topic through reading and writing will help students to become critical thinkers. Therefore, students read many short articles on the topic of freedom of speech and expression from varying points of view. Also, students wrote responses to these articles, to class discussions, and to real-world situations concerning issues of First Amendment rights. The final writing project assignment asked students to conduct a survey of college community individuals on some aspect of freedom of expression and to write a report of their findings and an essay for a particular audience interested in their results. Students were presented with a strict format for the report that included a narrative introduction, a description of their "methodology," a presentation of their survey results, and a reflective conclusion. They were then expected to take this report form and work it into an essay. In many ways, the report worked as a first draft for the essay, allowing students the opportunity to become familiar with and organize their survey results. I hoped that students would accomplish several things in the unit's final writing assignment:

1. They would learn to form a general research question that would turn their exploration into a topic.

2. They would learn to write a survey questionnaire and use the results as a source for writing.

3. They would learn to make generalizations based on specific information they obtained.

4. They would learn to use the same pool of information for different types of writing (format, purpose, audience).

The unit consisted of fifteen class days and exceeded the departmental course requirements with a total three journal entries and two major writing projects.

Designing a Hypertext

HyperCard offers its users a number of authoring and scripting capabilities in addition to word processing, paint, draw, and tools to create backgrounds, fields, and buttons. With these capabilities, users can create graphically complex cards with multiple scrolling fields within a rich network of links that can be specially scripted to meet particular needs. Also, scanned images, sound, and video can be incorporated into a user's stack. (HyperCard uses the term "stack" to refer to a collection of "cards" that are linked together.) HyperCard can be easily learned and used by those with little technological expertise. However, foregrounding my pedagogical objectives, I chose to narrowly focus what I taught students about HyperCard. I focused HyperCard instruction by:

1. designing a common card for all students to use that was clearly titled for the unit and contained a scrolling field and an area to store buttons. (See figure 4.1). Students accessed this common card easily

through the classroom network, and selecting "New Card" gave them a copy of the blank card I designed;

2. teaching students how to use the word processing features of the scrolling field. The word processing features were relatively simple in this program, but text created in Microsoft Word could be incorporated into HyperCard if necessary;

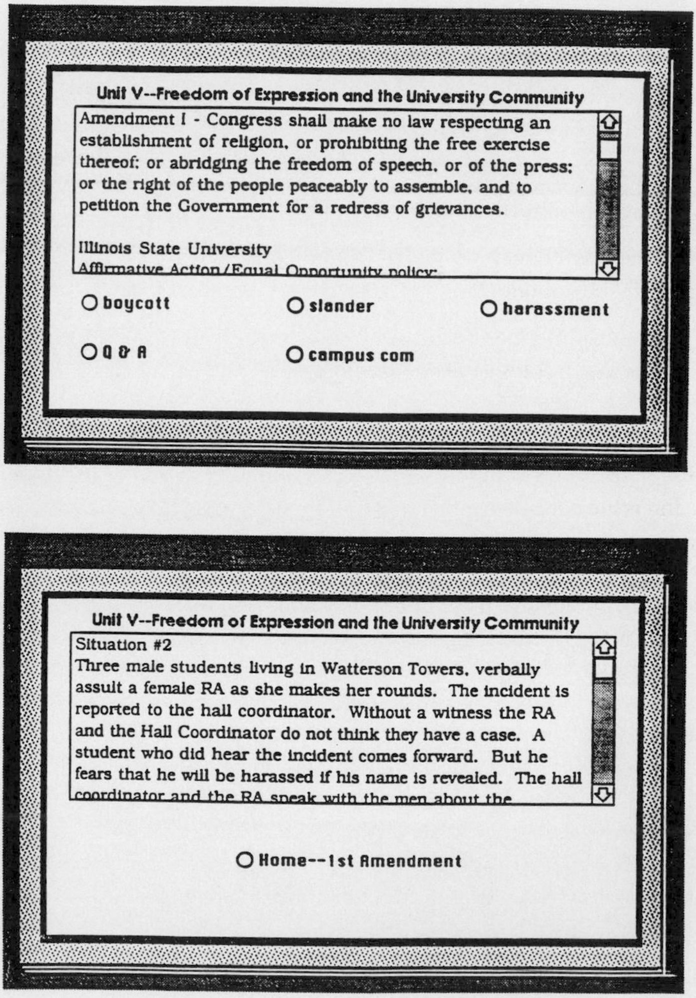

Unit V--Freedom of Expression and the University Community

Amendment I - Congress shall make no law respecting an establishment of religion, or prohibiting the free exercise thereof; or abridging the freedom of speech, or of the press; or the right of the people peaceably to assemble, and to petition the Government for a redress of grievances.

Illinois State University
Affirmative Action/Equal Opportunity policy:

○ boycott   ○ slander   ○ harassment

○ Q & A   ○ campus com

Unit V--Freedom of Expression and the University Community

Situation #2
Three male students living in Watterson Towers, verbally assuit a female RA as she makes her rounds. The incident is reported to the hall coordinator. Without a witness the RA and the Hall Coordinator do not think they have a case. A student who did hear the incident comes forward. But he fears that he will be harassed if his name is revealed. The hall coordinator and the RA speak with the men about the

○ Home--1st Amendment

Figure 4.1 HyperCard template

3. demonstrating for students how to navigate through their cards using the tools under the "Go" menu; and

4. instructing students on the basic steps necessary for creating buttons/links between cards.

Students were asked to create a HyperCard stack that included the following:

• A copy of the U.S. Constitution's First Amendment and Illinois State University's Equal Opportunity/Affirmative Action statement (they needed to find these on their own).

• A summary and a response to three assigned rhetorical situations about university life and freedom of expression. These situations focused on verbal harassment, libel, boycotts, protests, and demonstrations; each asked students to examine conflict from multiple perspectives; each presented a story that, on the surface, appeared to be a simple, cut-and-dried case.

• A written summary of "Chapter 2: An Open Community" from the Carnegie Foundation's *Campus Life: In Search of Community* (1990).

• A written response to the following question: "Consider your role in the university community at ISU. What do you feel is the most pressing issue concerning this role and First Amendment rights and freedom of expression?"

They were encouraged to include the following assignments in the stack, also:

• Written responses to two articles they were asked to find on their own on a topic of interest for the unit.

• Written responses to two articles from an alternative reading list of twenty-seven articles.

As students continued to build their HyperCard stack, they would create links, called "buttons," between texts where they saw relationships and connections in content. Students were instructed to give the button a name, a linguistic representation to cue users as to where the link would take them. After working with HyperCard, building their stacks, students were presented with the unit's major writing project. They were directed to their HyperCard stacks:

> For the past week (and actually, for the past semester), you have been writing about different issues of freedom of expression. And for the last week, you have stored and organized much of your writing on a HyperCard stack. From this writing, your HyperCard stack itself, and your own personal experience, you need to generate a topic for this paper.

In other words, students were asked to draw from their experiences creating their hypertexts. Also, they were asked to search their hypertext as a database to help generate a topic for the unit's major writing project.

This integration of hypertext in the current composition curriculum allowed me to fulfill many responsibilities expected of me in my position as writing instructor at the university. Students completed the department's requirements for the course. Writing that students completed for their HyperCard stacks was modeled after suggested assignments for writing about reading (journals). This included written responses to readings and summary writing. Because each of these writings was contained on a separate card within the stacks, I was able to evaluate them as separate pieces of writing (in fact, users of HyperCard will find that they can print "fields" of text, bringing their writing from an electronic writing space to print).

Overall, the integration of hypertext in this particular case reinforced the idea that the reading and writing that students completed for a unit in the classroom should not be viewed as a series of "assignments." Instead, I wanted students to view their work with hypertext as a means of inquiry, invention, exploration, forming content and formal schemata, or, in other words, as a process of coming to know, and that successful writers read and write a great deal before completing a desired end product. Indeed, some of the reading and writing *within* their stacks was graded and was considered a product worthy of meeting department requirements. However, the creation of the stack itself to facilitate invention was not evaluated. Never before was it possible, or desirable, to evaluate students' reading and writing as it related to invention. Grading students' inquiry would mean grading student process. Instead, the chunks were graded as product as they fulfilled a department requirement. The creation and use of the hypertext was treated as process: The hypertext itself was not graded and was treated solely as a space of exploration.

The five students I chose to act as participants for my study granted me interviews that took place on day twelve of the unit: The subjects' names were Devin, Daniel, Marie, Yvonne, and Matthew. The interviews focused on the students' use of HyperCard throughout the unit. I used the five students selected as research participants as a resource primarily in two ways. First, I closely analyzed their HyperCard stacks and their writing. Second, I closely analyzed how they described and reflected on their use of HyperCard in invention. While writing in class, the students worked directly on the classroom's network and used their floppy disks for backup purposes. Because of the classroom disk storage facilities and network of the computerized classroom, I was easily able to gather the work that they had stored in our class's folder. Within the designated class folder on the classroom disk, each student had his or her own folder designated by their last name. From their folders, I collected students' HyperCard stacks and the first drafts of their writing projects for the unit. Analyzing students' writing and their HyperCard stacks provided me with the data to begin answering my first two questions:

1. How would students organize and link their reading and writing using HyperCard?

2. How could the overall design of the students' stacks be described and classified?

Toward completion of the unit, the five students I selected as research participants granted me interviews concerning their experiences with Hyper-Card and the writing projects they were working on. These interviews were conducted with each individual participant at a computer workstation in the classroom during periods of the day when no classes were meeting. I recorded the interviews on tape with each one lasting approximately twenty-five minutes. These recordings provided me with an account of students describing their own experiences in the context of the learning environment, Analyzing the transcripts from these interviews provided me with the data to begin answering my next two research questions:

3. How would students describe how they organize and link their reading and writing using HyperCard?

4. How would students describe and classify the overall design of their own stacks?

Students were asked to define HyperCard in their own words to see if they had constructed a theoretical framework of the concept of hypertext. Next, students were asked to give a "tour" of their stacks and describe their rationale for constructing the stacks in the manner in which they did. Students described what they had written on a particular card, clicked on an available button, and explained where the link would take them and why. Also, they were asked to describe their link classification, or in other words, how they decided to linguistically represent the links within their stacks. This also added to the students' perceived theoretical framework of the concept of hypertext. And finally, students were asked to explain how they used the stack they created throughout their invention processes while working on their writing projects.

The information that I obtained while conducting this study (descriptions of the classroom learning environment, analyzing students' writing and HyperCard stacks, and interviewing students about their experience using Hyper-Card in the composition classroom) provided me with the data to answer my all-encompassing research question:

5. How would students use their HyperCard stack *throughout* the processes of invention?

In order to answer this final question, the most important of the five, I found that I needed to isolate a segment of my research design in a way that truly runs counter to my vision of invention presented in the first chapter of this book. I believe that invention occurs throughout the writing process and that our instruction needs to illustrate for students that invention is not a "step" in their overall writing scheme. However, I wanted to see how hypertext fed into and influenced students' invention; after a certain moment in the unit, many other factors besides hypertext played a role in their invention, to the point that I could no longer discern what was and was not directly related to their use of HyperCard. Considering writing instruction, I think this is a positive factor; student invention should be driven by multiple, diverse encounters and experiences. Considering research on hypertext and invention, however, I needed to limit my scope in order to capture what I could as it related to students' Hyper-Card experiences. Therefore, my analysis of students' writing examines the relationship among the students' HyperCard stacks and their chosen topics, the survey they constructed, and the *first draft* of the "report" required in the assignment, all of which took place early in the fifteen-day unit. The interviews, which were held on day twelve, represent more completely their invention and their reflections on using hypertext.

Case Portrait: Devin

Devin's stack design would best be described using a "web" metaphor. Devin's stack is rich in its connectivity with no discernible center or "starting point." When opening the stack, HyperCard places him at the card with the First Amendment and ISU's antidiscrimination policy, the first card he created. But he can quickly lose sight of this as a "beginning" since an option to return here from every other card is not always available. From the cards that hold his responses to the three rhetorical situations, Devin can always return to the First Amendment. But from his other cards, he must search the stack until he finds a button that will return him to the First Amendment if he so wishes. Furthermore, Devin has little or no regard for keeping constant the names of buttons on different cards that will take him to the same place. For example, from one of the rhetorical situations, Devin named a button "1 Amend." From another, he named a button that would take him to the same place, "First A." From another, the button is called, "ISU pol." Devin obviously did not copy and paste his buttons from card to card. Instead, he created buttons and named them according to the association that he was making at the moment. Only one card linked directly to the First Amendment/ISU antidiscrimination policy and to no other card—the card where Devin began to create the survey for his major writing project for the unit.

I asked Devin, "How has using HyperCard changed the way that you thought about this topic and how you approached the assignment?" And the following conversation ensued:

DEVIN: It made it all more about me. Like, I always looked at everything we did before an assignment as just, assignments, you know, what we had to do for class. But when I had to look at everything together because I had to make these buttons, it made all of my work more mine. Like, that question that you asked about our role on campus, I would not have thought about some of what I wrote if I didn't look at it in connection with like, the situations or with the article that we summarized. About racism.

SCOTT: Would it have made any difference if you had written these assignments on paper or in different files rather than on HyperCard?

DEVIN: Oh ya. I felt like I was at an advantage over all of my mixed up ideas when I had this to work with. I get really confused, and I forget things that I think or that I have written, and this let me keep it all together. I could manage better. I really don't remember getting all confused during this assignment like I have with others. And I think that I saw things different. Like, it really is all the same thing, free speech. I mean that it's all related, not the same. Just different ways of looking at it.

SCOTT: Did you get your paper topic from this writing? You have your survey written on one of these cards. How often do you think you went to the other cards when you were writing your questions?

DEVIN: I moved around a lot in, well, in my writing before I started writing questions. Then I went back to the First Amendment each time that I wrote a question. Being able to go back like that, I think that I stayed on the topic better. You always are pointing out where I stray from my topic. I think that using this program made me stay on track.

Devin focuses on the question at hand and explains how he believed using HyperCard facilitated his inquiry, problem formulation, and invention.

The first draft of Devin's report was entitled, "Report on the Level and Severity of Racism at ISU" in which he surveyed students about their opinions and experiences with racism on campus. His survey questions were as follows:

I'm conducting a survey to find out the level and severity of racism on ISU campus. I would appreciate it if you would take a few moments and fill out my questionnaire.

1. What year in school are you?
   A. Freshmen
   B. Sophomore
   C. Junior
   D. Senior
   E. Grad Student

   Gender?
   A. male
   B. female

2. Ethnic background?
   A. Caucasian   B. African-American
   C. Hispanic   D. Other

3. Are you a racist against any other group?
   A. yes
   B. no

4. Have you ever called someone a racist name out of frustration, anger, or fun since you have been attending this university?
   A. yes
   B. no
   C. comments

5. If yes, what name did you use? (please be honest)

6. Have you been called a racist name or been in a racist situation since you have been attending ISU?
   A. yes
   B. no

7. If yes, did this situation or name offend your freedom of expression as stated in the U.S. Constitution and the ISU Affirmative Action/ Equal Opportunity policy?
   A. yes
   B. no
   C. comments

8. Have you ever been with someone committing a racist act against someone of a different race since you have been attending ISU?
   A. yes
   B. no
   C. comments

9. If yes, did it offend you in any way?
   A. yes
   B. no
   C. comments

10. Did you join that person or group, or did you try to stop them in committing that racist act? (please be honest)

11. Would you consider ISU a racist campus in any form?
    A. yes
    B. no
    C. comments

12. Do you feel this campus allows a person or group to express themselves in any form, no matter what race they may be?
    A. yes
    B. no
    C. comments

13. How do you feel ISU should deal with people who have victimized a person or group with racist slurs or act?
    A. educate them
    B. expel them from the university
    C. other

First of all, it is clear why Devin chose to write about racism at the university. A good portion of the writing that he completed before starting the final writing project focused on racism and the academy. When asked to articulate his role at the university in relationship to freedom of expression, Devin writes:

My role in the ISU community consists of being a proud and educated African-American. Not to just stand for coming in second or third but to try and become first in whatever I do. Also, not to stand for just becoming a statistic but a leader of many. The most pressing issue about my role is that there are people trying so hard to keep myself and many more African-Americans from becoming that leader and trying to hold my people back in anyway they can. But the First Amendment allows us to express ourselves in any form. It also allows us to take advantage of education so we won't be held back, but so we can go on.

Also, in his summary of the chapter from the Carnegie Foundation piece, Devin observes that "on too many campuses, they believe incivility is a problem and, all too frequently, words are used, not as the key to understanding, but as a weapon of assault."

From his short, inventive writings, and from the survey questionnaire that he wrote for the major writing project, Devin wrote the first draft of an introduction to his report:

Racism has been one of the major problems for most universities across the world and the campus at Illinois State University is not an exception. By ISU being predominantly white with a percentage of 5.8 minority, the campus population views blacks and other ethnic minorities as the "other." This causes doubt and ignorance on the part of the mainstream student population. Therefore, I conducted a survey in the hope of finding a solution that would make the ISU campus equal and fair for everyone as stated in the First Amendment of the U.S. Constitution.

He concluded the report:

I also found out that 85 percent of the students I surveyed felt that education was the best way to deal with the students that commit racist acts or slurs against another person or ethnic group. Many feel that expelling them from the university will not solve the problem. Taking it a step further with education will solve the problem. I believe this could be a very effective solution to solve this problem. Many students that come to the university do not know any better, from the time they were able to walk all they learned was to hate anyone different from them because of the color of their skin. The only way to deal with these types of people is through education.

Although, the severity of racism at Illinois State University seems to be pretty steep, there is still hope. What this campus needs is for everyone to come together and treat each other as equals. For the university itself to stop treating the minorities as the "other" but as another distinctive student at this campus trying to succeed.

Although Devin's focus for his paper is narrowed to racial slurs, equality, and the university, his complex hypertext and his reading and writing experiences with HyperCard seem to reflect one another. His survey questions come from his own writing in his stack, some of which refer directly to freedom of speech and the university's antidiscrimination policy. Many other questions are inspired by the readings and written responses he completed for the unit. By writing his survey questions on HyperCard, he believes that he saw many connections between seemingly unrelated topics and was able to gain control through the program's linking capabilities in order to develop a focused topic.

Case Portrait: Daniel

To describe Daniel's stack design in terms of a metaphor, one may use the term "asterisk" to describe its apparent shape. In other words, there exists a distinct center from which specific stems extend. However, at no time do these stems connect with each other except at the center. Therefore, to move from one stem to the other, it is necessary to return to the center. At the center of Daniel's HyperCard stack is the card which contains the First Amendment of the U.S. Constitution and ISU's antidiscrimination policy. From this card, Daniel has a number of buttons that take him to different pieces of writing that he completed. On each card, then, he created a button, "1st Amend," that takes him back to the center card. Daniel says:

> All my buttons, if I hit a button, it will take me to one card and it has one button that will take me back to the same card. I did it like that because I felt you could read the situations and then you could come back and read the First Amendment and make a decision where you stand based on that, right away instead of having to go through all of the cards. So every time you are faced with a situation about freedom of speech, you should go back to the First Amendment and make your decisions based on that.

This design for Daniel results in an intentional and purposeful way to interpret different issues of free speech.

I explained to Daniel how I had constructed the unit that we were working on, that before beginning a major writing assignment, the class had completed short, inventive reading and writing assignments. The only difference with this assignment was the use of HyperCard. I asked, "Did that change the ways in which you approached the paper assignment at all?" and the following dialogue occurred:

DANIEL: Well, it made it a lot easier. I didn't have to sit down and write all of this on paper. It was a lot quicker to get it into the computer and to connect the points and the ideas than to sit down with a bunch of pieces of paper. It made it easier, I suppose. I was more organized. I knew where my writing was because of the buttons.

SCOTT: How was this different than just having all of this informa-
            tion on separate sheets of paper? Was there a difference in
            how you worked with these ideas on HyperCard than if you
            had them on paper?

DANIEL: It was a lot neater and easier to work with.

SCOTT: What makes it easier?

DANIEL: Once you have everything organized, you just click a but-
            ton to get what you need without having to shuffle through
            all of the sheets of paper every time. You can figure out
            what you are looking for. It helps you look ahead, like, how
            you are going to link things so that you can use them in
            your paper. Like, I had to decide on a paper topic so that I
            could make sure that I had my cards organized so that I
            could use them.

Daniel's response to the original question, "Did that change the ways in which
you approached the paper assignment at all?" in fact failed to answer the question. He claims that HyperCard made "it," the assignment, easier. However, he
then describes his completion of the short, inventive writing assignments using
HyperCard. When he finally comes to talking about the major writing assignment, he says that using the program helped him to "look ahead." Interesting,
though, is that Daniel felt pressured to decide on a paper topic in order to guide
his linking of cards rather than linking cards to create a database that would in
turn help him to discover a topic for writing.

The first draft of Daniel's report was entitled, "Report on How Students
Feel about Art Censorship" in which he surveyed students about their opinions
on, of course, art censorship. His survey questions were as follows:

I am conducting a survey on the feelings of ISU students about censorship of works of art. I would really appreciate it if you could take a few
minutes to fill this out. Thank You.

1. Do you understand the full meaning of "freedom of expression?"
   A. Yes   B. No

2. Do you feel the First Amendment (freedom of expression) should
   apply to art?
   A. Yes   B. No

3. Are you an art major?
   A. Yes   B. No

4. Are you offended by the nude form?
   A. Yes
   B. No

5. Do you feel that pornography is a form of art?
   A. Yes
   B. No

6. Do you feel that art should be censored?
   A. Yes
   B. No

7. Explain why you feel this way?

8. What aspects of art do you feel should be censored, if any?

9. How do you feel when you hear of art censorship?
   A. Angry
   B. Slightly upset
   C. Alright for censorship!
   D. Do not care

10. Do you feel that you have compromised your own art, because of censorship?
    A. Yes
    B. No
    C. Not into art

Daniel's exigency for writing about art censorship seems to stem more from his background as an artist and as an art major at the university than it did from any problem formulation that resulted from relationships he saw and connections he made while creating his HyperCard stack. He did, however, write directly on this topic when answering the question about his role at the university and freedom of expression:

> I view my role at ISU as a student of art and as a practicing artist. The First Amendment has become very important to me lately as I have heard of more and more art censorship. It has really forced me to understand what it means to have, or not to have, freedom of expression. People today are so upset about some of the art that is made. But I don't think they really try to understand it. They just see a nude, or sex, or something they think is violent and they want to censor it. What that means is that they think some art is ok, but

some art is not. As I have thought more about censorship, I have become very pissed off. I never used to get mad about things like this. Maybe I am just getting older and taking things more seriously.

There is no denying that this writing directly influenced the survey that Daniel wrote. In fact, there is a sequential relationship between the order in which he addressed topics in the above passage and the questions that he wrote for his survey.

Although the design of his HyperCard stack does not show many dynamic connections made within, Daniel certainly benefited from juxtaposing different topics in his HyperCard stack. Daniel did use HyperCard to write the first draft of his survey, and this card was linked only to the card that contained the First Amendment. His response to the question that asked him to discuss his role at the university was also connected to the card that contained the First Amendment. But there was no link that connected Daniel's draft of his survey and his writing about his role as an artist at ISU. He did say, though, that he purposely designed his stack in that way so that "you could come back and read the First Amendment and make a decision where you stand based on that, right away instead of having to go through all of the cards." He also said another piece of writing helped him to develop a topic: "If they are going to stop a comedian from telling jokes, no matter how racist, then they are going to stop artists from trying to paint what they are going to paint. That's what I did my survey on." But again, there is no link from this card to the card on which he wrote his survey. His summary of the Carnegie Foundation chapter makes no reference to art censorship.

From his short, inventive writings, and from the survey questionnaire that he wrote for the major writing assignment, Daniel wrote the first draft of an introduction to his report:

> Art is one of the few lasting forms of free expression left in the world. People are now trying to censor what artists can do. People have a variety of different opinions about the subject. Therefore, I decided to put together this survey.

He concluded:

> It looks to me like we are putting too much trust into our governing body in Washington, D.C. I have been told since I was a young child that in this country we have the freedom to worship in whatever church we wish, and the freedom of speech. Along with freedom of speech goes the freedom to express ourselves in any way we want whether that is through art, or speech, or music, it does not matter. However, in recent years our government has decided that we are not intelligent enough to figure out what we should see and should not see.

Although not conclusive, one could claim that Daniel's simplistic Hyper-Card design, his simplistic approach to the topic, and in fact, a simplistic style of writing run parallel. His stack is lacking in rich connectivity, and the survey questions he generates follow (i.e., "They just see a nude, or sex, . . . and they want to censor it" becomes "Are you offended by the nude form?," "Do you feel that pornography is a form of art?," and "Do you feel that art should be censored?"). On the other hand, Daniel does articulate connections between invention and hypertext by describing the pressure that was put on him to organize his stack according to his chosen topic.

Case Portrait: Marie

Marie's stack design can also be described in terms of an "asterisk" metaphor, but with one exception. Like an asterisk, there exists a distinct center from which specific stems extend. However, at no time do these stems connect with each other except at a center. Therefore, to move from one stem to the other, it is necessary to return to the center. At the center of Marie's HyperCard stack is the card which contains the First Amendment of the U.S. Constitution and ISU's antidiscrimination policy. From this card, Marie has a number of buttons that take her to different pieces of writing that she completed. On each card, then, she created a button, "US Const," that takes the user back to the center card. Marie says, "Even though this is the first card that we made in this class, I look at it as explaining everything that is coming up. It will give a general background to what is coming up in the rest of the cards."

However, one of the stems leaving Marie's center provides a different path. There exists a linear progression which users must follow if they select from the center a button called "Too far?" From the center card, selecting "Too far?" will take users to the first rhetorical situation that Marie responded to. On this card there is still another button, "Too far?," that takes her to the next situation. And again she created a button, "Too far?" On the third card of this progression there is, for the last time, a button called "Too far?," which returns her to the center card, the one that contains the First Amendment and ISU's antidiscrimination policy. Therefore, selecting "Too far?" from the center card, in effect, traps Marie into going through all three cards before returning to the center card. (Marie, of course, could use the "Go" menu commands to leave this linear progression. See *Yvonne.*) Marie used HyperCard to write the first draft of her survey questionnaire.

I asked Marie, "Did you see yourself approaching this writing assignment differently because we did all of this invention using the HyperCard program?" and the following exchange ensued:

MARIE: Um, like, I think so. I like to use the HyperCard because it's like, I can go through the cards and see how I responded and it kinda, not really refreshes my memory, but it's helped me realize a lot of things, that these are my responses, and when I write my papers I can see how, like, how I responded to the writing.

SCOTT: Why would it be any different if I had you answer all of these questions and you just wrote those out on paper and you had a stack of paper that had all of these responses on sheets of paper? Is there a difference between that and HyperCard?

MARIE: Ya, because you don't have all of that cluttering that you have to waste your time with. Here, you can just click buttons and it's there for you. It's more interesting to do the reading off of the computer. Sometimes your own writing gets sloppy, and you don't want to read it. But here you can just click a few buttons and it's there for you. These cards, too, don't limit how much you can write, you know? Like, on an index card, you only have so much space. And it's always saved. Your disk can't get damaged because you are using the classroom disk and it's always there for you.

For Marie, using HyperCard facilitated organization and ease throughout the complex processes of problem formulation and invention. Furthermore, she felt a sense of liberation from space constraints in comparison to paper index cards.

Marie titled the first draft of her report, "Report on Obscenity in the Music Industry," in which she explored students' feelings about record labeling. Incidents surrounding 2 Live Crew were prominent topics in the news. Her survey questions were as follows:

I am conducting a survey about freedom of expression in the music industry. I would appreciate it if you would take the time to fill out this questionnaire.

1. What gender are you?
   M
   F

2. What year are you?
   Freshman
   Sophomore
   Junior
   Senior

3. Have you ever heard any music done by 2 Live Crew?
   Yes
   No

4. Do you listen to 2 Live Crew on a regular basis?
   Yes
   No

5. Do you feel that 2 Live Crew is obscene?
   Yes
   No

If you answered yes, what are your feelings about their obscenity?

6. Do you feel that 2 Live Crew has gone too far in using their freedom to express the song lyrics they use?
   Yes
   No

7. Do you feel that 2 Live Crew has the right to express themselves in this way?
   Yes
   No

8. Do you feel that this type of music, or any music should be labeled with warnings?
   Yes
   No

9. What are your feelings about only letting specific age groups purchase certain records?

10. Do you feel that it was unjustified that the authorities arrested 2 Live Crew during a performance in Florida?
    Yes
    No

11. Please write any additional comments:

It's difficult to see any "direct" correlation between the writing that Marie completed in her HyperCard stack and her final writing project topic. At no time does record labeling come up in her final project, where she describes her "role" at the university as that of a freshman who believes that the residence hall check-in policy is too strict.

However, there are interesting relationships between the rhetorical situations that she grouped together with the buttons labeled "Too far?" She interprets each situation as someone pushing his or her limits in claiming to be protected by the First Amendment. The button label asks, "Have these people gone too far in claiming this protection?" Marie negotiates her feelings about this same question as she surveys students' opinions about the rap band 2 Live Crew. One question in her survey even asks, "Do you feel that 2 Live Crew has gone too far in using their freedom to express the song lyrics they use?" Another theme that Marie carries through her responses to these rhetorical situations is "choice" and whether or not all parties involved have been allowed equal opportunities of choice.

From her short, inventive writings, and from the survey questionnaire that she completed for the major writing assignment, Marie wrote the following first draft of an introduction to her report:

> During the past few years, obscenity in the arts has become the heated topic of many discussions concerning what is obscene and what is not. One of the biggest discussions has been about obscenity in the music industry. And the same question always comes up: Do these bands go too far when exercising their First Amendment rights? Although this has been a gigantic topic in the press, we really don't know how students feel about obscenity. Therefore, I have conducted a survey about how students feel about obscenity in the music industry.

In her reflective conclusion, she wrote:

> Reading through the survey's, I felt that most students didn't realize that there are two versions of 2 Live Crew's music that they could choose from: The Nasty As They Want To Be version and The Clean As They Want To Be version. If the press would advertise The Clean As They Want To Be version more, maybe students would know that they had a choice between two versions and would be more open-minded as to whether 2 Live Crew was obscene or not.

Because there is no direct reference between the topics that Marie wrote about in her HyperCard stack and the topic she pursued for her major writing assignment, we are pushed toward looking for more subtle relationships in content. Those relationships exist mostly between the individual choice in society that Marie writes about and the choice to buy a particular artist's music. But HyperCard plays a more significant role in how it illustrated for Marie similarities of various ways that freedom of expression is sometimes stretched "too far." She, in turn, manipulates the program to illustrate for herself the connection she made.

Case Portrait: Yvonne

Yvonne's stack, too can be described as an "asterisk." At the center of Yvonne's HyperCard stack is the card which contains the First Amendment of the U.S. Constitution and ISU's antidiscrimination policy. From this card, Yvonne has a number of buttons that take her to different pieces of writing that she completed. She said, "I set this up this way because I always wanted to return to the First Amendment. I never felt that I got to the point that I wanted to sub-link, or whatever. Really nothing that I wrote had much in common except with the First Amendment."

However, on the cards which stem from the center, there are no buttons that return her to the card that contains the First Amendment and ISU's antidiscrimination policy. Instead, Yvonne says that she relied on the "Back" command under the "Go" menu to return her to this card: "This command does the same thing as programming a button. And it has these commands so I don't have to use the mouse. I can just type." The command for "Back" is "Command+~." On the one hand, it can be argued that this key stroke command serves the same purpose as a button copied on each card in the stack that returns her to her center card. However, it can also be argued that she has missed the benefits of the ongoing summarizing and strategic backtracking that are necessary in order to create a link on each card that would take her back to the center. Yvonne did not use HyperCard to write the first draft of her survey questionnaire.

I asked Yvonne, "Did you see yourself approaching this writing assignment differently because we did all of this invention using the HyperCard program?" and Yvonne replied:

> I guess that I started looking at all of the things that you asked us to write about as parts of a wider topic. I guess HyperCard made it easier for me to do that. The topics that I wrote about on the cards don't really relate, not directly, to my paper topic about music. But I guess that I was thinking in more specific terms when I was using the program and relating them to the whole, like you have this written on top of each of the cards, "Freedom of Expression and the University Community."

Yvonne says that using HyperCard allowed her to view the issues we were covering in class in terms of general versus specific, but admits that the topics that we covered did not help her directly in developing a topic for writing. Also, she does not articulate a relationship between the writing that she completed in HyperCard and her invention processes for her writing project.

The first draft of Yvonne's report, entitled "Warning Labels on Records: Are College Students in Favor of This Action?" discussed general record labeling practices. Her survey questions were as follows:

This is a survey on freedom of expression. I would appreciate your time in answering the following questions.

General Information:

Gender:
  A. Female
  B. Male

What year in school are you?
  A. Freshman
  B. Sophomore
  C. Junior
  D. Senior

How old are you?
  A. 18–20   B. 21–23
  C. 24–26   D. 27 and older

Survey:

1. What type of music do you listen to?
   A. Rap
   B. R&B
   C. Pop
   D. Other

2. Should a certain type of music have a warning label placed on it?
   A. Yes
   B. No

3. Have you purchased a record affixed with a warning label?
   A. Yes
   B. No

4. What do you think is obscene about a record?
   A. Swear words in lyrics
   B. Degrading women
   C. Title of album
   D. Picture on cover of album
   E. Other

5. From your answer to question 4, do you think only this type of obscenity should have warning labels?
   A. Yes
   B. No

6. Do you feel certain types of music can cause a person to try one of the following?
   A. Suicide
   B. Satanism
   C. No Affect

7. If you answered C to question 6, go to question 8. If you answered A or B, answer the following question: What type of music do you think would cause a college student to try such an act as listed in question 6?
   A. Rap
   B. Rock
   C. R&B
   D. Other

8. Do you think warning labels are effective in letting parents know what records are unsuitable for younger audiences?
   A. Yes
   B. No

9. Do you feel that artists' creativity is being stifled by having warning labels placed on their records?
   A. Yes
   B. No

10. Has anyone told you that they find your music offensive?
    A. Yes
    B. No

It is interesting that Yvonne chose this topic to pursue for her final writing project considering the writing she did within her HyperCard stack. For example, in her HyperCard stack, a great deal of the writing focuses on her role as an African-American student at a primarily white university. She writes:

> This is a predominately white university. I feel that the minorities on the campus are not being represented on the committees that are for all the students. As a student and an African-American I believe that it's my responsibility to exercise my voting rights when school elections are held. I also believe in

supporting minority programs that are for the betterment of minorities. The *Vidette*, our school newspaper, is suppose to be for all the students. But very rarely do I see an article for or about minorities, other than those geared toward sports. It seems that we have been placed in a role as making that slam dunk, scoring a touchdown, and winning a track race. I am proud that we can accomplish these tasks. But I would like to see an article on a student who is excelling academically as well. I know that there are students like this.

When Yvonne responds to the rhetorical situation concerning a comedian invited to campus who was deemed offensive by many student populations, she writes:

The *Vidette* prints what they want people to read not what the students should. There are exchanges with anything that happens. The *Vidette* and the Entertainment Committee chose to ignore the people who would be offended by such entertainment. So the different organizations went to the students of ISU. The issue turned to money when ticket sales were below the expected amount. The issue of the different racial groups and how they would feel about having a comedian like Hay come to ISU was never a consideration. Hay's view of people that are different stimulates racism.

The examples she chooses as illustrations in her summary of the Carnegie Foundation piece are those about racial tensions. And when responding to the rhetorical situation about violent verbal harassment, Yvonne concludes, "The First Amendment is not intended for people to use offensive language towards another person. When the students were caught they wanted to become the victim for not being allowed to vocally express themselves."

Few direct relationships seem to exist between the short, inventive writings that Yvonne completed and the survey questionnaire that she completed for the final writing project. She introduces the first draft of her report:

The lyrics of rap and heavy metal artists have recently come under fire for being too obscene. The major recording labels have decided to place a standardized label on music that may be unsuitable for certain audiences. The purpose of the warning label is to let the parents know that this music may be unsuitable for younger audiences. But, with the label being placed on records, would this hamper the artist's creativity? I conducted a survey to see if the students at this university thought warning label were necessary on certain types of music.

  The rap artists 2 Live Crew were arrested this past summer in a Florida nightclub for their obscene rap lyrics. Ozzie Osborne was placed on trial for the suicide of a teenager who had been listening to his record at the time of his death. From a recent survey that I conducted, I found that the students at this institution believe that warning labels should be placed on records.

What becomes most evident in these collective data are contradictions in what Yvonne wrote and the connections she says that she did not see while using HyperCard. She said, "Really, nothing that I wrote had much in common except with the First Amendment." But much of the writing focused on racial issues and her role as an African-American student. She also points out that the topics she approached in the stack had little to do with her major writing project's topic. And finally, she did not use HyperCard to create her survey questionnaire. It would therefore be safe to say that Yvonne failed to gain from the short, inventive writing she completed in two ways. First of all, the inventive writing did not directly help her in terms of content feeding into and enriching her chosen writing project topic, and secondly, she did not allow HyperCard's dynamic linking capabilities to push her toward seeing connections in her ideas, and therefore she could not use it to illustrate connections that she had made.

Case Portrait: Matthew

Matthew's stack design was a "branch" with loops that return each stem of the branch to a distinct starting point. Matthew's stack is rich in its connectivity. It always begins with the card with the First Amendment to the U.S. Constitution and ISU's antidiscrimination policy and enables him to return to that point no matter where he is in the stack. Some cards offer linking choices that others don't. Also, button names that lead to the same card change depending on where he is in the stack. For example, from the beginning card, Matthew has choices, "Situation 1," "Situation 2," and "Situation 3." These are button names that take him to the different rhetorical situations that he responded to. But once he has moved from the beginning card and has accessed other cards in the stack, buttons that lead to those cards with the rhetorical situations are named according to the content of the card: "Slander," "Comedy?" and "Harass." Matthew used HyperCard to write his survey and connected this card to both the card with the First Amendment and antidiscrimination policy and to the card with the rhetorical situation about a comedian deemed offensive by many student populations on campus.

I asked Matthew, "Has HyperCard changed your way of thinking throughout this invention process or the way that you approached your writing assignment? And how did it help you begin your major writing project?" Matthew responded:

MATTHEW: I think that this totally related to the assignment. When I started this I was thinking that this was kinda stupid, that we were going to have to rewrite everything that we just wrote. I really wasn't in favor of having to learn this program. Here and there, I began to change my mind, slowly but surely. It helped me to sort out the ideas and everything here had to deal with freedom of speech, and that was this whole unit. Everything in this stack relates to what we were doing, but when it was alone, everything was really very different. And I don't know if the EXACT things in here, like actual words or sentences, are in the assignment that I wrote, but the big picture got my mind thinking about certain things and relating them to other things that seem very different.

SCOTT: Would it have made a difference if I had asked you to complete all of these shorter assignments on paper rather than using HyperCard? Did the program make any difference at all as to how you approached this assignment?

MATTHEW: I really don't know. Like I related the First Amendment and the ISU policy to all of my situations, and if you don't necessarily think, "Why does that situation deal with the First Amendment," this gets you kinda thinking about why are they related, why is that situation part of the First Amendment? I could have written my own interpretation of each situation and how I would feel about each of them, and I might never have come across why does the First Amendment relate to this, and how does the First Amendment relate to this, and does the First Amendment govern what's going on in the situation. I think that HyperCard helped me to see those things. It just lets you relate things differently. I don't know if you wrote them down on a piece of paper, I mean it might be as easy, I don't know, but this surely saved time for me. You can get from one thing to the other however or whenever you need, you're not going to lose it.

In Matthew's eyes, HyperCard did facilitate his invention processes by acting as a tool through which he could physically link like ideas. He believes that, for example, seeing the rhetorical situations in connection with the First Amendment made him consider each situation at a higher level. But he qualifies his statements by saying that he really cannot assume that HyperCard helped him make connections that he couldn't make reading from paper. And although he was not sure if he imported actual text from HyperCard into his final writing project, he was confident that there was a certain level of transfer between the two.

Matthew's first draft of his report was entitled "Report on ISU Discrimination in Comedy Situations," in which he asks student to answer questions about the types of comedy they prefer and avoid. His survey questions are as follows:

I am conducting a survey of ISU students on whether or not comedians should be allowed to use any type of language when they do their acts at ISU. Will you please take a moment and fill out this personal survey? THANK YOU!

1. Have you ever seen a comedy act on T.V. or in the movies?
   A. yes
   B. no

2. Have you attended a comedy act in person?
   A. yes
   B. no

3. Have you ever attended any type of comedy act at ISU?
   A. yes
   B. no

If you have answered yes to any of the above questions, please continue. If no, you are finished with the survey.

Answer the following questions based on the comedy acts you have seen.

4. The comedy acts I have seen contained profanity.
   A. never
   B. almost never
   C. sometimes
   D. often
   E. always

5. The comedy acts I have seen contained discriminatory language toward race, religion, sex, or sexual preference.
   A. never
   B. almost never
   C. sometimes
   D. often
   E. always

6. The comedy acts I have seen use profanity and/or discrimination of any kind.
   A. never
   B. almost never

C. sometimes
D. often
E. always

7. I make an effort to stay away from acts that use profanity or discrimination.
   A. never
   B. almost never
   C. sometimes
   D. often
   E. always

8. I believe any type of comedy movie or comedy program should be allowed on campus.
   A. never
   B. almost never
   C. sometimes
   D. often
   E. always

9. I believe ISU should be sponsoring these comedy events.
   A. never
   B. almost never
   C. sometimes
   D. often
   E. always

10. I would attend a comedy event that uses discrimination and /or profanity, sponsored by ISU.
    A. never
    B. almost never
    C. sometimes
    D. often
    E. always

11. A comedian has the right to use profanity and some forms of discrimination in his/her act just to be funny.
    A. never
    B. almost never
    C. sometimes
    D. often
    E. always

12. All is fair in comedy because if the people are willing to pay to see
    your act, the comedian can say whatever.
    A. never   B. almost never
    C. sometimes   D. often
    E. always

Comments to any questions?

Matthew's decision to write on this topic makes a great deal of sense when
looking at the writing that he completed in his HyperCard stack. First of all, he
wrote the first draft of his survey using HyperCard, and linked the survey to
three cards: the First Amendment/ISU antidiscrimination policy, the rhetorical
situation about a comedian invited to campus, and the rhetorical situation
about violent verbal harassment. Matthew's driving research question became,
"What is funny, and how can what is funny be restricted on this campus?"

When writing about his role at ISU and how it relates to freedom of expression, Matthew writes:

> The most pressing issue is the right to have people express their own opinion
> verbally or written. Students should also be able to protest different activities
> on campus. If groups of people want to protest or boycott an activity then they
> have that right. However, these people should not try to impose their own ideas
> on the other people who might be interested in this activity. Everyone has the
> right to chose what and how they are associated with an activity. Everyone still
> has the right to their own opinion. It is fine to express those ideas but it is not
> fair to use force to get your point across. Intimidation is used quite often by
> people on campus to get their one-sided views out to the public.

Matthew, when responding to the rhetorical situations, insisted that, of course,
students should have the right to boycott any performer who comes to campus,
but that

> it was stupid for people to protest the concert because it is just comedy, and
> you should have enough intestinal fortitude to laugh at yourself without tak-
> ing it personally. The fact that these groups were offended tells me that they
> feel inferior to another group that is different from them. I was not in any of
> the groups that the article said were being ridiculed, but I would not mind if
> he picked me out of the audience to just get a laugh.

He also felt that the female RA who experienced violent verbal harassment
from three male residents should "learn to work with others. This was obviously a joke by the guys. Granted it was mean, but come on, the RA is being
ludicrous."

Matthew and I discussed his simplistic approach to these issues, and I presented him with alternative means of thinking about the situations in hopes of problematizing the issues for him. I responded in writing, to the whole class, "If this is your idea of a joke, I do not much understand your sense of humor." And Matthew, in writing, responded back to me, again insisting that the matters were not as serious as I made them out to be. About the RA he said, "All in all, I think the RA totally overreacted. The statements were made in jest. These guys are mean, but in no way should such a fuss be made over the whole deal." He added this response to the original card in his HyperCard stack.

From his short, inventive writings, from the survey questionnaire that he completed for the major writing assignment, and from the exchanges he and I had concerning the topic of comedy, Matthew wrote the following draft of an introduction to his report:

> Comedy programs in the life of a college student keep the fun going through hours and hours of hard work. Students at Illinois State University know as well as anyone that laughter is the best medicine. However, many students ask, "Should comedy programs on this campus be allowed to use discrimination, prejudice, and vulgarity to create their laughs?" To investigate this issue, I conducted a survey of ISU students to discover how they feel about discrimination, prejudice, and vulgarity in comedy.

Matthew clearly used HyperCard to the fullest extent that his knowledge of the program would allow. He had a clear understanding of how the program could work for him and how he could manipulate the program to serve as a positive learning tool. On the other hand, he understood that the program did not make connections for him or solve problems for him. He thought that possibly he could have completed the same work writing on paper, but that HyperCard certainly had some influence on how he approached the reading and writing tasks of the unit.

Reflections and Conclusions

As I pore over the vast amount of data I collected in this study—student hypertexts and writing, my daily journals, interview transcripts—as well as other angles on this study published elsewhere, I see that my findings begin to question many of the promises and broadly accepted benefits forwarded by early research about the use of hypertext in composition. Consider, for example, the claim that hypertext offers students the opportunity to develop high-level thinking skills, those that are associative and hierarchical, as they encounter texts and make purposeful connections. With its associative and intuitive branching capabilities, hypertext mirrors the cognitive processes of the human mind, enhancing learning by working in tandem with students' cognitive processes. The most significant way in which hypertext enhances students' learning is giving them the opportunity to become consciously aware of their own learning processes. In other words, as students work within a hypertext system, there are numerous possibilities for them to develop a strong sense of metacognitive awareness that will allow them to consciously theorize about their own learning processes.

I resist the idea that hypertext itself will teach students advance-level thinking skills. But its concept can indeed augment sound pedagogy that does. Although, as a researcher, I also object to and am critical of blanket, technocentric promises of hypertext, I am comfortable going as far as to say that actual experience with the technology can extend invention instruction and promote metacognitive awareness. In other words, the technology is valuable to our students as it concretely represents their learning processes and facilitates what we might refer to as hypertextual thinking.

It is difficult in this research study alone to differentiate between how students were influenced by the pedagogy in invention and how students were influenced by hypertext as a technology that could facilitate invention. Again, it becomes necessary to identify specifically how students were actually influenced by hypertext, and how other factors may have been influential. Even in my attempt to limit the scope of the research design by looking at students' early experiences with hypertext, I cannot erase the fact that throughout the semester I had already introduced students to hypertextual techniques—without technological application. For any given unit, students read many essays and articles on the topic being pursued. These readings were written from varying perspectives and employed many different forms and conventions. Students completed short writing assignments about the readings, including response and summary writing. Students also participated in class discussions and some type of small group activity. In the end, they were asked to address the unit's major writing assignment, which required them to make connections among the reading, writing, and classroom activities they had participated in throughout the unit. In other words, the unit's short reading and writing assignments—intended to facilitate inquiry—created a sense of chaos for students, and the unit's major writing assignment forced students to make meaning by developing a sense of order from the chaos. This practice was well in place *before* the introduction of hypertext.

I reviewed the basic structure of each unit that students had already completed as I asked during our interviews how they felt hypertext changed their invention processes:

When we started this assignment, it was really no different from any other assignment that we completed over the semester. You did a great deal of reading, and you wrote responses to the readings and different situations. There were class discussions. And we did this so that you could begin to generate some ideas toward forming a paper topic. But in this case, you did all of the writing and brainstorming using HyperCard. Has this changed your way of thinking throughout this invention process or the way that you approached your major writing assignment?

All of the study's participants believed, to varying degrees, that HyperCard had in some way changed the way they approached the processes of inquiry and invention. Responses ranged from suggestions that HyperCard made the process easier to those that HyperCard actually made the students see connections that they normally would not have seen. Yet, if students believe that hypertext helped them to see and make relationships, what do they believe prevents them from seeing and making the same relationships without the use of hypertext? One participant claimed that hypertext helped her to gain access to her own writing. What normally prevents her from gaining—or how did she lose—access to her writing? I am not denying the validity—or better yet, the truthfulness—of students' self-assessments. I would argue, however, that equally important to their invention experiences with hypertext are their abilities to articulate, reflect upon, and assess their learning processes, specifically those processes that relate to invention.

As the study was designed, I am unable to analyze specifically how hypertext changed students' approaches to invention. But I am able to see that the technology did at that moment shed light on the pedagogy I used throughout the semester and more concretely illustrated or reflected students' learning processes for them. Because students were able, without hesitation, to describe how they thought HyperCard had facilitated their processes of inquiry and invention, they were consciously theorizing about their own learning processes. And the connection here is an important one: In the end, hypertext served as a model or a representation for their own thinking and learning processes. Specifically, hypertext served as a technological representation of what it means to participate in invention, and generally the concepts of hypertext facilitated the teaching of this skill.

Another aspect of invention outlined in the previous chapter was also visible in students' experience with the technology. In the study, I found a direct correlation between students' reading and the links that they made in their HyperCard stacks. The most significant finding is that students, when creating links and when searching their hypertexts as invention, spent a considerable amount of time rereading their own writing in order to make purposeful connections within their stacks. What deserves further attention, though, is how the type of reading students participated in while creating links was different from the type of reading they participated in while exploring their stacks after links had been made.

Both types of rereading required reflective thinking, especially that which allows a writer to feed forward, which is integral to invention. Obviously, when students searched their completed hypertexts as an information source, they reviewed their own writing. They returned to their stacks, reading for depth, meaning, and ideas. I was struck by the high level of familiarity students had for their hypertexts and by their ability to talk about the writing contained within them with no hesitation. Students were familiar with these hypertexts because they extensively searched their completed hypertexts. However, I also attribute their knowledge of and familiarity with their own written texts to the process of creating the links in their hypertexts. Students read for connections in order to create links, forcing them to summarize, synthesize, and backtrack in order to do so. However, to make purposeful links between cards, students had to be not only familiar with the text they had produced on the cards, but they also had to actively make connections in the content of the writing. I was concerned that students' linking would be less than purposeful, that they might link every card to every card using the simple "copy and paste" features for making links. However, no one made gratuitous links in their stacks; the students made links that represented connections in their ideas. They scrutinized the links they made, and the links, most importantly in their eyes, were purposeful.

As noted earlier, trying to isolate particular moments of invention that are purely "hypertextual" runs counter to my vision of invention—that invention is a layering of many different experiences, moments of invention that, when connected to other moments of invention, result in elaborate, rich discoveries in content. In fact, now that I review the material, I'm certain that my isolation of invention that was hypertextual was artificial. As I noted earlier, students had experienced a hypertextual approach to invention—sans the technology—in my pedagogy for a number of units before the one that was the focus of this study. Also, I have no idea what other experiences influenced students' invention, for example, outside of class or, for that matter, when I wasn't observing students in class.

The most striking variable that prevented me from isolating hypertextual learning, however, was the interview of my research subjects. Although my intended goal was to collect data, I realized that the interview itself became a moment of invention for the students. Part of the overall study analyzed how students defined hypertext after their experience with a classroom application of the technology. I purposely did *not* define hypertext for the students; I only showed them the mechanics of the program we were using. In many ways during the unit, I remained "hands off" in the classroom. I helped students with technical difficulties and with quick questions about their writing. However, I did not want my intervention to influence their constructed definitions of hypertext (see DeWitt, "Defining Links"). Students admitted in the interview that they were frustrated by this, that they felt somewhat abandoned by a teacher who throughout the term had continually intervened in their writing process.

A great deal of my intervening in their learning took place in a conference setting, and almost all of these conferences took place in front of a computer. My contribution to the discussion with students about their writing often took the form of invention questions that would help them to discover new ideas or force them to rethink the texts they were producing. I discovered that the interview setting mirrored these student conferences and that these interviews were the first in-depth discussion they had with me about their hypertext experience; they were both willing and eager to rethink and resee their experiences with HyperCard, and when questioned during the interview about, for example, how they had organized their HyperCard stacks, their responses often led to a revision of their hypertexts.

The student/teacher conference was not the only setting in which students had grown accustomed to collaboration. Throughout the term, students participated in collaborative activities whose purpose was to facilitate invention. During the studied unit, the students were offered opportunities to use hypertext on a classroom network in order to collaborate with a community of peers. On day eight of the fifteen-day unit, students were told how to gain access to each others' HyperCard stacks via the classroom network. They were encouraged to explore each others' HyperCard stacks and make links between their own stacks and their peers' stacks when they experienced connections between ideas. Students, once they had made these links, were then encouraged to respond to the writing of their peers by adding to the text, agreeing and disagreeing, and questioning the ideas expressed.

However, no student in the class took advantage of making links between their stacks and their peers' stacks via the classroom network. I was concerned that even though I had instructed and encouraged students to look into other people's stacks in hopes of gathering more information or alternative points of view, not one student took advantage of the networked hypertexts by making links to other students' stacks. At first, I was quick to blame the students for this. The students in the class were accustomed to being placed in collaborative learning situations; students often worked in small groups and shared their writing with others in the class. I assumed they viewed this collaborative activity using a new technological application as too complicated because they were still fairly inexperienced users of HyperCard. They were well adept at word processing and the Macintosh computer system, they were accustomed to using the classroom network for file and information exchange, and usually they were eager to exchange their writing via the network. It seemed clear, then, that their disinterest in accessing their peers' stacks lay with HyperCard itself.

I knew from past research experience that teachers play a significant role in the collaborative learning setting, especially in how they intervene in and direct the activity. But more importantly, they are responsible for designing the task in which they ask their students to participate. In the case of this study, I directed students toward using the network in accessing each others' writing without considering the nature of the writing they had completed. I needed to go back and review the tasks that I had asked students to complete, and these tasks started with the short writing assignments that students had responded to that became their HyperCard stacks.

Consider, for example, three very different writing assignments that students completed that were part of their HyperCard stacks:

1. The three rhetorical situations about freedom of expression: Each rhetorical situation asked students to give their "gut reaction," followed by a specific question about the situation. These specific questions asked students to articulate how the situation applied to the First Amendment and free speech. As students were asked to integrate their writing into their stacks, they were asked, "Rethink your responses to these situations and revise your answers to the questions at the end of each response. Add these responses to your HyperCard stack preceded by a brief summary of the situation. Your responses should be well thought out, your position should be clear, and your arguments should be followed by plenty of support from your own experiences and from your reading." Later in the unit, I responded in writing to the class as a whole about their responses to these situations. Students were offered a journal assignment to respond to my writing within their HyperCard stacks.

2. Students were asked to respond to the following question: Consider your role in the university community at ISU. What do you feel is the most pressing issue concerning this role and First Amendment rights and freedom of expression?

3. Students were asked to write a summary of "Chapter 2: An Open Community," from the Carnegie Foundation's 1990 *Campus Life: In Search of Community*.

As I began to critically view these assignments I had students complete in relationship to the classroom network, I asked: Who was the audience that students were writing for when they completed these assignments? What, if anything, about this writing would make it useful, interesting, and insightful for someone else other than the writer (or teacher) to read? Did students wish for other students to read their written responses to the above assignments? Did students expect that this writing would become public when they produced it?

I hypothesized that, in general terms, the writing that students produced in response to the above writing assignments was not, by definition, "public." For example, I looked at these assignments in the context of the semester that had passed to this point. These assignments were identical to other types of writing assignments they had completed for other units: summary, response to written text, personal reflection. But in other units, this writing was rarely made public, and often "writing for the teacher" was, unfortunately, reinforced. Students were expected to complete journal assignments, for the most part, outside of class. Students rarely sought feedback on this writing; drafting and revision were encouraged but not incorporated into the curriculum. This writing was turned in to me in final draft form for evaluation, and my written feedback in the form of dialogue about the writing was present, but minimal.

Therefore, when students were asked to explore each others' writing via the network and link their stacks to those of their peers, conflict occurred. First of all, much of the writing was not produced with a visualized audience other than that of evaluator. Secondly, students were not made aware that this writing could become public until after it was completed and located on the classroom network (network instruction came during day eight of the unit). And finally, students may have found very little use for the writing that their peers' had produced, and thus felt very little exigency for linking their stacks to the stacks of others. Overall, the writing that students completed in their stacks was expressive, and students viewed it as personal with very little account for other readers. For the most part, these writing assignments were not designed to be used with a network-supported hypertext system.

The conflicts that arose in this study—the importance of discussion as collaborative activity and the importance of assignment—become two important subjects of the next chapter, "Inventing Scenes." One other theme carries over nicely from this study of students writing in HyperCard to the next where students write for the Web: The learning text that students generate from their work with technology becomes as important as their work that meets various course requirements.

5

Inventing Scenes

The winter was long, the gray Ohio skies had become too normal, and any enthusiasm toward my work was fading quickly. I was overcommitted with campus and community service, I had four weeks left of the winter term and a major conference to get through, and then another ten-week spring term and another conference before I would see any kind of significant break—and this during the year I was granted tenure. I was tired. I could recognize that. A friend suggested that I was feeling good, old-fashioned burnout. Time for a sabbatical, she suggested. Maybe, I thought. But this didn't feel as extreme as the burnout overworked composition teachers often face, where the thought of the classroom evokes gloom and despair. I loved my job, I loved being in the classroom, and I especially loved my interactions with my students and my colleagues. No, I was not really interested in pursuing any type of work that would take me out of the classroom and away from campus.

Perhaps I was feeling something closer to simple boredom. I needed something new and intriguing to both me and my students, variety, something that wasn't more of the same. I did not have much choice about what courses I was going to teach during the spring term. These had long been on the schedule, and most students had already completed registration. My small campus allowed me a great deal of flexibility, but not enough to simply change my teaching schedule four weeks before the term began.

But one of my assigned courses could allow me to teach a "new" course. The university's second-year composition course (English 367) is designed to teach students to write in the context of an academic seminar, a content-specific course where a single, narrow subject is studied. Teachers develop such a seminar while incorporating rigorous writing instruction into the subject matter, illustrating types of critical inquiry that take place in various intellectual settings. The content, within reason, could be completely open. Perhaps, I thought, my restlessness could be eased by finding something new to explore in this one composition course.

The equation seemed simple enough: find new subject, use old assignments. And considering the amount of work that goes into new course development, the temptation was strong. After many years in the composition classroom, I felt that I had developed a series of assignments that, when sequenced carefully, gave my students a variety of opportunities to learn about and write a variety of texts while developing critical abilities that would serve them well in academic settings and beyond. Yet, these assignments were intimately tied to the content of my courses, the subject matter that I was asking students to investigate. The assignments I developed grew out of how I came to understand the content of the course and how I wanted my students to come to understand the content of the course. Traditional assignments and classroom activities were easily transferable, but in most cases, I believed, more sophisticated, complex assignments couldn't be lifted from one course and simply placed in another.

Furthermore, I wondered, really, if merely replacing content for content was going to restore the fervor that had vanished from my teaching. Doing so wouldn't really be an exercise in course development. Sure, I would gain an opportunity (or an excuse, in these busy times of teaching) to read and learn. But inventing a new course engenders much richer activity. Experimentation. Trial and error. Connections and relationships. Real invention in pedagogy is about new ways of thinking and seeing that can potentially produce new text forms. It forces the profession to progress and evolve.

Content alone, I convinced myself, would not allow for such change.

Generating a concept for a new course topic and pedagogy came to me, surprisingly so, rather quickly. A colleague suggested the obvious: Work with what you know. I wanted to teach Web design, I thought almost immediately. But my understanding of how such a course would work was much more grounded in technical writing or professional business writing than it was in anything I could do in a second-year writing course. I was certainly aware of Web texts that were literary or artistic in nature. As a Web designer myself, I was still very much locked into informative writing—Web sites that served as information systems.

"And documentary films. I know a lot about documentary films. I suppose I could use documentary films as the texts for the course, although I've never really taught a film studies course before." In fact, I've never even taken a film class, although many of my literature courses have included a study of film. I suppose I am more accurately described as an avid consumer of documentary films.

So I originally decided to use documentaries in my second-year composition course out of my love for these films, not necessarily out of a scholarly or technical understanding of the genre. Yet, even at the sophomore level, I felt challenged, almost pressured, for a theoretical lens through which we would read the films we were studying. I was uncomfortable with just "hitting the books," quickly reading documentary film theory and merely passing it onto my students in the form of reading assignments or class lectures. Instead, I wanted to find a theory of teaching film that would not only teach students to read films critically, but would also serve them well in what perhaps might be their last college writing course.

Work with what you know. My colleague's advice returned to me. If I were going to use films as my course's text, then I wanted to engage students in writing that would allow them to make strong reading and writing connections, in both content and in structure. A "complete" connection would ask students to study series of films and then ask them to create their own documentaries. This was a writing course, I reminded myself. Asking students to create films not only felt, at least initially, inappropriate for this course, but I am not a film-maker, and I certainly did not posses the necessary technical equipment for film-making. There were, however, important concepts about filmmaking that I wanted students to understand, and I wondered if there were writing assignments in which I could involve my students that would let them understand the genre more profoundly.

I tend to shy away from the factual, illustrative, instructive films one finds on public television. Instead, I gravitate toward the creative nonfiction film, or documentary as essay. Often, the story is told through direct narration—a voice-over or a clear, linear story line. At other times, however, this story is told through juxtaposition—strange groupings, fragmented scenes, odd parallels, clever asides, surprising takes on seemingly common themes. In fact, it seemed, these films were hypertextual. They were still produced and viewed on a reel or in a VHS tape case—a linear technology. But the techniques that the filmmakers used were clearly informed by the same notions of "text" that informed current theories of hypertext. And not only was I familiar with hypertext writing tech-nologies, but I also had them at my disposal. If students could "read" the hyper-textual elements in a documentary film, they could use hypertext writing technologies to create their own documentary texts.

I started at the end by writing the assignment for my students' final project:

Writing Project 3
Creating a Documentary Web Site

In collaborative writing teams, create a documentary Web site, a nonfiction "story" of sorts that adopts an angle that is new and refreshing to your audience. You should begin this Web site by considering the following initial requirements:

- You should plan to incorporate some "traditional" (read "library") research into your Web site. This research should be cited in your Web site using MLA documentation. You will receive guidelines for doing this and setting up a works-cited Web page. Although your project does require research, you are NOT writing a traditional research paper.

- Your project has an original photo requirement. Writing Project 2 outlines this requirement: "These final projects require that documentary Webs include at least ten (10) *original* photographs; funds have been designated to purchase film or disposable cameras and to cover the cost of photo processing."

- Your project has an original interview requirement. You should expect to conduct interviews with key players in the story you are telling; the texts from these interviews (direct quotations and paraphrases) should be incorporated extensively into your Web site.

- Your project should utilize an effective sense of organization. Whereas it might be appropriate at some point in your documentary to organize a short series of pages in a linear order, you should also try to present your readers with a series of choices so that they can explore a variety of linked pages in an order that meets their personal needs and curiosities. The last thing you want to do is to use a "filmstrip" effect for the entire Web site.

- Your Web site should include active "outward" links to pertinent and appropriate Web sites.

- Your Web site must include biography statements about the creative team, an "about us" type of page. It would be great to have your picture on this Web page.

A Sequence of Assignments

In the previous chapters in this book, I have illustrated an emerging theory of writing invention and computer technology by providing pedagogical scenes from various courses I've taught. Although I have tried to be careful to situate these scenes within their appropriate contexts, nonetheless, these examples were isolated from an entire course blueprint This chapter, with which I conclude the book, demonstrates a more complete picture, a course as it was designed from beginning to end.

In this second-year writing course, I assigned students to work on an extended class project that asked them to create "documentary Web sites," bringing together a study of documentary films and the creation of WWW sites. Students began this course much like a traditional film seminar: They read articles, essays, and books on filmmaking in order to develop a "critical lens" that they could use to study a series of documentary films, looking at the relationships among the subject, the audience, and the filmmaker while trying to better understand the filmmaker's "craft." At the same time they were studying film, they also closely examined a number of WWW sites, analyzing them in terms of their purpose, intended audience, structure and organization, and visual effect. Whereas the film and Web site texts that students were studying may not be considered "traditional" by many in the academy, a number of the writing assignments they were completing were rather conventional in form. Students completed summaries, thesis/support essays, proposals, and close reading responses.

After the midterm (about five weeks into a ten-week term), students were given an assignment where they were asked to create a collaborative "documentary Web site" about a subject of their choice. Although they were required to conduct extensive research (including interviews and other film verité techniques), they were instructed *not* to write a traditional research paper that had simply been cut into segments, linked, and uploaded to a Web server. Instead, the assignment asked them to create a short documentary: a nonfiction story that adopted angles that were new, refreshing, and relevant to their audiences. The project also had an "original photo" requirement; students needed to visually document images that would, in and of themselves, tell part of their story. At the time I taught this course, our department did not have video or audio capabilities; students were required to use written text and still images.

This documentary Web assignment, along with an analytical reading of my students' work, will be the sole focus of this chapter. My task here is twofold. First, I want to completely and fully describe the sequence of assignments that I have developed for this course. This sequence of assignments not only asks students to work on a wide range of reading and writing tasks, but it also carefully integrates the technologies and their associated theories that have been the subject of this book. I will illustrate how various Internet technologies available to my students—the WWW, e-mail, threaded Web discussions, and Web-writing software—facilitated collaboration and topic development and provided a foundation for the overall instructional goals of the course. Second, I want to use this opportunity to analyze and reflect upon the experiences I shared with my students in this class, deliberating on what they learned about new writing spaces and what I learned about teaching in them. In doing so, I hope to tie up loose ends, splicing together a number of scenes that will culminate in a written documentary of sorts, a classroom portrait that blends and exposes theory, practice, technology, and pedagogy.

English 367 is a second, required composition course for students who have at least sophomore standing (calculated by the total number of earned credit hours). Those who created this course believed, in theory, that students would benefit from a year between their first- and second-year writing courses that would allow them to apply what they had learned in their first composition course in other classes. This design represented a shift in traditional writing course sequences where Composition I and II are often taken back-to-back during freshman year. In practice, however, the scheduling of this course can pose problems. For example, students can take first-year writing during the last quarter of their freshman year, gain sophomore standing, and take second-year writing the first quarter of their sophomore year, defeating the purpose of the "application" period between the two courses.

Because students would spend the last half of my course creating Web sites instead of traditional academic texts, I had no qualms about inventing the sequence of assignments with very traditional beginnings. After profiling my students about their past experiences with English classes, I found most of them had had some type of introductory college literature course by the time they came to my class. However, for many of them, this course would offer them their first experience in reading *film* as text. Although they were eager to learn more about film, many expressed concern about their lack of background with film studies. Similarly, many of my students had used the Web for research and entertainment, but no one in the class had ever created a Web site. Their anxiety levels, along with their excitement, increased when they learned how these two elements would converge into their final projects.

For the first five weeks of the course, students were engaged in a number of simultaneously occurring activities. During class, in groups of four or five, students were asked to draft a "critical lens" through which we could read, examine, and better understand the documentary films we would be studying. They were offered a number of strategies for completing this task:

- Pull from a number of different sources: what you have read thus far in the textbook about making documentary films; what you already know about studying film; what you already know about studying literature.

- Think about how we typically write about something that we have read, viewed, or experienced. A first step is almost always description. From there, we move to evaluation. In other words, before you can formulate a response to a text or an experience, you need to be able to effectively describe or summarize it.

- Perhaps you would like to think of this critical lens as a list of questions that we can ask ourselves as we study these films.

Student groups created their critical lens using word processing and saved their work to disk. After they had completed their work, we combined files into one large document. Then, together, the entire class worked through this list, finding common strategies and eliminating any repetition. At the same time, we worked on a sense of continuity, attempting to achieve a seamless list of questions that everyone could use in the class as they began to read and analyze films. When our work was finished, I uploaded the critical lens to our class Web site:

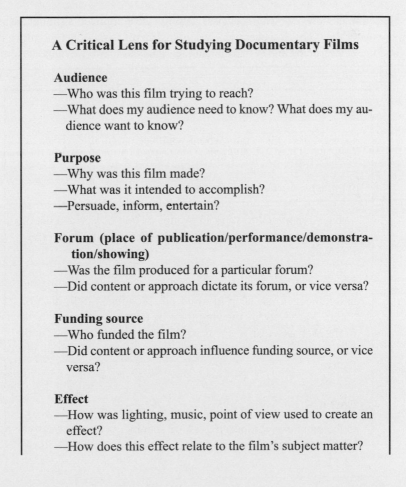

A Critical Lens for Studying Documentary Films

Audience
—Who was this film trying to reach?
—What does my audience need to know? What does my audience want to know?

Purpose
—Why was this film made?
—What was it intended to accomplish?
—Persuade, inform, entertain?

Forum (place of publication/performance/demonstration/showing)
—Was the film produced for a particular forum?
—Did content or approach dictate its forum, or vice versa?

Funding source
—Who funded the film?
—Did content or approach influence funding source, or vice versa?

Effect
—How was lighting, music, point of view used to create an effect?
—How does this effect relate to the film's subject matter?

Evidence
—What type of evidence does the filmmaker utilize to make a point?
—How does the type of evidence relate to the main point?

Historical perspective
—When was the film made?
—In what ways has the film's context changed throughout history?

Production details
—Title, filmmaker, date, etc.

Immediately following this class activity, we completed a similar assignment about the Web. However, with this assignment, I asked them to move beyond mere description and to think about their analysis in more evaluative terms:

Part I

I would like you to think about what seems, on the surface, to be a rather simple question:

What makes a Web site effective?

Today, I want you to work in groups as you compose a list of 6–8 *statements* (not questions) about what constitutes an effective Web site.

I have a few suggestions that may help you get started with this assignment. First, keep in mind our broadened definition of "text." Just as we are viewing films as text, I want you to think of the Web as a text—as a piece of writing, of sorts. Now, with that in mind, ask yourself, "What makes a piece of writing effective?"

Part II

Once you have composed a list of statements about effective Web sites, I would like you to apply your work. This will require that you multitask. Keep your list of statements open on the screen in Word. Then, open Netscape.

Each group is going to be assigned a Web site to analyze in terms of its effectiveness. You may want to begin working individually, browsing your assigned location, keeping in mind your list of "what makes an effective Web site."

After you have spent time visiting your assigned site, return to your group and compose a short passage where you apply your criteria for effective Web sites to your assigned site.

Group 1: http://www.cnn.com
Group 2: http://www.nicsl.coled.umn.edu/
Group 3: http://www.interlog.com/~mercer/

How does your lens work? Does it provide you with an effective approach toward describing and evaluating a Web site?

The three sites student groups explored were very different from each other: CNN, the National Service-Learning Clearinghouse, and Mercer Union: A Centre for Contemporary Visual Art. Students' lists included typical issues of audience, purpose, accuracy of information, and reliable source material. At the same time, they were confronted with issues of graphic design and navigation, concepts very new to them as they talked about writing. Whereas their ideas were not necessarily sophisticated in their presentation, students, when asked to consider design, were able to identify some key, albeit general, issues:

- The graphics used should point out information and not distract the user from what is important.

- The design should have something to do with the audience and the subject matter. It shouldn't be too colorful or flashy, unless that would appeal to the audience.

- An effective Web site should have a readily apparent sense of organization, which should be clear from links that are easy to read and find.

- The Web site should be easy to get around in. And if the user does get lost, it should be easy to get back home.

Two other classroom activities were taking place in this first part of the quarter. First, we screened a number of documentary films. I used these films much in the same way that I would use readings or print texts. Not only did these films illustrate for students the different theories of documentary film-making that I wanted them to understand and appreciate, but they also served as models of the technique and craft that I wanted students to utilize in their own documentary projects later in the term. I used the following films when teaching this course:

Screenings

Common Threads: Stories from the Quilt (1989) Robert Epstein and Jeffrey Friedman
Living Proof: HIV and the Pursuit of Happiness (1992) Kermit Cole
Color Adjustment (1992), Marlon Riggs
Brother's Keeper (1992), Joe Berlinger and Bruce Sinofsky
Roger and Me (1989), Michael Moore

Discussion of these films took place primarily in two arenas: in class and on threaded discussion Webs. In both spaces, students were asked to apply, as often as possible and when appropriate, their readings of the films using the critical lens they had earlier created. They were also encouraged to talk about the film's content as long as they could advance their discussions beyond superficial readings of "plot."

The second activity students participated in was what I called "The 3Cs of the World Wide Web: Consume, Critique, and Create." Students were instructed that it was perfectly acceptable, if not necessary, in this course to surf the Web, visiting and taking in as many sites as possible. However, they were also instructed to move beyond a passive point-and-click approach to surfing the Web. Instead, their "reading" needed to be critical of what they saw, read, and heard, focusing on issues of design, function, purpose, and meaning. Often in class, students were given time to participate in this activity. They worked individually and in small groups, often adding URLs/Web addresses to a class list of sites they found particularly interesting (both positively and negatively). After a great deal of practice with applying "what makes an effective Web site" lists, they were asked to complete a short writing project:

Using the lists you generated in class, write a descriptive evaluation of a Web site of your choice (I suggest that you review a site that includes multiple pages, even if you don't review every page). Your descriptive evaluation need not be "exhaustive"—there is no need to cover everything from the list you created in class. Instead, be selective and choose what you believe is most important for the type of site you are reviewing. I would much rather see you write at length about two items from your list than merely scratch the surface of them all.

The first half of the term concluded with a traditional academic essay assignment. Most of the work on this essay took place outside of class.

Writing Project 1
Writing a Critical Response

Responding to other people's ideas, arguments, and work will play an important part in the writing that you do in college—and beyond. Frequently, you will be asked to evaluate, assess, examine, explore, judge, criticize, and add to the ideas and arguments of others. Formulating written responses to the texts you read will force you to think critically, to question rather than simply accept what you see. (For the purpose of this class, *text* and *read* refer to documentary films.)

Assignment: The Critical Response

Write a critical response to an idea, position, or a filmmaker's approach presented in a documentary film of your choice (excluding any film that we view as a part of this class). Your writing should exhibit a clear sense of purpose and should be directed toward a specific audience. Your writing should demonstrate your understanding of the film by making clear and specific references to it. Also, you should make reference to at least two (2) sources, in addition to the film itself, in the text of your paper (these sources must be documented using MLA style). Above all, your writing must be supported by strong evidence and thoughtful reasoning. Whereas I rarely prescribe page lengths for assignments, I am looking for a paper that is narrow in focus and approximately four (4) pages in length.

Starting Places: Finding a Film

There are a number of ways to find a film to review. Public television broadcasts three to four documentary films a week, usually between 8–11:00 p.m. Your local video store and your local library should also stock a collection of documentary films. I also own and have access to videos that I can lend you.

"Write a Critical Response . . ."

Whereas this assignment seems prescriptive in what it is asking you to do, there are options available to you. First, consider what you are responding to: "an idea, position, or a filmmaker's approach." Also consider that I am looking for a paper that is "narrow in focus." Therefore, I am *not* expecting an exhaustive examination of an entire film. Instead, I want you to find an aspect of the film about which you can generate a response. That can include the film's content, the film's intended agenda, or the film's approach toward reaching that agenda.

Also, your readers may or may not have seen the film you are writing about; they definitely will not have the film at their easy disposal to view as they read your paper. Therefore, you will need to provide a brief, contextualizing summary of the film early in your paper. Again, you are not expected to retell the entire story. Then, as you develop your argument, you will need to make specific reference to the film—citing dialogue and describing scenes—to connect your writing to the film's text.

Purpose and Audience

The most effective way for you to establish your purpose for writing a critical response is to include an *explicit* thesis early in your paper. I want you to work with the following definition of thesis: *an articulated point or position—an assertion—that is in need of exploration and defense.*

By the time your audience finishes your introduction, it should have a clear sense of the position you are stating about this film. If your thesis sets up an argument, then the rest of the paper is an exploration and defense of that argument.

You can make one assumption about your audience for this paper: Your audience is made up of readers who are intellectually engaged by critical analysis in general and are interested in your thinking about the film you choose. Beyond that, your audience is directly tied to your purpose. Perhaps you are informing your audience of something that was left out of the film. Perhaps you are trying to convince your audience that the filmmaker's agenda is skewed or that a "character" in the film presents an inaccurate view of the subject matter. You need to negotiate how you are going to address this audience based on your purpose for writing.

Strong Evidence and Thoughtful Reasoning

Being able to formulate an effective written response to others' writing requires that you *support* your own ideas instead of merely asserting them. "Because that's just the way I feel"/ "Because that's just the way it is" is not acceptable support. "Support" is loosely defined here, and you should feel free to use a wide range of support: carefully formulated opinions, interviews, library material, WWW sources. You need only cite three (3) outside sources in this paper.

Students were given two opportunities to receive feedback on their work: a mandatory draft on which they received written feedback, and a voluntary draft on which they could receive verbal feedback in a conference. Because of the traditional nature of this assignment, feedback mostly focused on narrowing topics, articulating claims, providing clear examples and other types of evidence to support those claims, and structuring arguments.

Once we had completed the first part of the term, I gave students their last two assignments. Although I had been talking a great deal about the assignments on which we would spend the last half of the term, students had only seen a short summary of their task in the course syllabus. I began by giving them their final assignment—the documentary Web site—first. Two classroom activities ensued immediately. The first was an introduction to Microsoft Front-Page, the software that students would be using to create the documentary Web sites. I constructed a short assignment where students would create a series of three pages. These pages would included internal links, external links, text, and graphics. Whereas I feel that students truly learned what it means to write in a

Web-based environment once they started their projects, and whereas I typically believe that students learn software applications best within the context of real projects, I wanted students to feel comfortable with the basics of the software before they faced some of the very sophisticated challenges of this assignment.

The second activity was topic development and the formation of collaborative groups. I set up a discussion Web for students where I posted the following directive:

Getting started
From: Scott DeWitt
Date: 4/24/98
Time: 9:18:32 AM
Remote Name: 140.254.112.181

Comments

This discussion Web is designed so that you can begin to explore, with your classmates, possible topics for the class Web project. You can also use this discussion Web to begin putting together collaborative teams based on common interests and learning styles.

These Web projects will be collaborative ventures. I'm going to suggest groups of at least three and no more than four. Many of you have ideas of how many people you'd like to work with as expressed in your first short writing project.

You'll want to choose a topic that is both narrow and manageable. Also, remember that although your project will require extensive research, you are NOT writing a research paper. You are creating a short documentary, a nonfiction "story" of sorts that adopts an angle that is new and refreshing to your audience.

The possibility for topics is truly endless. I'd suggest you think locally. That means that you want to find a topic that is centered in the local area or that has a local angle that you can discover. Are you aware of any local stories?

How about local legends? How about a local angle on a topic of broad scope? Do you have a personal story that others might share or have their own angle on? I have many ideas for potential topics. However, I want to see what you can come up with first before I jump in.

Of course, like all distance-learning ventures, students who can meet face-to-face will almost always do so. For those students who did not have that option, the discussion Web became an important starting place:

Crystal Lake

From: Trinda
Date: 4/28/98
Time: 10:12:53 AM
Remote Name: 128.146.255.214

Comments

About one hundred years ago there was a theme park in Marion that was actually about the equivalant of Cedar Point. In fact, Crystal Lake was one of the only theme parks around with a roller coaster. I've seen pictures of the once up and running theme park, and they are amazing. The name of the theme park was Crystal Lake, and it used to be out at the Rt. 423 and Rt. 4 split where the old bargain city used to be. A girl I went to high school with did an extensive research project on Crystal Lake and could probably get a group headed in the right direction. I am very interested in using Crystal Lake as a topic, but I'm not sure how much information is actually available. Most of the people around when Crystal Lake existed, have died, or are too old to remember anything. Also, current pictures of what is left of the theme park are really hard to come by because the current owner of the land won't allow anyone behind the front gate of the property. If there are other people really interested in this project, please let me know here because I won't be around tomorrow. If people are interested, then I'll talk to my friend to see where we can begin to look.

Re: Crystal Lake

From: Christy
Date: 4/28/98
Time: 2:44:52 PM
Remote Name: 128.146.189.85

Comments

Wow! I had no idea there was a theme park in Marion. That sounds like a really interesting topic. Where did that other girl get her information on it?

Re: Crystal Lake

From: Josh Hall
Date: 4/29/98
Time: 11:18:51 AM
Remote Name: 128.146.255.237

Comments

Sounds like a great workable topic. Along with Crystal Lake I know that there was an amusement park at Indian Lake in Logan county (not too far away). From what my Grandma told me it was pretty big too. Like Crystal Lake it also had a roller coaster. Maybe there were others around that other people know about.

Re: Crystal Lake

From: Trinda
Date: 4/30/98
Time: 10:46:15 AM
Remote Name: 128.146.189.96
Comments

Josh, that sounds like a really cool project!!! My parents have a cabin at Indian Lake and they spend a lot of time there. I had no idea there was once a theme park there. I just thought it was a place for old people to go and fish. So, what do you say we get a group together to start the investigation?? It sounds like a really cool project to me!!

The discussion Web also became an important place for me to talk to students about their topics early in the assignment:

Topic Ideas

From: Karie
Date: 4/27/98
Time: 1:42:33 PM
Remote Name: 128.146.189.239

Comments

I have a child with special needs. The public education system is really failing to meet its legal and moral responsibilities. A piece about the role of education in the lives of kids like him could be interesting. (He has Tourette Syndrome.)

Re: Topic Ideas

From: Scott DeWitt
Date: 4/27/98
Time: 4:58:50 PM
Remote Name: 140.254.113.39

Comments

I think that a Web site on the needs of kids with special needs and current educational systems that are failing them is a great topic. What becomes interesting in this case, Kristinne, is whether or not you choose to make your son part of the Web site. Remember, the Web is a public space. I'm not suggesting you don't include your son or that you not take on this subject. I just want you to begin thinking of some of the implications involved with writing for the Web.

Their second major writing assignment in the course was an exercise in practicality, but students found this to be an exceptionally challenging piece of writing to complete. They were asked to write a proposal that would "fund" a component of their documentary Web sites:

Writing Project 2
Proposal for Final Project Funding

Professor Scott Lloyd DeWitt was recently awarded $140.00 by the Ohio State University at Marion Small Grants Program. These funds will be distributed to students enrolled in English 367.01C who are working on documentary Web projects (see Writing Project 3). These final projects must include at least ten (10) *original* photographs; funds have been designated to purchase film or disposable cameras and to cover the cost of photo processing. All final projects will be collaborative endeavors involving groups of three to four students.

In order to have access to this money, your group must write a collaborative proposal that describes your project and articu-

lates how you plan to use the funds you are requesting. Proposals must include the following:

- General description and purpose of the project
- Targeted audience and scope of the project
- Plans for using funding
- Specific request for film/disposable camera and photo processing

Use this list as subheadings in your proposal to help your sense of organization.

Your proposal will be evaluated by a small panel of readers who will ask the following questions:

- Do the writers take a creative and innovative approach toward the subject matter?
- Do the writers carefully consider the project's audience and scope?
- Do the writers articulate a logical relationship between the subject matter and the intended audience?
- Do the writers use clear, descriptive prose in their proposal?
- Do the writers carefully prepare and present the final proposal?

The idea of "funding" and how it played into whether or not a film was made and its success was a topic frequently brought up by students in class: Where did Michael Moore get his money to make *Roger and Me*? How was Marlon Riggs able to secure the rights to the scores of television video clips he integrates into his film? How did Dustin Hoffman's narration of *Common Threads: Stories from the Quilt* contribute to the film's overall success? Also, Rosenthal's *Writing, Directing, and Producing Documentary Films and Videos*, the text for the course, offers its readers a chapter entitled, "Writing the Proposal," in which the writer states:

> A proposal is, first and foremost, a device to sell a film. . . . Its central purpose is to convince someone or some organization that you have a great idea, that

you know what you want to do, that you are efficient, professional, and imaginative, and that you should therefore be given the contract for the film against any competition and be financially supported in your endeavors. (25)

The first challenge that students faced with this assignment was audience. If the purpose of a proposal was to convince someone to fund their projects, then I wanted to give my students "someone" to convince. I arranged for a panel of readers to review their proposals: Lynda Behan, the campus director of the writing center, Robert Thompson, a news reporter from the Columbus, Ohio, CBS affiliate, and myself. They were told, "This is the audience for your *proposal*, not necessarily the audience for your *project*. Their job will be to assess whether or not you have a thoughtful perspective on your project and to assess the potential of your project. The only evidence they will have to formulate this assessment is your proposal itself." Students found it difficult to imagine an audience and purpose for their project that they would then have to describe to a different audience for a very different purpose. This complicated notion of audience, I hoped, would strengthen my students' overall awareness of audience when they worked on their final projects.

This assignment was also difficult in that students were describing something that didn't yet exist: their documentary Web sites. Instead, they were being asked to visualize what the final project would look like. Anyone who has ever written a grant proposal knows the difficulty of this task. What allows writers to create them, however, is an understanding of sorts that proposals are early inventions, imaginations of what *might* become the final product. We momentarily suspend our disbelief as we create an idea while emphatically stating, "This is what *will* be." Furthermore, no one expects that what we say in a proposal and what actually occurs will be identical. Close, we hope, but not identical. Being a part of this discourse community and having this understanding allows us to resolve this conflict. Our students, however, are typically not a part of this community. Therefore, they needed a great deal of feedback on this assignment:

- You need to spend much, much more time describing the topic, especially in terms of its history and its background. You are still not considering the audience for *the proposal*: The reviewers, very likely, are not familiar with the subject matter at all. If they are, they still expect to see that YOU are familiar with the subject matter, and they expect to see how you *understand* that subject matter.

- Also, you need to separate *your topic* and *your project*. Of course, you are going to describe the Web site itself—the project—but the proposal reviewers need to understand the subject matter first. Therefore, you don't want to begin with statements like, "Spring Quarter we will produce a Web site that . . . ." This type of statement, one that tells the proposal reviewers what you are going to do, is completely appropriate for this type of writing. However, it needs to come much later in the general description of the project. Describe the topic first, then describe the project.

- You need to spend much, much more time describing your audience, especially in terms of its relationship to the subject matter and its relationship to the intended purpose of your Web site (many of you have glossed over or completely omitted any type of discussion about the purpose of your site—to persuade, to inform, to entertain). Don't worry about being too extensive at this point—no one is even close at this point. We can always cut back. Again, the proposal reviewers want to see that you are thinking in depth about your subject, your purpose, and your audience.

Students needed this funding in order to complete their final projects, so there was an exigency built into this assignment beyond "the grade." Furthermore, this assignment had an audience that they perceived to be much more "real" than any other assignment they had completed in the past. I perceived a significant commitment on their part to do well on this assignment. All proposals were funded, although two were sent back to the writers due to their carelessness in presentation; they revised and resubmitted to acquire funding.

Understanding Students' Inventions: Reading Their Work

Without question, creating a new course—or, I might say, creating and *teaching* a new course—is labor intensive. The necessary effort not only involves the creation of new assignments and new course materials, but it also includes learning new course content and understanding how to impart that content to various levels of student ability. Implementing a new course requires an analytical cognitive activity while a course is being taught and after its conclusion, the purpose of which is not only to assess students' learning, but more specifically to find connections between their learning and the new pedagogies that have engaged them. My work as a researcher of student writing and writing instruction adds another layer of complexity as I reflect on my classroom experiences for other teachers who might find themselves in similar situations or who might be interested in embarking on a similar course design.

I would like to offer here a reading of this course beginning with my students' work on their documentary Web sites. This reading will include an analysis of their final products, the documentary Webs, and of their writing processes, the work they engaged in to produce their documentary Webs. By the time this work began, students had created their own collaborative writing teams, they had developed topics appropriate to class assignments, and they had received funding (cameras, film, photo processing) from successful grant proposals that reviewers had accepted. My reading will look at the following documentary Webs:

Nontraditional Students: We Are Unique

This documentary Web looks at the lives of a growing population on our college campuses. Nontraditional students are usually defined by a certain number of years between graduating from high school and beginning college. The writers present a significant amount of information about these students' academic lives as well as stories from their personal lives.

Welcome to the Fabulous Short North

Once considered one of Columbus, Ohio's most run-down neighborhoods, the Short North represents a success story in urban renewal. The documentary looks at the revitalization of this neighborhood that is home to art galleries, restaurants, shops, and coffee shops, not to mention a large population of Columbus' gay community.

Ohio's Thrills

Ohio's rich history often overlooks its past with amusement parks. Many are aware of current parks that keep today's families entertained throughout the summer. However, most have no idea that Ohio's amusement parks date back as far as 1870. In fact, one of these early amusement parks, Crystal lake, was located in Marion, Ohio. This site presents a state history of amusement park failures and successes.

A Dream, a Colt, and the Little Brown Jug

Each September, the population of Delaware, Ohio, triples as more than fifty thousand people flock to the county fair to witness a horse race that is not only world famous, but rich in tradition and brimming with history. The Little Brown Jug Race is one part of what is known as the Triple Crown of Pacing with the Little Brown Jug Race setting the standard in excellence, tradition, and speed of track. This documentary is informative not only in its history of the Little Brown Jug, but also in its history of the sport of harness racing.

Welcome to the Egg Farms of Central Ohio

Agri-business caught central Ohio by surprise as large egg farms moved into the neighborhood—literally. This documentary examines the devastating effects of agri-business on one community that has

had to deal with, among other things, waste runoff contamination and
. . . flies. The writers of this documentary were able to capture vivid
photographs of the farm's condition. (Note: Concerned Citizens of
Central Ohio lists this site in its newsletter as a resource for readers.)

Drive-ins: The Dinosaurs of Movie Theaters

America's love for the automobile and its love for the movies con-
verged into one of the country's most memorable pasttimes. Much like
its history with amusement parks, Ohio was once home to some 165
drive-in theaters. Most wouldn't be surprised to find that Marion, Ohio,
was home to X drive-ins. But why these outdoor screens disappeared
from the local community is not necessarily common knowledge.

Consolidation: Marion General Hospital and MedCenter Hospital

Duplication of jobs was the most cited reason for middle management
cutbacks throughout the 1980s and 90s. Similarly, duplication of health
care services drove the consolidation of Marion's two hospitals. But
the community soon realized that eliminating health care services also
eliminated choices in health care providers. This documentary Web reveals the issues confronting local communities with the consolidation
of two hospitals.

River Valley Cancer Scare

A relatively new school cluster compared to other schools in Marion
county, River Valley Middle and High Schools were built in 1967 on
grounds that had national recognition during World War II: a Ger-
man prisoner-of-war camp at the Marion Engineering Depot. However, the site was also later used by the U.S. Army to build bombs
during the war. After an alarming number of cancer cases were documented among the school district's graduates, research was conducted that revealed the school was built on buried hazardous
materials, a fact that the government refused to acknowledge played
a role in the graduates' illnesses. This documentary looks at a small
school district's fight to find answers and calls into question the
local media's role in the "River Valley Cancer Scare." (In May 2000,
after a long, controversial investigation, the Army Corps of Engineers agreed to relocate the school.)

Children's Literacy Awareness

When the public hears the word "literacy," it usually thinks of the ability to read and write and the clichéd "Why Johnny Can't Read." But
typically, when scholars talk about literacy, they are more concerned

with a culture where not only reading and writing activities are encouraged, but where different types of knowledge are valued. This site seeks to translate scholarship in literacy out of an academic setting and into one where both parents and educators can join to talk about these issues.

I have also developed a series of lenses through which I will read my students' work. I will begin by looking at issues of purpose, where students had difficulty negotiating between Web sites that were service/resource oriented and sites that documented real stories. Next, I will look at how students invented structures and organizations for their Web texts. Students also struggled with differences between writing traditional research papers and writing the type of text the assignment was calling for: a documentary hypertext. And finally, I'm interested in fleshing out the differences between research papers/documentaries—text forms—and researching/documenting—text processes.

Service Web Site versus Documentary. When my students first began this project, it became apparent to me that our field's application of schema theory was firmly grounded in practice (Alba and Hasher, 1983; Andre and Phye, 1986; Tierney and Leys, 1986; Kucer, 1987). Schema theory, in short, claims that writers create "frames" for understanding the texts that they read and write. These frames signify text forms, rhetorical aims, composing approaches, and critical thinking strategies. For example, if I were to ask students to write a business letter, they would pull on their schemata, their frames of reference, in order to create this text. They would make decisions about the appearance of this letter, purpose, audience, organization, and appropriate language based on their past experiences with this text form. Also, even if they had never read or written a business letter before, they would pull on their schemata from other experiences that would help them approach this new task. They would consider what they already know about audience and purpose, and they would seek out text forms that they believe to be closely related to a business letter.

Similarly, teachers use schema theory as a way to teach students about new text forms. Students entering the academy, for example, are expected to write texts that are more complex than those to which they are accustomed or with which they are completely familiar. Teachers use schema theory as a way of helping their students to create new frames that they can use to compose these complex texts. Often, teachers use written texts as models that students read in rhetorically critical ways (reading for more than content) and then they ask their students to apply these learned concepts to their own writing.

Because of the connections and relationships that student see between past experiences and current situations, schema theory plays a significant role in students' invention processes. I noticed a trend among my students when we first started work on our documentary Web project. For over five weeks, we had been studying documentary films, a text form with which they had very little experience. (Actually, I should note that they had very little experience with the types of film I was asking them to study. In their syllabus, I wrote, "This course will take up the study of documentary film as a genre and as an art form. We will avoid those films that people typically think of when they hear the word 'documentary'—sometimes dry, purely informative films about nature or historical events that are shown on Sunday afternoon television. Instead, we will study films where the filmmaker is an essayist of sorts, where he or she projects a story that is deserving of careful analysis and vigorous discussion.") Although the stories told in these films were rich and engaging, we studied these text forms beyond their content. Students had become well versed in looking at films' narrative structures, their approaches toward audience and purpose, and their use of "effect" as a way to connect content and form.

Similarly, they analyzed Web sites using the same concepts. Some of these sites I chose for them, while others they chose on their own. At the time I taught this class, I was not able to find exact examples of the types of documentary Web sites that I was asking them to compose. I did, though, direct them toward sites where the writing was essaylike in form, where the writers employed a sense of "craft" like that we had witnessed in the documentary films we watched. We compared these sites with others where the purpose was merely to inform or to report, a genre that is most prevalent on the Web and with which these students had had extensive experience. (A class discussion revealed that even though students read the Web for "entertainment," the sites they most often turned to are primarily informative in purpose with very little presence of a writer. In fact, one student admitted that she rarely read sites where a writer's presence was obvious, perceiving it as a "personal" site that lacked authority, a clear bias in these students' Web reading habits, one that was reinforced by how they are asked to use the Web for academic research—my own courses included.)

When they were first presented with the assignment and just beginning their process of topic development, many student groups proposed "service-oriented" projects: sites that were completely informative in nature and could be considered resource or instructional sites. Even after our study of documentary films and our discussion of various text forms found on the Web, students' schemata of informative and service Web sites—the texts with which they were most familiar—were stronger than, and thus overpowered, the yet unrealized text forms that I was asking them to create: the documentary Web. After more in-class discussion about these issues, most student groups abandoned those topics altogether and began to develop topics that were more in line with the assignment. Two groups, however, continued to work with their original topics and struggled through changing their focus and their purpose for writing.

In *Nontraditional Students: We Are Unique,* the writers attempt to profile the changing face of today's college campuses, a face that does not necessarily include an overwhelming majority of new, eighteen-year-old high school graduates. All of the writers themselves were nontraditional students, all were women, and all had significant extracurricular family and/or work responsibilities. In our initial conferences, their collective identity was driving the development of their project. Of course, I praised them for this; collective identity was a characteristic that drove the development of all of the documentary films we watched. However, their identity also told them that women returning to school often lacked the resources necessary to make a smooth transition into a college environment. What nontraditional students needed most was *information*, they believed, and they planned to provide a service for those students returning to college.

I believe that these writers, after a number of conferences, fully understood the difference between what the assignment was asking of them and what they initially proposed—a documentary versus a service/resource site. However, even in its final draft form, one can note a tension between the assignment's charge and their personal desires for creating this site. Indeed, the site contained numerous profiles of characters who are nontraditional students and who are responsible for helping nontraditional students on our campus. However, before readers of the site ever get the opportunity to meet any of these players, they must wade through a great deal of information: comparison bar graphs, definitions of "multiple role strain" and its management, external links to the U.S. Census Bureau and the "Stress Free Network." Also, one of the key pages to the site still employed what one might refer to as a "rhetoric of service":

> Over age 25 and been out of school a while? Thinking about college? Don't panic!! You'll be right at home on the Marion campus of the Ohio State University! About one-third of our students are "non-traditional,"—people just like you who have been away from formal education for a few years. Most older students have jobs, families, and varied responsibilities—and really love taking classes.

In fact, to apply schema theory here, one might argue that the frame they pulled from for this text was an admissions brochure for nontraditional students.

Welcome to the Fabulous Short North struggled with the same difficulty between intention and assignment, although its intention differed slightly from that of the nontraditional student site. These writers were interested in profiling the highly successful neighborhood revitalization, yet their proposal for their project was more concerned with "promotion" than it was with "profile." In fact, what these writers initially proposed was "the definitive Web site promoting the Short North." During one of our conferences that took place at the computer, I showed them the official site of the neighborhood's association as a way of illustrating that not only did their site not meet their assignment, but also that the site already existed.

What became apparent to me is that once again, these writers allowed their collective identity to drive the development of this project. None of these students lived in this neighborhood, and only one of the writers considered it to be a regular "hangout." Instead, they were "visitors," the very population the neighborhood association targets with its promotion of shopping, art galleries, and restaurants. Upon approaching the Short North neighborhood, it doesn't take long for a visitor to be confronted with these promotional texts—brochures, neighborhood maps, posters, welcome signs—and clearly, these texts served as frames for the students' writing, especially in its early draft form:

> The *fabulous* Short North. Shopping. Restaurants. Night clubs. Art galleries. What else do you need from a neighborhood? The Short North is located just blocks from Columbus's downtown and is eager to have you visit! Morning to night, there is always something happening in this popular neighborhood.

Also, the rich history of the neighborhood, which is not free from controversy and not promoted by the association, was nearly invisible from early drafts of the site. The students were writing from the perspective of what they knew and had conducted very little research into their topic. After I directed them to a few key players in the neighborhood's revitalization, the promotional rhetoric nearly disappeared, and their perspective shifted:

> Displacement is a factor in gentrification of a neighborhood. Due to the increase in property value in the Short North, some individuals using low-income housing were forced out of the area. When asked about the city's stand on the displacement of individuals in the Short North, Michael Wilkos, Business and Development Specialist for Housing and Community Services in Columbus, said that the city is not directly involved in any displacement. If there is a situation where individuals will be forced to move, the city provides other housing for them. He adds, "The Short North project has actually brought an increase of housing. Many empty buildings were redone and apartments were made available."
>
> While the city will provide housing if it is involved in any displacement of individuals, it does not require investors to do so. Do investors have an obligation to provide housing or business space to people they are forcing out? Or is displacement just a side effect of progress?

Whereas the rhetoric of promotion was revised out of their written text, students in the class noted that their photography certainly mirrored what one might expect in promotional materials. (One of the students on this team was an amateur photographer and computer graphics artist.) As a result, a tension exists in this site between its written text and its graphic images. This neighborhood's path to revitalization began with a core block on its main street and spread outwards, and all of the photos focused on this area. There were photo opportunities that would have depicted untouched areas of the neighborhood or displacement on its peripheries, but none of these opportunities was seized. The group's photographer explained that she was uncomfortable venturing into these areas, especially alone or with the only other woman on the writing team, unsure of the neighborhood's crime (I fully supported this choice, especially after instructing student groups to take caution in how they conducted their research). She was also concerned about the exploitative nature of such photographs, citing Michael Moore's work on the film, *Roger and Me*. She said, "He filmed those people and then made them look really bad just to make his point. It felt really unfair to me."

Table of Contents/Index versus Choice. In his article, "Reading Hypertext: Order and Coherence in a New Medium," John Slatin fuses the theory/literature of hypertext with the theory/literature of reading, positing a "basic point . . . [that] is almost embarrassingly simple: Hypertext is very different from more traditional forms of text" (1990, 870). Slatin uses this comparison of hypertext and traditional text as a means of structuring his argument about sequence, prediction, and coherence. Reading texts, in traditional reading acts, necessitates sequence: "The reader's progress from the beginning to the end of the text follows a route which has been carefully laid out for the sole purpose of ensuring that the reader does indeed get from the beginning to the end in the way the writer wants him or her to get there" (1990, 871). Sequence is of paramount importance for a writer as he or she devises "a sequence that will not only determine the reader's experience and understanding of the material but will also seem to the reader to have been the only possible sequence for that material" (1990, 872). Hypertext disrupts, to a certain extent, our notions of reading: Memory is utilized in tandem with the machine; meaning is constructed still by making relationships, but indefinite choices are possible; connections are made both cognitively and electronically; and all electronic links are audience-based. In the end, Slatin concludes, a comparison of reading traditional texts and reading hypertexts strives to reconceptualize "coherence."

In chapter 4, I describe a number of different "shapes" of hypertexts that students constructed using a freestanding program called HyperCard. Their assignment was considerably different from the documentary Web assignment. Instead of creating an end product as a hypertext, the students using HyperCard created a personal hypertextual database of their own writing that would eventually aid them in the writing of a traditional documented essay.

These hypertexts did not have a "public" audience; instead, students created hypertexts for their own personal use. I identified three shapes that could describe their hypertexts:

- Asterisk: a distinct center from which specific stems extend with no stems connecting with each other except at the center.

- Branch: a distinct starting point that moves progressively outward with points of departure that always offer the choice to move back to that point of departure.

- Web: a richly connected design with no discernable center or starting point.

At the time that students worked on the HyperCard project, there were no models on which they could base their hypertexts. There was no accessible World Wide Web, and there were no commercial hypertexts available to illustrate even the most basic of concepts to them. In fact, as a part of my research study, I refrained from "defining" hypertext for them, instead opting to interview them after the project's conclusion to discover how they constructed their own definitions of hypertext. These shapes, then, grew out of their personal notions of organization, their understanding of the assignment, and their experience with the technology (these shapes were more than likely a result of the design of the software itself, also). The software didn't offer a "mapping" feature like most current hypertext programs do, a way to see a picture or a graphic representation of the hypertext's shape (StorySpace is probably the best known hypertext program that utilizes this feature). Instead, HyperCard forms a series of linked "cards" into a "stack" and allows users to view the cards lineally. Because there was no mapping feature, I gleaned these shapes from my own reading of the students' HyperCard stacks.

Students who worked on the documentary Web project used Microsoft FrontPage '98, the same Web design software the department uses to design its instructional Web materials. FrontPage uses two main work spaces. The "Editor" is where students actually write their Web pages; it utilizes menus and tool bars almost identical to other Microsoft writing tools. Although there are templates and predesigned pages available for writers, I began students working with a blank page. The program is WYSIWYG ("what you see is what you get") with HTML code created "behind" the page. Under the "Window" menu of the program, users can see a lineal list of all of their open pages. The "Explorer," on the other hand, is where the writer manages Web pages within a Web site. It lists all of the site's pages, yet it also offers the site's map, or a graphic representation of what FrontPage calls a "Web." The Explorer shows the relationships of pages to other pages by illustrating their links.

Students who worked on the documentary Web project produced hypertexts that followed designs similar to those by students who created personal databases using HyperCard. However, in early drafts of the project, one design feature appeared in every documentary Web project: a table of contents or an index, a home page from which all other pages could be accessed. In fact, individual pages were only accessible through the table of contents/index, and the only option available once on these pages was a "home" button that returned the readers to the table of contents/index. In other words, in their early draft forms, all documentary Webs utilized an asterisk shape.

As I conferenced with individual writing teams, I better understood their thinking behind these early designs. To their credit, all student groups cited one or both of two reasons that drove the design of their documentaries:

1. Audience: Students did not want their readers to get lost in their hypertexts, and they understood from their experiences writing traditional, academic papers that readers expected a clear, logical progression through the texts they were reading.

2. Past experience: Students in this class had extensive experience reading the Web, and their frame of reference was a professionally designed Web site that was highly structured and that almost always used a home page as its core.

Students, therefore, were actively engaged in inventing an audience for their projects as well as pulling on schemata, frames that were utilized to create a text which they had no experience writing.

After I identified this trend across numerous student groups, I pulled the entire class together for a rather impromptu discussion. I wanted not only to introduce them to some user-friendly hypertext theory, but also to remind them of a text form that we had been studying for over six weeks: the documentary. I found myself in the middle of what is often called a "teachable moment." Ultimately, I would have found a student-friendly essay on hypertext to introduce them to how hypertext has the power to "encourage and enable an audience . . . to control the transformation of a body of information to meet its needs and interests" (Conklin, 1987, 11), an audience who then creates a mental text, a whole, from the pieces. I would have also found a reading that would explain the political issues of choice that surround blurred terms such as reader and writer. This issue was exposed early in a two-hour class period; the importance of this issue and seizing the moment immediately forced me to relate this theory to them in our discussion rather than in a reading assignment.

Of more concern to me, though, was how students failed to learn from their weeks of studying documentary films when structuring their hypertexts.

Film is a linear medium because of its physical existence, a continual band that intends its viewers to view a text from beginning to end. Without using the fast forward and rewind of a VCR to clumsily pinpoint an exact location in a video, the viewer is forced through the entire text at the hands of the filmmaker. However, many of the filmmakers we studied did not tell their stories in a linear fashion. Instead, they used fragmented, episodic scenes that, as the film progressed, coalesced into a whole. For example, in *Living Proof: HIV and the Pursuit of Happiness*, Kermit Cole takes the viewer through rapidly changing scenes, from interview to photography studio to the streets of New York while the film's complex themes about living positively with HIV develop. Even films that tell a linear story, like Berlinger and Sinofsky's *Brother's Keeper*, the account of Dilbert Ward who was accused of murdering his brother in their one-room rural home and the trial that ensued, weave their narrative through a number of carefully constructed but not necessarily traditionally structured scenes.

(As one might imagine, the potential for DVD, digital video display, is enormous as a teaching tool for bringing together studies in film and hypertext. Typically, the film is stored on CD and is accessible by scene and a specific counter with options to view directors' and actors' interviews as well as "behind the scenes" and "making of" clips. Unfortunately, I don't expect that most documentaries will be produced on DVD for some time to come.)

After our discussion of both hypertext theory and the approach to structure in the films we studied, I sent students back to their documentaries to begin thinking of alternative ways of organizing them. I saw primarily two approaches to structure emerge. The first closely resembled what I described earlier as a "Web" shape. These hypertexts maintained their central core—the table of contents/index as a home page—and once readers accessed a specific page, they were still offered the option of returning home. However, they were also provided a list of links to every single page in the hypertext. Yet, these links merely replicated the table of contents/index at the bottom of the page. Readers could move from page to page or return to the home page, but these choices at the bottom of the page were identical in link name and in order to the table of contents/index.

The second approach to structure was a variation on the "Web" shape, or perhaps a more complex "Web." These hypertexts still relied heavily on a table of contents/index and a replicated list of links at the bottom of the page. However, these writers also offered their readers links to various pages throughout their text, most often in the form of highlighted words that indicated to the readers where they would be taken. Often, these highlighted words would be identical to the replicated table of contents/index at the bottom of the page. However, at times the highlighted word would appear to be a choice not offered by any other link at the bottom of the page, but it would still take the readers to a listed page.

No student group attempted what might be considered an alternative or experimental variation on the asterisk- or Web-shaped hypertext. Again, I asked student groups to describe their choices for revising their hypertexts. Their replies were nearly uniform. They were interested in attempting a more scenic, episodic approach to their hypertexts, and they were encouraged by my request for a less rigid sense of structure. However, in the end, they were still constrained by notions of audience and by texts they were familiar with on the Web, both of which were related in their minds. During our discussion, one student revealed, "We didn't want our audience to get confused because our documentary wasn't well organized. Won't they just stop reading?" Another student added, "I hate Web sites that don't let me easily return to the home page. I like the ones that have frames at the bottom or on the side that have the same links present all the time." And in our discussion, a newly invented audience emerged: "And we wanted to make sure you could find all of our pages. We didn't want to get a bad grade because you couldn't find some of our writing." As they revised their hypertexts, considering audience at a deeper level, these students were still very much aware that they were completing an assignment for a course that would later be assessed by their teacher.

Research Paper versus Documentary.   The documentary Web assignment asked students to conduct extensive research that attempted to put them in the role of a documentary filmmaker. They were asked to find and (re)construct stories, conduct interviews, and shoot original photography. They were also asked to conduct, when necessary, traditional library research and online research, but these would play secondary roles in their projects. Regardless of the type of research students were asked to conduct, they strained to find appropriate ways to *present* that research. By the time students registered to take this particular class, they had thought of research in terms of a very narrow audience. Often, their teachers were the audience for their research. But more often than not, they were asked to consider their research in terms of audience and subject matter—what does my audience *need* to know, and what does my audience *want* to know? Regardless of how they were taught to approach audience, they were almost always asked to consider an *academic* audience. Certainly, the instruction they received in research was focused on an academic audience. This consideration, above all others, drove their approach and tone towards presenting their research to their audience. This is not to suggest that students at this level were completely comfortable and proficient at dealing with audience in their academic writing, only that their experience with, and instruction in, research and presenting that research was very narrow in focus.

The tension between what students knew about writing academic research papers and what they were being asked to do with the documentary Web assignment presented a number of difficulties. In short, the documentary

Web project asked students to invent an audience, a general task with which they had experience in their composition courses, but within the context of this assignment, one with which they had very limited experience. The presence of a "real" audience as perceived by the students and made possible by the Web heightened their awareness of this new sense of audience ("This is *really* going to be on the Web?"). They were still confronted with the questions of what their audiences needed and wanted to know, but they were asked to approach and address an audience they had never written to before. As a result, they were faced with a new question tied specifically to the documentary: In what compelling ways can I convey this research to this audience I know little about?

The writers of *Children's Literacy Awareness* Web Site, for example, were all education majors who had been studying how children learn to read and write. They were all familiar with academic research in their major and believed that this scholarly theory could translate well into a documentary that both parents and teachers would find appealing. In fact, making this theory "real," as they put it, for parents who typically would not be interested in scholarship, was their primary goal in creating this site. As a result, we find pages where the writers successfully present their research to their intended audience:

> A child's world is full of print. In their home, children observe messages jotted down on paper, shopping lists that hang on the refrigerator, birthday cards that are made out to friends, and the recipes we use to cook. Away from home, children observe cashiers who are using registers which print out what we buy, people who are writing checks to purchase items, librarians who are using computers which print out what books we have checked out, and teachers manually taking attendance and sending home newsletters. Even when we drive up to our children's favorite fast food restaurant, we read from the written menu, and what we have ordered is printed onto a monitor to review for accuracy. Children see all of these interactions daily. They take in all of this various information to help them gain knowledge about the power of print.

However, in the very next page, we find that the research they know best—the academic—returns to their writing:

> Whereas most infants and toddlers enjoy looking at the pictures in books, preschool children begin focusing on the print. According to renowned author of literacy for children J. Mason, there are three stages of reading behavior (Morrow, 80). The first stage of reading behavior is understanding the functions of print (Morrow 80). Children become familiar with print such as those found on environmental signs, logos, and the names of people they know. The second stage occurs when children become curious about the forms of print

such as letter names, what they look like, how they sound, and how the letters make up words. Some children will begin to ask, "What's that letter?" or "What's that word?"

J. Mason also proposes that the third stage involves developing conventions about print. This means that children learn how to read from left to right. They also discover that "Punctuation serves certain purposes in printed material" (Morrow, 81).

Interestingly, this shift happens from one page to the next, never within the same page. These students were able to maintain their approach to audience within the constraints of a Web page, but not within the constraints of an entire Web site.

Similar difficulties faced the writers of *A Dream, a Colt, and the Little Brown Jug.* Twice during this project, we held Web site "critiques," peer response activities where students reviewed each other's projects in progress. The authors of the *Little Brown Jug* conducted a significant amount of research on their topic, a combination of traditional "source" research and oral history. However, their writing failed to effectively illustrate a blend of these. Instead of shaping their library research into something which more closely resembled the oral history, their Web site "sounded" much like a research paper, according to their peers:

> The American pacer descended a different path from that of the trotter. Pacer heritage fuses the blood of the Narragansett pacer, a saddle horse that disappeared by 1850, and the Canuck of French Canada. The trotter began in the East, but the great growth of the pacer was in the Midwest and the South. Before the pacer gained popularity late in the 19th century, it was a despised horse. The horse who popularized pacing was Dan Patch, one of the fastest ($1:55 \frac{1}{4}$ for the mile) and most popular standardbreds ever.

When told by the class that their writing seemed very "research-paper-like," the writers attempted to add "voice" to their introduction. The result is what most would consider to be a highly unsuccessful piece of writing:

> Been to the races lately? What races, you ask. Why the harness races of course. You know, horses go around an oval track pulling a little man on a cart. Yes, the Little Brown Jug, see you know what I'm talking about. Many people in today's world of computers, professional sports, technology and fast-paced society in general have lost touch with the many good, old-fashioned pleasures of harness racing.

These inconsistencies in audience existed within a single page. Unlike the *Children's Literacy Awareness* site, these students were not able to address their audience consistently within the constraints of a single page. Much of the writing, organization, and design of this site was strong (and often viewed by the other students in the class as "the best" site). However, their method for responding to their peers' criticism was what Birnbaum would label "impulsive." Instead of thinking of their peers' feedback in relationship to their entire site and how they presented their research, they often went for the quick fix, adding chatty, conversational phrases in hopes of developing a sense of what many of the students called "voice."

Researching versus Documenting. The differences between "the research paper" and a documentary Web—the text forms—were clear in my mind. My students struggled until the end of the assignment with producing texts that illustrated these differences, though I believe they, too, understood the two different text forms, regardless of what they were producing (a case of "I know what I'm supposed to do, but I'm having a hard time doing it"). As my students approached bringing their hypertexts to closure, a number of issues became evident to me:

- I was asking students to juggle a number of different text forms while synthesizing them into a yet unrealized text form. In the course of the quarter, students were required to process academic prose, film theory, documentary films, and hypertexts.

- I was asking students to participate in a number of different processes in order to interpret these text forms, the most significant of which were conducting original research and writing hypertext, both of which were completely new to them.

Students were clearly uncomfortable with the work they were producing toward the end of the quarter. One student adamantly stated in class, "I think we're all better writers than this." I had to agree. Students' written text often broke down unexpectedly in the middle of otherwise strong prose. We all confirmed that the design of some of the sites was less than appealing, often cluttered, inconsistent, conflicting. And as I began to review my students' work, I saw that what they had produced were certainly not research papers, nor did they fulfill my expectations of these preconceived, imagined text forms—documentary Webs.

I have to admit that I was feeling a certain pressure to have student products that were strong and that illustrated not only their writing abilities but also my teaching abilities. And I shared an unsettling awareness with my students: These projects were going to become public, on the Web, for anyone with the technology and the desire to see them. I am always uncomfortable with these feelings of uncertainty as I grow close to the end of a course, even though I know how important this discomfort can be to learning. This uncertainty, I knew, would force me to reexamine what I had hoped to value in my students' work. But with one week remaining in the term, and the students' work and their attitude toward their work in flux, I was even more uncertain how to approach this task.

During class for our last days together, I was immediately overwhelmed with requests by students to provide feedback on their hypertexts. Three groups had just received their photographs, a significant requirement of the assignment:

* The students working on *River Valley Cancer Scare* were debating whether or not a "photo gallery" was an effective way to use some of their photographs. One student insisted that the photographs should be spread out more evenly throughout their site and integrated more carefully with their writing. The other three, however, pointed out that there were other photographs throughout the site. More important, however, the photos in and of themselves would tell a story that their words couldn't. These photographs consisted of sections of the school grounds roped off by the Army Corp of Engineers because of possible leukemia-causing contaminants, endless public town meetings, and a "press-only" tour of restricted school grounds areas. These three students also compared this approach to the films we watched in class: "In some of those films, you could turn off the sound and still pick up the story." Finally, one student insisted that these photos only strengthened their main point by showing a stark contrast: As the publicity continued to grow over this controversy, the students themselves became indifferent to the possible dangers at their school.

* The team working on *Drive-ins: The Dinosaurs of Movie Theaters* had expressed concern over their site having any documentary value. They had constructed an interesting history of drive-in theaters, one that included the Marion area where they had all grown up. However, they all felt that their site lacked substance. They split their duties over the weekend. Two students would try to contact a former owner of one of the extinct drive-ins while the other two would try to photograph what was left of the site. When they came together in class, the students were eager to share their experiences. Everyone had succeeded at finding the information that would give their documentary the substance it was missing. They shared that Regal Cinemas, a multiplex theater company which operates out of the local mall, had purchased the last of Marion's drive-in theaters and immediately destroyed the projection equipment and the sound boxes. Only the large screen and an aban-

doned building remained. They also learned that Regal Cinemas had recently sold the land with a stipulation in the contract: No drive-in theatre could be built on the land for ninety-nine years. At the same time that they conveyed their findings, the other team flipped through their newly processed photographs. "This is it! You drive around this old dirt road around these trees, and there's the old drive-in." Their findings, we agreed, were both thrilling and heartbreaking.

* *Welcome to the Egg Farms of Central Ohio* was not intended to present a biased argument. Their documentary even began by explaining to readers that, "The purpose of this Web site is to present an unbiased view of the impact the Buckeye Egg Farms have made on the environment and the citizens of Northwest Ohio." Their recent findings, however, would force them to think otherwise. They called me over to express this concern. Their entire Web site, based on "factual" information, tried to remain "neutral" on the issue of agribusiness, but over the weekend, the entire student group had gone to Buckeye Egg Farms and its surrounding neighborhoods to shoot photographs and interview local residents. "I'm not so sure we're neutral on this anymore. Look." The photos told a story more powerful than anything they had read or heard about the local egg farm. The chickens. The flies. The manure trough. Even the sign they found as they approached the area: "This property is an agricultural district. At times dust, noises, spraying, insects, and odors occur due to normal farming activities. Anyone interested in locating near this property should take its current use into consideration." The students had obviously gotten very close to the farm. Their photos suggested that perhaps they actually found a way into the building. I didn't want to know. They insisted they didn't do anything illegal. "It's really unfair," one student started. "How do you fight THIS if you're THEM." She laid out two photographs: one of the mammoth factory-farm building, the other of the couple they interviewed who called the area home and now devoted their lives to fighting the conglomerate that had ruined their neighborhood.

Yet another theory from our field became evident to me. In their book, *The Psychology of Written Communication,* Carl Bereiter and Marlene Scardamalia introduce the premise of knowledge *telling* versus knowledge *transformation*, concepts that play significant roles in my theory of invention in this book (1987). Overly simplified here, knowledge telling describes the *processes* of reporting and restating (1987, 9). Knowledge transformation, on the other hand, describes the processes of finding something compelling to say about and making meaning of found content (1987, 10–12). Bereiter and Scardamalia are careful to point out that these concepts describe *processes*, not texts (1987, 13). I want to emphasize this distinction, one that I was privy to as the instructor in the class but that is not necessarily evident in the texts my students produced.

Our profession is deeply concerned with teaching our students the process of research. We are also deeply concerned that students' research processes are meaning-making activities that result in something more than "information dumping." In fact, this entire book has been about getting students to avoid such a superficial approach to research and moving them toward meaning making and knowledge constructing. That said, I, for one, am well aware (mostly from personal experience) of how well-intentioned instruction in research often results in students' patchwork quilting of multiple quotations, statistics, and historical facts.

To read my students' documentary Web sites in isolation of any classroom experience, one would find it easy to classify much of their work as "information dumping." Often, photographs and text didn't speak to each other. Factual information was layered on top of factual information. In many ways, their hypertexts looked like research papers, and not very good ones at that. However, I would argue that my students created a deep learning text from the whole of their experience working on this project. First, I find it impossible to deny the importance of the learning that transpired when text, research, collaboration, and conversation came together during class meetings. Again, this learning text was a complex fabric that I was privy to as an instructor in my classroom, not as a reader of their hypertexts.

More important, however, is the realization that my students were not necessarily engaged in the process of *researching*, but instead were engaged in the process of *documenting*: the finding, capturing, and coming to understand content. The act of creating their documentary Web sites represents a sense of their coming to know about their subjects, a process of knowledge transformation, in ways that traditional research often does not allow. They were pushed to develop content by finding and transforming material, making meaning by documenting and shaping a story.

Certainly, assignments that ask students to conduct "real" inquiry—interviews, field work, surveys, anything that gets them beyond the classroom and the library—are nothing new in composition studies. The recent emergence of "service learning" projects in various composition programs is evidence of this. Yet, I think we need to carefully consider to what end is this inquiry taking place. I may ask students to interview a local politician about recent policies that restrict skateboarding in the town square. I may also suggest that students interview local skatepunks. Students could then compare the agendas of these two groups to better understand this issue. But if those interviews result in nothing more than transcribed quotations that are used merely to fulfill research paper requirements or to make a piece of writing "look" academic, then the students may as well have pulled the quotations from an issue of *Newsweek*.

For this reason, I am finding myself increasingly uncomfortable with the term "research" to describe these acts in which we would like our students to become engaged. As I review the assignment for the documentary Web project, I found that I had asked students to meet traditional research requirements:

- You should plan to incorporate some "traditional" (read "library") research into your Web site. This research should be cited in your Web site using MLA documentation. You will receive guidelines for doing this and setting up a works-cited Web page. Although your project does require research, you are *not* writing a traditional research paper.

The contradiction of terms alone in this passage is enough to confuse students: Conduct traditional research, but do not write a traditional research paper. But more problematic is the rhetoric I used to describe these requirements, a rhetoric that runs counter to the type of text I was asking students to create. Even the vocabulary I used to describe the documentary features of the assignment denote traditional notions of academic research (emphasis added):

- Your project has an original photo *requirement*. Writing Project 2 outlines this *requirement*: "These final projects require that documentary Webs include *at least ten (10) original* photographs; funds have been designated to purchase film or disposable cameras and to cover the cost of photo processing."

- Your project has an original interview *requirement*. You should expect to conduct interviews with key players in the story you are telling; the texts from these interviews *(direct quotations and paraphrases)* should be *incorporated extensively* into your Web site.

Regardless of these shortcomings in my original assignment, and regardless of the final products they produced, students, in the end, were able to transcend *experiencing* the mere creation of an electronic research paper.

So what made their experience so different from any other research project I have taught in the past? What contributed to their learning texts that hasn't been a part of my coursework in the past?

I would argue that my students' experience with documenting technologies allowed them to prevail over a superficial treatment of their subjects. The first and most obvious is hypertext technology. I've already argued in an earlier chapter that hypertext writing allows students to see connections between seemingly unlike ideas, resulting in invention, or the formation of new content. Also, the necessity for creating links between small chunks of text requires students to participate in extensive rereading of their text, resulting in more frequent moments of invention. Whereas I have not read my students' documentary Webs in these terms, I would argue that their experiences would mirror these concepts.

The second piece of documenting technology that I had not considered to its fullest extent in my pedagogy is the camera and photo processing. Most students took their documentary photographs with ten-dollar disposable cameras. Aside from one skilled photographer in the class, no one used any camera more sophisticated than an auto-focus, point-and-click 35mm. Regardless of the sophistication of the technology, nothing for these students represented the act of documenting more concretely than did capturing an image in a photograph. Of course, this entailed framing a subject in a lens and activating a shutter that would allow an image to be inscribed on film. But this also entailed a physical and intellectual engagement with their subject. Sitting through hours of town meetings in order to get one photo of an angry citizen losing her temper. Choosing to identify children by face and name in a public forum like the Web. Understanding that the only photo opportunities you might have are actually meta-photographs—photographs of photographs that are available only at the local historical society because the actual landmarks were long ago destroyed. Facing the disappointment that the film was exposed because the plastic disposable camera case was cracked.

Today, it seems that a majority of Web writing—both in education and corporate settings—has more to do with manipulating content than it does finding content. Web writers are often *given* content by their clients, or they merely upload content from print sources to a hypertext. Images are often borrowed from other sources, and photographs are often staged or montaged (Brugioni). Talented Web writers employ sophisticated design theory where great care is taken in the enhancement and placement of every image. But in the end, their experience with the content is often one of knowledge telling.

Concluding Reflections

At the end of each term, regardless of the course I'm teaching, I typically ask my composition students to write a "reflective" essay where they look back at their own development as readers and writers in the course. Such an exercise is mostly relevant to how I ground my students' learning in metacognition—the final push toward asking them to think about *how* they learned something, not just *what* they learned. At the same time, I have a secondary agenda: I want to see my pedagogy reflected back to me through the words of its subjects—the students. This is especially true when I teach a new course or use a new sequence of assignments. The reflective essay gives me an additional level of "data" to use as I assess and revise my pedagogy.

What we ask of students in the reflective essay is rhetorically tricky. They know this isn't necessarily a course evaluation where they assess the course and the teacher. This essay is going to be evaluated to become a part of the teachers' assessment of the student. Their writing is far from anonymous; in fact, the essay is often a "cover letter," responsible for setting the tone of their portfolio or final collection of work which subsequently often receives the majority of weight when determining their final grade in the course. And then, after we ask them to consider all of this rhetorically, in addition to being descriptive and reflective, we tell them to write critically, to be honest. Indeed, the reflective essay is tricky.

I would be less than honest if I suggested that all of my students' reflective essays were able to effectively juggle the rhetorical complexities that were required of them. In fact, after ten weeks, some students still struggled with the course's basic content issues: hypertextual concepts of linearity and documentary matters of narrative. For others, the power of novelty and the rush to finish final projects completely eclipsed not only the types of writing they were composing for the course and our discussions of this writing, but also the shear volume of writing they had generated by the end of the term. They seemed to suffer from a kind of academic shock and were left wondering how a class that asked them to create documentary Web sites could be defined as a *writing* course.

"They *know* this," I thought aloud. "We talked about this in class." I had to laugh at my own words. Yes, they probably *did* know more than their reflective essays revealed. I could hope they would experience one of those "a-ha" experiences some time in the middle of summer, waiting on customers at the mall, watching swimming lessons, sitting under the stars in the back of a pickup listening to Dave Matthews and Sarah McLoughlin, when their minds had cleared a bit from the world of academe, allowing for a large, coming-to-know moment of invention.

Then I came to Karie's final essay:

> I tried to be aware of the ways in which the documentary and the World Wide Web could work together. I thought of writing for the Web site as self-contained "scenes" that were able to stand on their own, while at the same time stringing them along on a thread connected to the whole project. However, in film, the director moves the viewer through the story, deciding which characters or situations get revisited. The threads of the Web site are rewoven by the viewer, who may revisit or skip over segments they wish.
>
> Allowing linearity to become a more flexible concept helped me to write as if each piece were to be its own small story. This "scenic" approach, more like film than the usual writing-course writing, is a great way to rethink the purposes of writing. The idea was new to me since college writers are most often trained from very early on that writing must have a beginning, a middle, and an end. The three components are still there. It is just possible to

manipulate the boundaries in this context. As cubism did for painting, the Internet allowed me to write using components of the whole and to see the segments of the work rearranged without losing the essence of the project.

Quite frankly, I couldn't ask for a more insightful reflection, one that took the remaining end-of-the-course loose ends and tied them together so thoughtfully and beautifully.

I have come to see great value in teaching Web writing in a variety of composition courses. One common theme that recurs whenever the topic of Web writing instruction is discussed is "student preparation." More and more, corporations, small businesses, and nonprofit organizations rely on the Web as a means of representing their missions and providing information to the general public. And someone needs to create these Web sites. These same businesses and organizations expect employees to produce meaningful, effective writing that will be incorporated into, for example, an annual report, and increasingly, these reports and the like are being written for the Web. In this case, an emerging technology is creating an emerging genre, and, quite simply, this change in forum for this type of writing—from print layout to screen layout—will dictate a significant change in how we teach business, technical, and professional writing if we expect these courses to truly prepare students for what they will face in the workplace.

Whereas I have taught courses that would speak to the concerns above, I am more intrigued by the possibilities of teaching Web writing in lower-division composition courses, like the first- and second-year writing courses I regularly teach. However, the value I see in Web writing for these courses has much more to do with learning and learning development than it does with learning how to create a product that resembles what they might be asked to do outside of my class. Certainly, students will be able to take specific skills they learned from us to a professional writing course or to their family's small business or to a social service agency where they volunteer. But more so than at that level, teaching Web writing allows us to illustrate important writing concepts to students—like invention—in ways that otherwise might not be possible. Providing instruction in Web writing can also push students toward being highly self-aware of their own learning and learning processes.

In many ways, I taught hypertext writing in my study where I asked students to create HyperCard stacks of their writing that they would later search as they were inventing topics for a class writing project. The writing these students produced represented hypertextual writing in a number of ways: Students needed to develop a logical organizing structure for writing that didn't fit their definition/schema for "logical organization," a schema already developed from years of traditional print reading and writing instruction; they needed to understand the mechanics and operations of a computer program that was not designed to produce the types of written texts they were used to; and with this program, they needed to create links between chunks of text and represent the connection between the two texts linguistically (a "button," in the case of HyperCard). But in the end, this writing is really not what I envision when I speak of teaching hypertext writing. First, students were not asked to write this hypertext as an end. Instead, they worked on a number of shorter writing assignments that were then worked into their HyperCard stacks. They created a hypertextual database that was *used to another end*. In this case, creating links and later searching the stack led to invention for a traditional print text.

I don't think this point necessarily negates someone's experience as "writing a hypertext." What does differentiate my students' work with Hyper-Card and my students' work with documentary Web sites is a point that has been the foundation of this entire book. When teaching students to write in Hy-perCard, I did not invent and bring to class a specific pedagogy for teaching hypertext writing. I had a carefully designed and sequenced pedagogy in place within the framework of a course, one that reflected what I knew about teaching reading and writing and what students had learned to date in my class about reading and writing. And I spent a great deal of time learning the technology and understanding the best way to teach its operations to my students. However, I did not invent a pedagogy that bridged the two, a pedagogy that was grounded in how students read and write hypertexts. With the documentary Web class, I used the technology and my prior interests in documentary film to imagine and invent a new pedagogy.

With all its technological necessities and various "crude" manifestations, Web writing raises a simple but serious question: Why should teaching Web writing be the job of compositionists?

This, I believe, is one of the most pressing questions facing the field, one that deserves a volume in and of itself. Although inventing a pedagogical stance toward teaching students to write hypertexts has been a logical step in *my* research agenda, I don't mean to suggest that we have even begun to answer the multitude of questions that arise when students read the Web, engage in discussions using e-mail, or create hypertexts using freestanding computer software. As I argued in the introduction of this book, all too often our research agenda moves as quickly as the computer industry, trying to keep up with new innovations and the latest upgrades, without fully exploring one technology before we move into the next (for years, published research might have us believe that we have asked and answered all of the questions we can surrounding word processing, a point that is obviously not true as is evidenced in Christina Haas' 1997 title, *Writing Technologies*). I do believe, however, because of its size and its rapid acceptance and use by popular culture, Web technologies, or variations of them, are going to be a part of how we write for a long time to come. This alone should draw our attention toward better understanding this technology.

I do, without hesitation, hope to see the teaching of Web writing taken up by compositionists. I do not mean to suggest that such a task shouldn't be taken up by other disciplines at the same time. Anyone who sees the value of writing across the curriculum would understand the reciprocal, synergistic verve that results from students' writing in all subject areas; I believe this would be true of Web writing, also. But compositionists, I believe, deeply understand that writing entails more than simple skill acquisition and service course teaching, more than a "show me what you know" vision of school. We see language as a complex system that simultaneously reflects and constructs reality. We teach writing as an activity that results in the production of artifacts, in this case written texts, but also as an activity that results in learning, the discovery and formulation of knowledge. Our craft includes a theory of intervention and a theory of assessment. Composition is one of the few disciplines in the university whose subject is indeed pedagogy, the imparting of instruction. This vast background of what we know and do as a field is all necessary for inventing an effectual pedagogy for writing for the Web.

Aside from the practice and theory described within these pages, one more reason firmly grounds why I see compositionists involved in teaching Web writing: We have an acute understanding of the role writing plays in how we come to know ourselves. Writing in this way is often described as "personal," where individuals have invented and disclosed a great deal of their identity, sometimes exploring a particular incident or set of circumstances in their lives. But writing need not be "personal" in appearance for it to have played a significant part in individuals coming to know themselves. Writers also learn about themselves by creating "distanced" texts where they investigate various issues or topics, internalizing what they learn and comparing that to what they already know about themselves, often reseeing or reestablishing their "take" on the subject at hand.

I am often struck by how much of the writing on the Web can be described as personal in its form. The amount only increases when one considers the writing that is not personal in form but where a great deal of self-realization has occurred for the writers. What further makes the personal nature of Web writing so striking to me is that the writing is always *public*. In fact, the notion of "public" is inherent in a Web text, for its very purpose is to allow/encourage access to the text. No one would create a Web text that they didn't eventually want launched on the Web. Likewise, composition teachers would seldom ask students to create Web documents that would never eventually make it to the WWW. Whether we like it or not, this attitude stands in stark contrast to other class writing where students are usually quite satisfied with never seeing their traditional print texts published, especially those texts that are academic in nature. Not so with the WWW; students would be frustrated, if not completely stupefied, if a Web writing assignment did not culminate in a launched page.

At first, one might think this culmination of the personal and the public would undeniably result in a positive writing experience for our students, a powerful "teachable moment." As techno-compositionists, however, I feel it is our responsibility to come to understand the complexities of how computer technology can or cannot facilitate learning within our classes. I am not speaking narrowly of learning here to mean the content of the course. I wish to include the complexities of how students come to know themselves and the opportunities in our classrooms that allow them to do so.

Until recently, all of my teaching experiences where students have come to know themselves through their writing have involved traditional, print texts: writing to learn followed by a required final hard copy to fulfill the assignment. What is key to these texts is an element of privacy and control that is allowed not only by the text form, but also by a pedagogy attached to the text form. For example, in my course syllabi, I tell students that they will be writing with real purposes for real audiences while imagining real forums, or places of publication, for their work. Nothing about my assignments or my course design, however, requires students to actually make their work public beyond the class. So whereas students may, for example, write to an imagined audience made up of young voters and visualize its publication in *Rolling Stone* after a careful forum analysis, their actual readership rarely extends beyond me, their classmates, and possibly a writing tutor. Many writing courses, particularly creative writing courses, require students to submit their work for publication. I can see pedagogical value in such a requirement. However, as I consider my own writing, I feel uneasy about forcing anyone to submit for publication work that they feel is not ready for "public" consumption. I especially feel uneasy about pushing students to publish a piece of writing that discloses information for which they do not wish a large-scale readership.

I imagine that as I continue to incorporate emerging technologies into my writing classes, students will increasingly use the Web to explore subjects that are personal. Again, this includes both reading from and writing for the WWW. We know that writing, both the act and the artifact, in the medium of the WWW is different from writing traditional print texts. Considering what we already know about technology—that it indeed changes the very nature of the composition classroom—I feel safe in saying that the Web will alter much of what I know about teaching and creating a pedagogical environment for students to learn about these personal subjects. I like to think that I provide a safe, inviting space in my writing classroom for all of my students. I believe that students make the choice to explore the personal based in part or totally on their perception of the classroom space which is created by the individuals in the class, the types of assignments students are asked to complete, and the tone of feedback that they receive on their writing from the teacher and their peers. As our students begin to write for the Web, we need to recognize that the nature of the audience for student writing changes as the writing space changes from physical to virtual. As a result, the space that I have in the past been able to create in the classroom is potentially out of my hands. And students, once realizing the Web's inherent public nature, may choose not to explore the personal, or may choose to do so at a "distanced" level so as not to identify with their subject matter. What seemed to be a teachable moment, this union of personal and public, may actually never be realized.

There should be no doubt in any readers' minds of my excitement about computer technology in the writing classroom. This book itself has been yet one more invention of my professional identity. Yet, as I have increasingly more access to more powerful computers waiting every day in my classroom, I'm careful to ensure that my enthusiasm does not overpower the critical sensibility with which I approach all of my teaching.

Bibliography

Alba, Joseph W., and Lynn Hasher. "Is Memory Schematic?" *Psychological Bulletin* 93 (1983): 203–31.

Andre, Thomas, and Gary D. Phye. "Cognition, Learning, and Education." *Cognitive Classroom Learning: Understanding, Thinking, and Problem Solving.* Ed. Gary D. Phye and Thomas Andre. Orlando, FL: Academic P, 1986. 1–19.

Arnheim, Rudolf. *Visual Thinking.* Berkeley: U of California P, 1969.

Atwan, Robert. "Introduction: Reading, Writing, and Class Discussion." *Our Times/4.* Ed. Robert Atwan. Boston: Bedford, 1995. ix–xvi.

Augustine, Dorothy, and W. Ross Winterowd. "Speech Acts and the Reader-Writer Transaction." *Convergences: Transactions in Reading and Writing.* Ed. Bruce T. Petersen. Urbana, IL: NCTE, 1986. 127–48.

Ayto, John. "Text." *Dictionary of Word Origins.* New York: Arcade, 1990.

Baird, Patricia. "HyperCard Opens an Electronic Window on Glasgow." *Electronic Library* 6 (1988): 344–53.

Bartholomae, David. "Inventing the University." *Journal of Basic Writing* 5 (1986): 4–23.

Bartholomae, David, and Anthony Petrosky. *Facts, Artifacts, and Counterfacts: Theory and Method for a Reading and Writing Course.* Portsmouth, NH: Boynton/Cook. 1986.

Beach, Richard. "Experimental and Descriptive Research Methods in Composition." *Methods and Methodology in Composition Research.* Ed. Gesa Kirsch and Patricia A. Sullivan. Carbondale, IL: Southern Illinois UP, 1992. 217–43.

Beach, Richard, and Jo Anne Liebman-Kleine. "The Writing/Reading Relationship: Becoming One's Own Best Reader." *Convergences: Transactions in Reading and Writing.* Ed. Bruce T. Petersen. Urbana, IL: NCTE, 1986. 64–81.

Bell-Gredler, Margaret E. *Learning and Instruction: Theory into Practice.* New York: Macmillan, 1986.

Bereiter, Carl, and Marlene Scardamalia. *The Psychology of Written Communication.* Hillsdale, NJ: Lawrence Erlbaum, 1987.

Berthoff, Ann E. *Reclaiming the Imagination*. Portsmouth, NH: Boyton/Cook, 1984.

Bevilacqua, Ann F. "Hypertext: Behind the Hype." *American Libraries* 20 (1989): 158–62.

Birnbaum, June Cannell. "Reflective Thought: The Connection between Reading and Writing." *Convergences: Transactions in Reading and Writing*. Ed. Bruce T. Petersen. Urbana, IL: NCTE, 1986. 30–45.

Bleich, David. "Cognitive Stereoscopy and the Study of Language and Literature." *Convergences: Transactions in Reading and Writing*. Ed. Bruce T. Petersen. Urbana, IL: NCTE, 1986. 99–114.

Bolter, Jay David. *Writing Space: The Computer, Hypertext, and the History of Writing*. Hillsdale, NJ: Lawrence Erlbaum Associates, 1991.

Booth, Wayne C. "Forward." *The English Coalition Conference: Democracy through Language*. Ed. Richard Lloyd-Jones and Andrea A. Lunsford. Urbana, IL: NCTE, 1989. vii–xii.

Bowen, Betsy. "Telecommunications Networks: Expanding the Contexts for Literacy." *Literacy and Computers: The Complications of Teaching and Learning with Technology*. Ed. Cynthia L. Selfe and Susan Hilligoss. New York: MLA, 1994. 113–29.

Brandt, Deborah. "Social Foundations of Reading and Writing." *Convergences: Transactions in Reading and Writing*. Ed. Bruce T. Petersen. Urbana, IL: NCTE, 1986. 115–26.

Bransford, John, et al. "Teaching Thinking and Problem Solving." *American Psychologist* 41 (1986): 1078–89.

Brent, Doug. *Reading as Rhetorical Invention: Knowledge, Persuasion, and the Teaching of Research-Based Writing*. Urbana, IL: NCTE. 1992.

Brodkey, Linda. "Writing Ethnographic Narratives." *Written Communication* 4.1 (January 1987): 25–50.

Bronski, Michael. "Magic and AIDS: Presumed Innocent." *Our Times/3*. Ed. Robert Atwan. Boston: Bedford, 1993. 445–54.

Brother's Keeper. Dir. Joe Berlinger and Bruce Sinofsky. Creative Thinking International. 1992.

Bruffee, Kenneth A. "Collaborative Learning and the 'Conversation of Mankind'." *College English* 46 (November 1984): 635–52.

Bruner, Jerome. *Actual Minds, Possible Worlds*. Cambridge: Harvard UP, 1986.

Burkland, Jill N., and Bruce T. Petersen. "An Interactive Approach to Research: Theory and Practice." *Convergences: Transactions in Reading and Writing*. Ed. Bruce T. Petersen. Urbana, IL: NCTE, 1986. 189–203.

Burns, Hugh. "A Writer's Tool: Computing as a Mode of Inventing." *The Writer's Mind.*
Ed. Janice N. Hayes, et al. Urbana, IL: NCTE, 1983. 87–94.

———. "Recollections of First-Generation Computer-Assisted Prewriting." *The Computer in Composition Instruction.* Ed. William Wresch. Urbana, IL: NCTE, 1984. 15–33.

Bush, Vannevar. "As We May Think." *Atlantic Monthly* April 1945: 101–08.

Byles, Torrey. "A Context for Hypertext: Some Suggested Elements of Style." *Wilson Library Bulletin* 63.3 (1988): 60–62.

Cahalan, James M., and David B. Downing, eds. *Practicing Theory in Introductory College Literature Courses.* Urbana, IL: NCTE, 1991.

Carnegie Foundation for the Advancement of Teaching. *Campus Life: In Search of Community.* Princeton, NJ: Princeton UP, 1990.

Carr, Clay. "Hypertext: A New Training Tool?" *Educational Technology* 28.8 (1988): 7–11.

Carter, Michael. "The Idea of Expertise: An Exploration of Cognitive and Social Dimensions of Writing." *College Composition and Communication* 41 (1990): 265–86.

Collins, James L. and Elizabeth A. Sommers, eds. *Writing On-Line: Using Computers in the Teaching of Writing.* Upper Montclair, NJ: Boynton/Cook, 1985.

Color Adjustment. Dir. Marlon Riggs. PBS. 1992.

Common Threads: Stories from the Quilt. Dir. Robert Epstein and Jeffrey Friedman. Tellings Pictures. 1989.

Conklin, Jeff. "Hypertext: An Introduction and Survey." *IEEE Computer* 20.9 (1987): 17–41.

Cooper, Marilyn M. "The Ecology of Writing." *College English* 48 (1986): 364–75.

Cooper, Marilyn M. and Cynthia L. Selfe. "Computer Conferences and Learning: Authority, Resistance, and Internally Persuasive Discourse." *College English* 52 (1990): 847–69.

Coover, Robert. "Finding Your Way in Hypertext: A Guide to the Software." *New York Times Book Review* 21 June 1992: 24.

Cozby, Paul C. *Methods in Behavioral Research.* Mountain View, CA: Mayfield, 1989.

D'Angelo, Frank J. "Paradigms as Structural Counterparts of *Topoi.*" *Rhetoric and Composition: A Sourcebook for Teachers and Writers.* Ed. Richard L. Graves. Upper Montclair, NJ: Boyton-Cook, 1984. 202–11.

Delaney, Paul, and George P. Landow, eds. *Hypermedia and Literary Studies.* Cambridge: MIT P, 1990.

DeWitt, Scott Lloyd. "Hypertextualizing Composition Instruction: A Research Study." *DAI* 53 (1992): 2279. D.A. diss., Illinois State U.

———. "Emerging Technologies, Changing Discussions: Using Computer-Mediated Discussion in the Writing Classroom." *Our Times/4 Instructional Resources*. Ed. Robert Atwan. Boston: Bedford, 1995. 30–40.

———. "The Current Nature of Hypertext Research in Composition Studies: An Historical Perspective." *Computers and Composition* 13 (April 1996): 69–84.

———. "Defining Links." *Contexts, Intertexts, and Hypertexts*. Ed. Scott Lloyd DeWitt and Kip Strasma. Creskill, NJ: HamptonP, 1999. 117–54.

DeWitt, Scott Lloyd and Kip Strasma. "Introduction: An Emerging Research." *Contexts, Intertexts, and Hypertexts*. Ed. Scott Lloyd DeWitt and Kip Strasma. Creskill, NJ: HamptonP, 1999. 1–13.

Dickson, Marcia. *It's Not Like That Here: Teaching Academic Writing and Reading to Novice Writers*. Portsmouth, NH: Heinemann, 1995.

Doheny-Farina, Stephen. "Writing in an Emergent Business Organization: An Ethnographic Study." *DAI* 45 (1984) : 11A. Rensselaer Polytechnic Institute.

Duin, Ann Hill and Craig Hansen. "Reading and Writing on Computer Networks as Social Construction and Social Interaction. *Literacy and Computers: The Complications of Teaching and Learning with Technology*. Ed. Cynthia L. Selfe and Susan Hilligoss. New York: MLA, 1994. 89–112.

Ede, Lisa. "Methods, Methodologies, and the Politics of Knowledge: Reflections and Speculations." *Methods and Methodology in Composition Research*. Ed. Gesa Kirsch and Patricia A. Sullivan. Carbondale, IL: Southern Illinois UP, 1992. 314–29.

Ehrlich, Diane Berger. "A Study of the Word Processor and Composing Changes in Attitude and Revision Practices of Inexperienced Student Writers in a College Composition Class." *DAI* 45 (1984) : 07A. U of Iowa.

Eldred, Janet. "Computers, Composition Pedagogy, and the Social View." *Critical Perspectives on Computers and Compisition Instruction*. Ed. Gail E. Hawisher and Cynthia L. Selfe. New York: Teachers College P, 1989. 201–18.

Faigley, Lester. *Fragments of Rationality: Postmodernity and the Subject of Composition*. Pittsburgh: U of Pittsburgh P, 1992.

Flood, James, and Diane Lapp. "Reading and Writing Relations: Assumptions and Directions." Ed. James R. Squire. Urbana, IL: ERIC and NCRE, 1987. 9–26.

Flower, Linda. "Cognition, Context, and Theory Building." *College Composition and Communication* 40 (1989): 282–311.

Flower, Linda R., and John R. Hayes. "A Cognitive Process Theory of Writing." *College Composition and Communication* 31 (1980): 365–87.

Fontaine, Sheryl I., and Susan Hunter. "Introduction: Taking the Risk to Be Heard." *Writing Ourselves into the Story: Unheard Voices from Composition Studies*. Ed. Sheryl I. Fontaine and Susan Hunter. Carbondale, IL: Southern Illinois UP, 1993. 1–17.

Forman, Janis. "Literacy, Collaboration, and Technology: New Connections and Challenges." *Literacy and Computers: The Complications of Teaching and Learning with Technology.* Ed. Cynthia L. Selfe and Susan Hilligoss. New York: MLA, 1994. 130–43.

Franklin, Carl, and Susan K. Kinnell. *Hypertext/Hypermedia in Schools: A Resource Book.* Santa Barbara: ABC-CLIO, 1990.

Gardner, Howard. *Frames of Mind.* New York: Basic Books, 1983.

Gerard, Philip. *Creative Nonfiction: Researching and Crafting Stories of Real Life.* Cincinnati: Story, 1996.

Greeno, James G., et al. *Associative Learning: A Cognitive Analysis.* Englewood Cliffs, NJ: Prentice-Hall, 1978.

Halio, Marcia Peoples. "Student Writing: Can the Machine Maim the Message?" *Academic Computing* 4 (1990): 16–46.

Haas, Christina. *Writing Technology: Studies on the Materiality of Literacy.* Mahwah, NJ: Lawrence Erlbaum, 1996.

Hawisher, Gail E. "Research and Recommendations for Computers and Composition." *Critical Perspectives on Computers and Composition Instruction.* Ed. Gail E. Hawisher and Cynthia L. Selfe. New York: Teachers College P, 1989. 44–69.

Hawisher, Gail E., and Charles Moran. "E-Mail and the Writing Instructor." *College English* 55 (1993): 627–43.

Hawisher, Gail E., Paul LeBlanc, Charles Moran, and Cynthia L. Selfe. *Computers and the Teaching of Writing in American Higher Education, 1979–1994: A History.* Norwood, NJ: Ablex, 1996.

Hawisher, Gail E. and Cynthia L. Selfe, eds. *Evolving Perspectives on Computers and Composition Studies: Questions for the 1990s.* Urbana, IL: NCTE, 1991.

Holdstein, Deborah H. and Cynthia L. Selfe, eds. *Computers and Writing: Theory, Research, Practice.* New York: MLA, 1990.

Howard, Alan. "Hypermedia and the Future of Ethnography." *Cultural Anthropology* 3 (1988): 304–15.

Howe, Neil, and Bill Strausse. *13th Gen: Abort, Retry, Ignore, Fail?* New York: Vintage, 1993.

Hull, Glenda, and Mike Rose. "Rethinking Remediation: Toward a Social-Cognitive Understanding of Problematic Reading and Writing." *Written Communication* 8 (1989): 139–54.

Hull, Glenda, et al. "Remediation as Social Construct: Perspectives from an Analysis of Classroom Discourse." *College Composition and Communication* 42 (1991): 299–329.

Irmscher, William F. "Finding a Comfortable Identity." *College Composition and Communication* 38 (1987): 81–87.

Jennings, Edward M. "Paperless Writing: Boundary Conditions and Their Implications." *Writing at Century's End: Essays on Computer-Assisted Instruction.* Ed. Lisa Gerrard. New York: Random House, 1987. 11–20.

Jonassen, David H. "Designing Structured Hypertext and Structuring Access to Hypertext." *Educational Technology* 28.11 (1988): 13–16.

Joyce, Michael. "Siren Shapes: Exploratory and Constructive Hypertexts." *Academic Computing* 3.4 (1988): 10–42.

———. *Of Two Minds: Hypertext Pedagogy and Poetics.* Ann Arbor, MI: U of Michigan P, 1995.

Kaplan, Nancy. "Ideology, Technology, and the Future of Writing Instruction." *Evolving Perspectives on Computers and Composition Studies: Questions for the 1990s.* Ed. Gail Hawisher and Cynthia L. Selfe. Urbana, IL: NCTE, 1991. 11–42.

Kaplan, Nancy, and Stuart Moulthrop. "Other Ways of Seeing." *Computers and Composition* 7 (1990): 89–102.

Kearsley, Greg. "Authoring Considerations for Hypertext." *Educational Technology* 28.11 (1988): 21–24.

Kemp, Fred. "The User-Friendly Fallacy." *College Composition and Communication* 38 (1987): 32–39.

Kerrigan, William J. *Writing to the Point: Six Basic Steps.* New York: Harcourt Brace Jovanovich, 1979.

Knutson, Deborah. Telephone interview. 27 May 1992.

Kucer, Stephen B. "The Cognitive Base of Reading and Writing." *The Dynamics of Language Learning.* Ed. James R. Squire. Urbana, IL: ERIC and NCRE, 1987. 27–51.

Landow, George P. "Hypertext in Literary Education, Criticism, and Scholarship." *Computers and the Humanities* 23.3 (1989): 173–98.

———. "The Rhetoric of Hypermedia: Some Rules for Authors." *Hypermedia and Literary Studies.* Ed. Paul Delaney and George P. Landow. Cambridge: MIT P, 1990. 81–103.

———. *Hypertext: The Convergence of Contemporary Critical Theory and Technology.* Baltimore: John Hopkins UP, 1992.

Lauer, Janice M., and J. William Asher. *Composition Research: Empirical Designs.* New York: Oxford UP, 1988.

Leahey, Thomas H., and Richard J. Harris. *Human Learning.* Englewood Cliffs, NJ: Prentice-Hall, 1985.

LeBlanc, Paul. *Writing Teachers Writing Software: Creating Our Place in the Electronic Age.* Urbana, IL: NCTE, 1993.

LeFevre, Karen. *Invention as a Social Act.* Carbondale, IL: Southern Illinois UP, 1987.

Living Proof: HIV and the Pursuit of Happiness. Dir. Kermit Cole. First Run Features. 1992.

Lloyd-Jones, Richard, and Andrea A. Lunsford, eds. *English Coalition Conference: Democracy through Language.* Urbana, IL: NCTE, 1989.

Lundsford, Andrea A. "Alexander Bain's Contributions to Discourse Theory." *College English* 44 (1982): 290–300.

———. "Composing Ourselves: Politics, Commitment, and the Teaching of Writing." *College Composition and Communication* 41 (1990): 71–82.

Mabrito, Mark. "Electronic Mail as a Vehicle for Peer Response: Conversations of High- and Low-Apprehensive Writers." *Written Communication* 8 (1991): 509–32.

McDaid, John. "Toward an Ecology of Hypermedia." *Evolving Perspectives on Computers and Composition Studies.* Ed. Gail E. Hawisher and Cynthia L. Selfe. Urbana, IL: NCTE, 1991. 177–202.

McKnight, Cliff, Andrew Dillon, and John Richardson. *Hypertext in Context.* New York: Cambridge UP, 1991.

Mitchell, Felicia. "Balancing Individual Projects and Collaborative Learning in an Advanced Writing Course." *College Composition and Communication* 43 (1992): 393–400.

Moulthrop, Stuart. "The Politics of Hypertext." *Evolving Perspectives on Computers and Composition Studies.* Ed. Gail E. Hawisher and Cynthia L. Selfe. Urbana, IL: NCTE, 1991. 253–71.

Moxley, Joseph Michael. "Five Writers' Perceptions: An Ethnographic Study of the Composing Process and Writing Functions." *DAI* 45 (1984): 06A. State U of New York at Buffalo.

Myers, Linda, ed. *Approaches to Computer Writing Classrooms: Learning from Practical Experience.* New York: State U of New York P, 1993.

Nelson, Theodor Holm. "Replacing the Printed Word: A Complete Literary System." *IFIP Process.* (October 1980): 1013–23.

———. *Computer Lib: You Can and Must Understand Computers Now!* Redmond, WA: Microsoft, 1987.

———. *Literary Machines.* San Antonio, TX: Theodor Holm Nelson, 1987.

Newkirk, Thomas. "The Politics of Composition Research: The Conspiracy against Experience." *The Politics of Writing Instruction: Postsecondary.* Ed. Richard Bullock and John Trimbur. Portsmouth, NH: Boynton/Cook, 1991. 119–35.8.

Payne, Lucile Vaughan. *The Lively Art of Writing.* Chicago: Follett, 1982.

Phelps, Louise Wetherbee. *Composition as a Human Science: Contributions to the Self-Understanding of a Discipline.* New York: Oxford UP, 1988.

———. "Images of Student Writing: The Deep Structure of Teacher Response." *Writing and Response: Theory, Practice, and Research*. Ed. Chris Anson. Urbana, IL: NCTE, 1995.

Roger and Me. Dir. Michael Moore. Warner Bros. 1989.

Ronald, Katharine. "The Self and the Other in the Process of Composing: Implications for Integrating the Acts of Reading and Writing." *Convergences: Transactions in Reading and Writing*. Ed. Bruce T. Petersen. Urbana, IL: NCTE, 1986. 231–45.

Rose, Mike. "Rigid Rules, Inflexible Plans, and the Stifling of Language: A Cognitivist Analysis of Writer's Block." *College Composition and Communication* 31 (1980): 389–401.

———. *Possible Lives: The Promise of Public Education in America*. New York: Penguin, 1995.

Rosenthal, Alan. *Writing, Directing, and Producing Documentary Films and Videos*. Carbondale, IL: Southern Illinois UP, 1996.

Schwartz, Helen. "Teaching Writing with Computer Aids." *College English* 46 (1984): 239–47.

Selfe, Cynthia L. *Creating a Computer-Supported Writing Facility: A Blueprint for Action*. Houghton, MI: Computers and Composition, 1989.

Selfe, Cynthia L. and Susan Hilligoss. "Introduction." *Literacy and Computers: The Complications of Teaching and Learning with Technology*. Ed. Cynthia L. Selfe and Susan Hilligoss. New York: MLA, 1994. 1–7.

Selfe, Cynthia L. and Kathleen E. Kiefer. "From the Editors." *Computers and Composition* 1 (November 1983): 2.

Selfe, Cynthia L., Dawn Rodrigues, and William R. Oates. eds.. *Computers in English and the Language Arts: The Challenge of Teacher Education*. Urbana, IL: NCTE, 1989.

Shirk, Henrietta Nickels. "Hypertext and Composition Studies." *Evolving Perspectives on Computers and Composition Studies*. Ed. Gail E. Hawisher and Cynthia L. Selfe. Urbana, IL: NCTE, 1991. 173–76.

Shneiderman, Ben, and Greg Kearsley. *Hypertext Hands-on: An Introduction to a New Way of Accessing and Organizing Information*. Reading, MA: Addison-Wesley, 1988.

Slatin, John M. "Hypertext and the Teaching of Writing." *Text, Context, and Hypertext*. Ed. Edward Barrett. Cambridge, MA: MIT P, 1988. 111–29.

———. "Reading Hypertext: Order and Coherence in a New Medium." *College English* 52 (1990): 870–83.

Smith, Catherine F. "Reconceiving Hypertext." *Evolving Perspectives on Computers and Composition Studies*. Ed. Gail E. Hawisher and Cynthia L. Selfe. Urbana, IL: NCTE, 1991. 224–52.

Smith, Karen. "Hypertext—Linking to the Future." *Online* 12.2 (1988): 32–40.

Sperling, Melanie. "Dialogues of Deliberation: Conversation in the Teacher-Student Writing Conference." *Written Communication* 8.2 (April 1991): 131–62.

Spitzer, Michael. "Writing Style in Computer Conferences." *IEEE Transactions on Professional Communications* 29 (1986): 19–22.

Sternglass, Marilyn. "Writing Based on Reading." *Convergences: Transactions in Reading and Writing.* Ed. Bruce T. Petersen. Urbana, IL: NCTE, 1986. 151–62.

Tierney, Robert J., and Margie Leys. "What Is the Value of Connecting Reading and Writing?" *Convergences: Transactions in Reading and Writing.* Ed. Bruce T. Petersen. Urbana, IL: NCTE, 1986. 15–29.

Tresselt-Wharton, Kim. "The Rhetoric and Design of Online Resumés." Conference on College Composition and Communication. Washington, DC, 24 March 1995.

Warren, Howard C. *History of the Association of Psychology.* New York: Scribner, 1967.

Wesley, F. "Association." *Encyclopedia of Psychology.* Ed. H. J. Eysenck, W. Arnold, and R. Meili. 3 vols. London: Seabury P, 1972. 86–88.

Wiener, Harvey S. "Collaborative Learning in the Classroom: A Guide to Evaluation." *College English* 42.1 (January 1986): 52–61.

Williamson, Michael McKay. "The Function of Writing in Three College Undergraduate Curricula." *DAI* 45 (1984) : 03A. State U of New York at Buffalo.

Woods, William F. "Nineteenth-Century Psychology and the Teaching of Writing." *College Composition and Communication* 32 (1985): 20–41.

Woods-Elliott, Claire Ann. "Students, Teachers and Writing: An Ethnography of Interactions in Literacy." *DAI* 42 (1981) : 2376A. U of Pennsylvania.

Worley, Demetrice. "Visual Imagery Training and College Writing Students." *Presence of Mind: Writing and the Domain beyond the Cognitive.* Ed. Alice Glarden Brand and Richard L. Graves. Portsmouth, NH: Boyton/Cook, 1994.

Wright, Robert. "The Man Who Invented the Web." *Time* 19 May 1997: 64–68.

Young, Richard E. "Invention: A Topographical Survey." *Teaching Composition: Ten Bibliographical Essays.* Ed. Gary Tate. Fort Worth: Texas Christian UP, 1976. 1–43.

Young, Richard E., Alton L. Becker, and Kenneth L. Pike. *Rhetoric: Discovery and Change.* San Diego: Harcourt Brace Jovanovich, 1970.

Zeni, Jane. "Literacy, Technology, and Teacher Education." *Literacy and Computers: The Complications of Teaching and Learning with Technology.* Ed. Cynthia L. Selfe and Susan Hilligoss. New York: MLA, 1994. 76–86.

Index